ACCLAIM FOR ELEVEN TWO

MIKE CLARK
Friend and award-winning television journalist:

"Frank Kravetz's personal story of honor and courage is a must-read for every American who wants to understand the heartbeat of the 'Greatest Generation.' Frank's heroic love of God, country, and family pulled him from the valley of death, back home to Pittsburgh. *Eleven Two* is the story of a man of steel, who will melt your heart with the moving real-life tale of survival and patriotism. We salute you, Frank, and all of your POW comrades. God bless you all."

U.S. CONGRESSMAN MIKE DOYLE

"*Eleven Two* is a fabulous account of Frank Kravetz's journey in the Army Air Corps during World War II. Frank showed his bravery and love of his country, as well as the deep appreciation of those who helped him along the way. This is a great memoir of his service time that is indicative of thousands of other American servicemen just like him. I'm glad he survived to share his story with us in this book."

JEFFREY PETERS, M.D., DFAPA
Associate Professor of Psychiatry,
University of Pittsburgh School of Medicine

"I find *Eleven Two: One WWII Airman's Story of Capture, Survival and Freedom* to be an excellent book. The many men of his generation and the families of those who served and suffered are offered well-deserved tribute in his book. It has been my honor for the past 25 years to provide psychiatric care to men who served in WWII and Korea, faced combat and military captivity, and returned home. I have been blessed with the opportunity to meet many of their family members over the years.

It is moving to see, in detail, the true story of one man's journey in life, which is typical of the experiences of many others. I have been profoundly moved in my professional career by the resilience, patriotism and honor that Mr. Kravetz and so many other veterans display.

ROBERT F. ("ROCKY") KRAVETZ, JR. ESQ.

"For my entire life, my grandfather, Frank, has been my hero. His continuing service to God, his family, and his country is truly inspiring. I am thrilled that, with the publishing of his memoirs, others will get to learn about this great American."

ELEVEN TWO

ONE WWII AIRMAN'S STORY
OF CAPTURE, SURVIVAL AND FREEDOM

FRANK A. KRAVETZ

To Briane

Peace be with you

Enjoy the Book

Frank G. Kravetz

SILVERBEAR GRAPHICS
Stahlstown, Pennsylvania

To obtain permission for reprint of passages of this book, or to contact the author, use one of the contact points below:

Frank A. Kravetz, Author
Cheryl Werle, Coauthor
Lynne Kravetz Hartnett, Editor
www.eleventwothebook.com
info@eleventwothebook.com

Published by Silverbear Graphics
647 Jones Mills Stahlstown Road
Stahlstown, PA 15687
www.silverbeargraphics.com

Earl Needhammer, Contributing Editor

Cover Art, Graphic Design and Layout by Mark Werle
Werle Creative
www.werlecreative.com

First Edition Published 11-02-2010
Paperback
Printed in the USA

ELEVEN TWO:
One WWII Airman's Story of Capture, Survival and Freedom
Frank A. Kravetz
ISBN: 9780982716144
Library of Congress Control Number: 2010938281

ELEVEN TWO

Not just two words, not just two numbers.
Rather… two numbers, combined to form one date.
One significant date – three times by chance –
the fourth time by choice, with the publishing of this book.

The month is NOVEMBER.
The day is the SECOND.
The story of the importance of the day
follows in the pages of this book.

One Date.
One Story.
One Life…
Changed Forever.

DEDICATION

This book is dedicated to my crew, my friends –
brave heroic young men…whose selfless acts of courage
amidst the clouds and chaos gave me the opportunity to live
and not die over the skies of Germany on 11-2-1944.
My debt of gratitude is beyond words.

S/SGT.
HARRY J.
CONNORS
TOP TURRET
ENGINEER

S/SGT.
VIRGIL H.
SMALLEN
RADIO
OPERATOR

S/SGT.
FRANK A.
KRAVETZ
WAIST
GUNNER

S/SGT.
WILLIAM E.
RHODES
WAIST
GUNNER

S/SGT.
JOHN
SIMMEN
TAIL
GUNNER

S/SGT.
HERBERT E.
BRAYMAN
BALL
TURRET

LT.
GEORGE H.
KELLER
COPILOT

LT.
KENNETH E.
GUPTILL
PILOT

LT.
EDMOND C.
McNAMARA
NAVIGATOR

LT.
THOMAS
DUNN
BOMBARDIER

ELEVEN TWO
One WWII Airman's Story of Capture, Survival and Freedom

Dedication i

Introduction v

Ch. 1: Growing Up in Small Town, USA 1

Ch. 2: Pearl Harbor – Entering the Military 15

NOVEMBER 2ND, 1943:
   Frank Leaves Home To Begin Military Training 23

Ch. 3: Into the Wild Blue Yonder –
   Flight Training 24

Ch. 4: Ordered Overseas – 457th Bomb Group 43

Ch. 5: Fighting a War from the Air 52

NOVEMBER 2ND, 1944: The Mission 63

Ch. 6: Mission Number Six 64

Ch. 7: Shot Out of the Sky 69

Ch. 8: Freedom Lost – a Prisoner of War 75

Ch. 9: War Wounded and More 83

Ch. 10: Enemy Interrogation 90

Ch. 11: The Long Recovery – Obermassfeld
POW Hospital, Germany 97

Ch. 12: Barbed Wire and Bugs –
Nuremberg Prison Camp; Stalag XIIID 118

Ch. 13: Steps to Survive –
The March to Moosburg 141

Ch. 14: Hell's Journey Continues –
Moosburg – POW Camp – Stalag VIIA 152

Ch. 15: Liberation – Freedom Gained 158

Ch. 16: Lady Liberty – Home Sweet Home 170

NOVEMBER 2ND, 1945: Frank A. Kravetz
Honorably Discharged From The Military 181

Ch. 17: Mending a Broken Body 182

Ch. 18: A Civilian Again 197

Ch. 19: Finding My Way 211

Ch. 20: Moments to Remember 225

Ch. 21: A Story To Share – Coming Full Circle 239

Ch. 22: A Wife Looks Back 247

Ch. 23: Reflections: My Experience; My Promise 275

NOVEMBER 2ND, 2010: Frank Publishes His Story 289

To My Dad 290

Frank's Personal Photo Collection 291

Acknowledgments 301

References 304

INTRODUCTION

I received a warning through my radio headset that enemy fighters were spotted at 3:00 high headed straight for our plane. In the next instant, three single-seat German fighters were zooming around, hell bent on their hunt to zero in on our crippled B-17.

There was no time to avoid their concentrated attack. Flying at blazing speeds of 200 mph, the enemy FW-190s were quickly in my range of vision and I opened fire, rapidly exchanging shots, blasting my .50 caliber machine gun with great intensity. The firefight lasted only moments. Soon the fighters were spiraling out of sight – gone in a flash.

Within seconds and without notice, I saw a second wave of three fighters again attacking our plane from the rear. I saw the face of the pilot seated in the cockpit of the lead fighter plane coming directly at me, 20 mm bullets blazing from his wing guns. A shot came bursting through the plane's exterior, ripping deep into my leg, the explosion filling the tail compartment with thick black smoke...

ELEVEN TWO

ONE WWII AIRMAN'S STORY
OF CAPTURE, SURVIVAL AND FREEDOM

Chapter One

GROWING UP IN SMALL TOWN, USA

My story begins in the Oakhill section of North Versailles, Pennsylvania, a small town located ten miles east of Pittsburgh. My parents, George Kravetz and Susan Chalata, immigrated to America from the small village of Hermanevce in Slovakia, now officially known as Slovak Republic. George and Susan were married August 30, 1915, at St. Michael's Roman Catholic Church in Braddock, Pennsylvania.

World War I began in the summer of 1914 in the European countries. My oldest brother, George, was born February 28, 1917, and the United States entered the conflict by declaring war on Germany in April of that same year. Many young men joined the armed forces and were sent overseas to serve their country. Consequently, a labor shortage was created and the farming industry was hit particularly hard. Workers were needed to help the farmers sow and harvest their crops, so draft deferments were offered by the government in exchange for working on the farms. My father took advantage of this opportunity and was assigned to a farm in Minnesota. In early 1918 he took his wife, who was expecting again, and their young son, and together they moved west, far away from their home in Pennsylvania. It was while they were living in Minnesota that my brother, Mike, was born September 15, 1918.

After the war ended, the family returned to Oakhill and bought a home near the Westinghouse plant in East Pittsburgh where my father was able to return to his former job. My brother, John, was born January 27, 1920, and I, the fourth child, was born October 25, 1923, and named Francis Albert. When I was only 26 months old, on January 15, 1926, my mother died. Of course, I was not aware of what happened at that young age and did not find out for many years. In my memory, I honor her because she gave me life.

On November 26, 1926 my father married a woman named Susan Kollar, and they moved the family into a brand new house located at 110 Bessemer Avenue in East Pittsburgh, Pennsylvania. Even though I was just a small boy, I remember that the new house was large and clean, with lots of space. It had a huge bathroom upstairs and a bathroom in the basement. There was a spacious kitchen and a big dining room and living room. On the second floor, I shared a nice-sized bedroom with my three older brothers, George, John, and Mike. It was a comfortable place to call home. While my three older brothers were away at school, I spent the day amusing myself with small toy trucks and cars while my new mother kept a watchful eye on me. For all intents and purposes, she was the only mother I ever knew. I always felt a real sense of security with her and completely cared for by her. It all seemed to be enough and I was content.

It was an interesting time to be alive, or so it seemed to a young boy. The Pittsburgh Railway with its streetcars came right past our house, and I was fascinated by

Left to Right: George, Mike, John, Frank and their father George, Sr.

the low, rumbling sound that alerted all to the fact that a rail car was coming. As each car approached, I ran eagerly to the window to enjoy the sight and sound of this impressive machinery going right past our front window. It was also an era when milk was delivered to our doorstep by the Brown Dairy Company, and a horse-drawn wagon came every day with fresh-baked bread, cakes, and cookies.

Our family continued to grow with the births of Katherine, born May 7, 1928; Ed, born December 7, 1929; and Tom, January 20, 1932. There was also another person introduced to our household at that time, Anna Kollar. I didn't know who she was because it seemed like she just appeared at our home one day and began living with us. I found out much later that my mother had been working to save money to bring Anna, her daughter, to America from Europe where she had been living. Anna, born in 1912, was now old enough to find employment doing housework, so she worked for families in our area until she was able to gain employment at Westinghouse.

Soon it was my turn to start school, and I proudly ventured off into this new world, anticipating all that lay ahead for me in my little-boy life. My older brothers and I walked five blocks to Bessemer Avenue Grade School which housed grades one through eight. We went home every day to have lunch with Mom, a welcome break in my day. I liked going to school because there were so many opportunities for interaction with my peers and so much to learn and discover in my classes. I was a good student and I approached my classroom work with intensity and a desire to excel.

At home, when we had time to just be kids, we enjoyed playing the common childhood games together such as Hopscotch and Run, Sheep, Run. As we got older, there was a wooden basket erected on a telephone pole outside of our home where we gathered for a game of spirited basketball. We also played our own family version of baseball that used a rag ball and was played on any empty field we could find. There was much joy in the time we spent together, and we grew to realize that we were not only brothers, but also great pals.

Quite often, our family would load up the car with lots of delicious picnic food and spend the day at various parks in the area where we would run around playing and having a great time with each other. We also went to the school picnic that was held at Kennywood Park every year. One of the largest amusement parks in the United States at that time, Kennywood was a beautifully clean, sparkling place full of unlimited fun for us kids and for all ages who went to the park. The Westinghouse Company sponsored a whole day at Kennywood every year for their employees and families. It was such a big deal! We would bring a big basket full of food for a picnic and then spend the whole day enjoying the rides, swimming, eating ice cream and cotton candy – just playing. It was wonderful!

We didn't have much interaction with our extended family until one day we all had to get dressed in our good clothes. We got in the car and were told we were heading for Ohio to visit an uncle. I wasn't even sure what an uncle was! We were admonished to be on our best behavior; we couldn't run around and play because we might ruin our good clothes. Our destination was the home of Uncle Steve, my dad's brother; his wife, Aunt Sophie; and their daughter Mary who was my first and only cousin. They lived near several lakes and took us fishing with long bamboo fishing poles. It's a good thing Uncle Steve caught some fish, because we certainly didn't have the time to master his fishing skills. This visit was the first of many wonderful times that we spent with them through the years and the beginning of a great relationship.

Coinciding with school and family activities was our religious life that spilled over into every aspect of my youth. We attended St. Helen's Slovak Roman Catholic Church, the church home to the large Slovak population which had settled in the region to work the factories and steel mills. From my very earliest recollections, we all knew that our parents required us to attend all church functions. We understood, and there were no questions asked and no exceptions made. Essentially, if the doors were open, we were there.

It was mandatory that we attend catechism classes where we learned to pray in Slovak. It was rote memory type of learning. The teacher would say something in Slovak and we would repeat the words. We didn't understand what we were saying, but we could recite the prayers. It was short-lived though, because as we grew older and the catechism class was no longer required, the prayers in Slovak went by the wayside.

The church Holy Days were strictly observed, as well as the seasons of Lent, Easter, and Christmas. As a way of service within the church, I took part in May Day programs and Holy Day processions. I still recall the solemnity involved and the seriousness my participation required.

As a result of the importance my parents placed on our religious upbringing, religion and faith were very important to me and became a defining way of life. I developed a great reverence for the things of God, and I always remember that God made me to know Him, to love Him, to serve Him, and to be happy not only while in this world, but also forever with Him in the next.

The Stock Market crashed in 1929, and by 1932, when I was nine years old, over a quarter of the American work force was unemployed, my father among them. I recall that everybody was poor. In our home, the meals were meager, but we were fed and we were thankful. Items needed for existence and sustenance, such as flour and potatoes, were provided to families from government welfare-type distributions. My father planted a small garden in our backyard and worked and tilled it to produce food to add to our diet during those years. As well, both my parents were very good bakers. It seemed like there were always fresh baked products in our home such as bread, cakes, and pies.

My mother got hand-me-downs from other families and distributed the clothing to each of us to ensure that we had clothes that fit and were in reasonably good condition. Mother, in turn, gave clothing that we had outgrown to other families in need. Winters were very cold, and mother did all she could to make sure her family was warmly clothed.

Work was hard to come by, but eventually Dad got called in for a couple of days per week at the Westinghouse East Pittsburgh plant. He worked on punch presses that produced various components for many finished Westinghouse products. He would take sheared metal of all different shapes and sizes and punch holes out of them; these pieces were used in all kinds of electrical apparatus. My older brothers also found employment during this time working in grocery stores as stock boys or selling newspapers, and they were expected to contribute the income they earned to help support our family. Those were tough years for my parents, difficult years. They both worked hard to provide necessities for us and to make sure that we also had some special treats during that challenging time. Being a young child, I didn't fully grasp the severity of the times, but somehow I knew that everything would be all right.

Finally, the pronouncement came that the depression was over! I wasn't really sure what that meant, but I soon saw that life improved within our home.. Dad got called to work full time at Westinghouse, and my mother found employment working for the Dillworths, a wealthy family who had many luxuries, including their own chauffeur. They hired my mother to be a nanny to their children as well as a chambermaid of sorts.

It was during this time that Mother was exposed to the good things in life that her employers enjoyed, which she became accustomed to. Desiring them for her family, she diligently saved her earnings to buy many of them for us. She provided nice living room and dining room furniture, a china closet, real silverware, good dishes, and a chandelier. We also received new beds and mattresses, a new stove, an electric washing machine, an electric mangle for ironing clothes, an electric refrigerator, and a gas furnace. These were luxury items to us, and we were glad to have them. On special occasions – holidays and times like that – we would have dinner in the dining room, and my mother went all out by using the good china, silverware, and cloth napkins. Otherwise, we ate our meals in the kitchen.

I was about ten to twelve years old during this post depression time, and I recall that my brothers, George, John and Mike, were all working as butchers in local stores and driving delivery trucks part time until they got full time jobs working at Westinghouse. East Pittsburgh was bustling with businesses, and jobs were plentiful thanks to the Westinghouse Electric Company.

I was busy, too, as I had chores that I was responsible for around the house, including taking out the garbage and helping my mother with cleaning the house. One of those chores was sweeping soot from the porch and sidewalk. The soot from the local steel mills was so thick I had to clean it up by the shovelful.

A highlight on my list of chores came in the fall when my folks made homemade sauerkraut from sacks of cabbage bought in the Strip District in downtown Pittsburgh. My parents' part in the process was to prepare the cabbage by washing and shredding it. Then I was summoned to take my turn at stomping the cabbage. What a ritual it was to get this done!

I was required, first of all, to get a bath – and not just any bath, but a bath that ensured that I was literally scrubbed from head to toe. Behind the ears? Check. Between the toes? Check. After finally passing inspection, I then dressed in clean, white underwear, barefoot and ready for my task. I climbed onto a chair on top of a table and then jumped into a whiskey barrel full of freshly shredded cabbage. Thus began the stomping process which lasted about six hours. It seems to me that I must have been bribed with cookies, or money for candy and the movies to get me to do all that!

After I completed eight grades of school, it was time to go on to East Pittsburgh High School, which included grades nine through twelve. Our high school nickname was the Shamrocks, and our school colors were green and white. I can honestly say that those years were some of the best years of my life. I really enjoyed interacting with other students my own age who had the same interests, hopes, dreams, and youthful excitement trying to find their place in this world, like I was. During these transition years, I received no advice from my mother or father about which direction my life should take, what I should be thinking about for the future, or what career I should pursue.

My mother was a very intelligent person and could speak German, Hungarian, Slovak, and perfect English. She wanted me to do well in high school, so she always saw to it that I did my homework. As a result, I was an above average student. For the most part, I chose the academic courses for my curriculum, and I especially liked the math and science courses, including physics and chemistry, and received good grades in those classes. I also enjoyed the language, literature, and poetry classes. Along with these courses I took woodworking and shop classes, which later proved to be helpful and rewarding.

Besides my schoolwork, I got involved in extracurricular activities that kept me busy. I participated in all of the intramural sports that were available – softball, baseball, and swimming. I never played any varsity sports, but not because I didn't want to. My older brother, Mickey, broke his arm while playing varsity basketball, and the medical expenses incurred due to that injury were too much of a burden on the family budget, so I wasn't permitted to play varsity sports. I was selected to be a member of the glee club, so I must have had a decent voice – I sang baritone. I also joined the camera club, and worked on the stage crew where I really enjoyed working with wood and building the stage sets for the school musicals and plays. Each year, a special gymnasium dance, prom and hops were held for each class. I always attended these events and had a lot of fun at them.

I also ventured out into the work world during my high school years. One of my first jobs was working for O'Hara's Gas Station after school and on Saturdays. I enjoyed this job because I loved cars. I was a "grease monkey" and my job description was quite broad – pump gas, fix flat tires, change the oil, put the cars up on the racks – everything that involved getting dirty, but I thoroughly enjoyed it. It was exciting to experience driving the different cars that came into the station for repairs, so the job wasn't really like work at all. Plus an added bonus was that I got out of doing chores at the house – what a great thing that was!

Perhaps one of the reasons why the job was such a good trade-off was that I didn't have to clean the chicken coop anymore! Before I was a "working man", I would have to take turns with my brothers doing this most disdainful chore. It required "shooing" the chickens all to one side of the coop while shoveling out the droppings from that side (or whitewashing that side of the walls of the coop) and then "shooing" the chickens back to the other side and repeating the process. As I recall, the chickens weren't any happier with the arrangement than I was.

I completed my junior year of high school in the summer of 1940. That summer I saw a notice in the Pittsburgh Press newspaper that the University of Pittsburgh was offering a tuition-free Engineering Program through the Department of Defense. I applied to the program and was accepted. I also applied at that time to the Westinghouse Electric Corporation Trades Training Program to be an Apprentice Machinist.

The day after Labor Day, 1940, I started my senior year at East Pittsburgh High School. I had taken extra courses during my junior year and was planning to double up again, hoping to earn enough credits to meet my graduation requirements early. I was also looking forward to enjoying everything about high school – like football games, senior hop, dating, meeting "TC girls" (Turtle Creek) and having some of the best times of my life.

October 16, 1940, was the day 17 million men aged 21-35 were required to register for the Draft. Once registered, men received a number that was then used in a lottery type system where numbered pills were put in a container and drawn randomly by the draft board. These proceedings didn't mean a lot to me since my older brother George was married and probably would not be called to serve. My brothers Mickey and John were waiting to receive notice from the draft board to find out when they might be inducted. There was no talk of war at this time. I was waiting to hear if I got accepted to the Westinghouse Trade Training course. Life was good, full of hopes and plans for the future.

After completing midyear exams, I learned that I was finished with my senior year in December, 1940. I had completed enough credits and wasn't required to attend any classes after the Christmas break. So, after the start of the New Year, I continued to work at O'Hara's gas station and was able to add more hours. A few hundred dollars could buy a pretty good used car at the time, and I was hoping to make enough to buy one. I graduated with the rest of my class from East Pittsburgh High School on June, 6, 1941, at 17 years of age. I was happy and proud of my accomplishments and achievements, and must admit that my high school years had passed by quickly and very enjoyably.

Frank's High School Graduation

The summer of my graduation year was a "Summer of Fun." It was a carefree time filled with the joys of being a teenager – no school for the time being, some extra cash in the pocket, lots of friends, and plenty of good times. I admit that I was interested in wooing the opposite sex, and I worked hard at it. I shopped for neat, fashionable, dressy clothes in order to put my best foot forward – and I succeeded. I had a camel hair coat that was beautiful, and I looked pretty good in it, even if I do say so myself! I wore that coat when I drove vehicles for O'Hara's gas station to transport folks to Lanigan's Funeral Home in East Pittsburgh for funeral visitations. Behind the wheel of a big Buick, I would drive through town wearing my Sunday best – a dapper suit and my camel coat – tooting the horn at all the girls I passed – big stuff!

The movies were a big deal back then with the glamour of the Hollywood stars of the 1940s and the big production movies they made. Among my favorites were "Gone with the Wind," "Stage Coach," "From Here to Eternity," all of Mickey Rooney's movies, and any movie about airplanes! Of course, we guys were always hoping to have a special girl to take to the movies, or to dinner and a dance, or to see a live stage show, or a band performance, or maybe spend the day picnicking. And speaking of special girls...

During those magical days spent in a small town, filled with friendship and fun, I would often jump on my bicycle and head out for adventure. My friends, Al Cinna and Jim Seese, liked to go to the local roller skating rink, where I quickly discovered that I didn't enjoy roller skating. What I did enjoy was meeting lots of kids my age from other neighborhoods. Meetings led to friendships and soon, we were attending dances that took place on top of the bank building in Turtle Creek and at St. Williams. We would also all get together at each other's houses to listen to music and just hang out.

There was one particular house party that stands out in my memory. I found myself participating in the ever-popular social activities commonly known as *Spin the Bottle* and *Post Office*, and it was there that I first met a beautiful, dark-haired, special young lady with a sparkle in her eyes. Her name was Anne Cerjanic and she attended Turtle Creek High School. Meeting Anne made my heart skip a beat – life just didn't get any better! It was full of innocence, wonderful friends, good times, and summer romance.

Also during the summer of 1941, I was attending the University of Pittsburgh's Engineering Program. Classes started at eight o'clock each morning, Monday through Friday, and finished at four in the afternoon. The curriculum consisted of shop engineering, engineering drawing, and other introductory classes. I was hoping to get a job at Westinghouse, but had to wait until my 18th birthday in October before I would finally be old enough to apply. In addition to my classes, I started working for a Chrysler/Plymouth auto dealership in Wilkinsburg after responding to an ad in the paper that they wanted a "flunky" to work around the shop. My job was to help repair cars, and I really liked the work.

My friends and I continued to enjoy a carefree, happy-go-lucky life, not concerned about anything in the newspapers regarding world affairs. There were no storm clouds gathering on the horizon yet or any talk about the United States getting involved in the war going on in Europe.

At the end of summer, in August 1941, I graduated from the University of Pittsburgh's Engineering program. During this time, my brother Mickey who had been working for Westinghouse received his draft notice. The military service requirement at that time was supposed to be only one year, so Mickey and many other young men left on August 15, 1941, thinking they would be home in a year. I remember hearing people say, "Good-bye dear, I'll be back in a year," and the song, "You're in the Army now, you'll never get rich, you son-of-a-bitch, you're in the Army now!" was heard everywhere. A large crowd was at the East Pittsburgh train station to see the men off, the high school band played, and there were a lot of tears shed by mothers, fathers, wives and other friends and relatives. In the months to follow, this scene would be repeated often.

I received a call from Westinghouse in October 1941, shortly after my 18th birthday, notifying me that I had successfully passed the entrance exam and was accepted into the apprentice trade training program. It was a two-year program consisting of classroom training and machine shop training. Everyone at home was glad about my opportunities for work. All the older folks said that working for Westinghouse was a good deal, including John Cerjanic, my friend Anne's father. John was already employed at Westinghouse Electric as a builder of large motors. He encouraged me to be an apprentice because the mindset of that time was that apprentices always got the better jobs down the road. So, I began my apprenticeship on Thursday, December 4, 1941.

Chapter Two

PEARL HARBOR –
ENTERING THE MILITARY

Three days later on Sunday, December 7, 1941, the Japanese Empire attacked Pearl Harbor. At home, we were visiting with my brother, Mickey, who was on a weekend pass from his duty station at Fort Eustis Army Base in Virginia. We were sitting at the dining room table eating Sunday dinner and listening to the radio when we heard President Franklin D. Roosevelt boldly state that the United States of America had declared war on Germany, Japan, and Italy. Mickey then learned that all military personnel were ordered back to their duty base immediately, and the declaration of war became a reality in our family. Worry and sadness overwhelmed us all, and we began to cry because we knew that Mickey would now be in for the duration of the war instead of the one-year requirement that we had expected.

Things changed quickly. People everywhere were sad and frightened as the news that our country was at war became more of a reality. As we all listened attentively to the radio and carefully read the newspapers, we began to understand that many of our young men would have to go to war. The bombing of Pearl Harbor was an event that was going to affect all of our lives in many different and important ways. We had studied about Hawaii in school, but at the time, of course, we had no idea where a place called Pearl Harbor was or what it would mean in our lives. Little did we know that during the next five years everyone would be experiencing a geography lesson about the whole world.

In early February of 1942, my brother, John, took his girlfriend Agnes Dudash from Duquesne, Pennsylvania, to a theater in downtown Pittsburgh to see a popular movie at the time, "From the Halls of Montezuma." It showed the Marine Corps in action, and Johnny joined the next day. He was now the second son from our family to be going to war. After receiving his basic training in the United States, he was sent overseas to New Zealand for jungle training in preparation for combat in the South Pacific. As a Marine, John made landings on several beaches, including Bougainville, Munda, Tarawa, and also fought in other war zones. When he came home from overseas, he was sent to Walter Reed Hospital in Washington, DC, for medical treatment.

My oldest brother George wanted to enlist in the Army, but was given a medical deferment from military service because of a heart condition. He and his wife, Myra, were living in a small apartment in East Pittsburgh at the time, and Myra gave birth to the first grandchild in the Kravetz family on June 16, 1942. They named him Henry, but we all called him Henny.

When John went into the Marines, he put his car, a 1937 Plymouth, into my care. All of Mickey's and John's suits, sport coats, gabardine slacks, and shoes were left for me to use, and everything fit me perfectly. In the summer of 1942, I was the best dressed dude on The Terrace, the local name given to the top section of East Pittsburgh where we lived.

Frank wearing his favorite camel hair coat

By this time, many of my friends and classmates and neighborhood buddies from Bessemer Terrace had enlisted or been drafted into one branch of the service or another. I began to think seriously that I, too, should be helping with the war effort. I starting dropping hints to my parents about my desire to enlist in the Army Air Corps, and in January, 1943, I went to the US Army Air Corps enlistment headquarters at the downtown post office in Pittsburgh.

The war was hot and heavy now, and each man's draft status was reviewed yearly. I really believed that Uncle Sam was not going to grant me another deferment. The draft process was very confusing for my parents, and they didn't understand that I was likely to be drafted when I turned 18 in October of 1942. My thought was that if I was going to be in the service, I wanted to choose which one. So, I prepared all the paperwork necessary and applied for admission to the Army Air Corps Aviation Cadet Program. Other guys felt the same way and were joining the Navy or the Marines so they would have a say in where they served.

I brought papers home for my parents to sign giving me permission to join, but they refused. They said it was out of the question. As far as they were concerned, they already had two sons serving, and they would not sign for another son to go off to war.

In fact, Pap, my father, made *sure* I wasn't going to go in the service by going to the draft board and requesting that I be given a deferment from the military. This would allow me to contribute to the family income by working and attending school instead of going off to war. My parents still had three little ones at home to care for – my brothers, Ed and Tom, my sister Katherine, plus my stepsister Anna. The deferment would also allow me to finish the training for my trade as a machinist which consisted of two six-month courses of study. Because of my apprenticeship program, I was classified 1-A until June of 1943 when my occupational deferment would expire. So for now, I gave up the idea of enlisting in the service any time soon, and I continued with my school work and apprenticeship at Westinghouse.

My dream was to be in the Army Air Corps flying program. And, I have to admit, that the thought of maybe someday being able to fly an airplane, well… that was enough to keep me going. At this point, nothing else compared to the thought of flying someday.

As a young boy I was fascinated with airplanes, always looking in the air when I heard the sound of approaching aircraft. One of my favorite hobbies was making model airplanes. I purchased kits containing balsa wood, tissue paper, a propeller, and a rubber band. I would cut out the parts of the plane with a razor blade, glue them together to make the body and wings, and cover them with the tissue paper. Using the rubber band to power the propeller, I would launch it off our back porch, and what a great satisfaction it was to see it fly! I was always trying to find a way to go to an airport so I could watch the planes. I remember going to the Bettis Airport in West Mifflin, Pennsylvania to see small planes taking off and landing, but the first large plane I saw was at the old Allegheny County Airport when a Trans Continental Western Airlines DC-3 landed there. Thousands of people came to see this huge plane, and it was a great thrill for me. I wondered if I would ever be able to fly.

Also during this time, I was dating Anne Cerjanic more often. We went to dances, movies picnics, parties, and baseball games. She graduated from Turtle Creek High School in June, 1943, and went to work at the National Biscuit Company in East Liberty, Pennsylvania. She made many friends at work, and she and I shared many good times with them. In July of 1943, the United States Army Air Corps recruiting office in Pittsburgh sent me a letter explaining that now that I was over 18 years of age, I did not need parental authorization to join the service. I asked to be allowed to take the Air Corps exams, and since they already had my preliminary paperwork on file, I was ordered to report to the old post office building recruiting station in Pittsburgh to take the necessary exams and screening test for entry into the Air Corps program. I also needed three letters of recommendation, so I requested one from Judge Samuel Weiss; one from my Westinghouse Trades Apprentice School Supervisor, S.J. Dearbeck; and one from the East Pittsburgh School District Supervisor, Charles F. Young.

Frank and Anne – happy teenagers

WESTINGHOUSE
ELECTRIC & MANUFACTURING COMPANY

EAST PITTSBURGH, PA.

September 13, 1943

To Whom This May Concern:

Mr. Frank Albert Aravata is a Machine Tool Operator student in our Trades Apprentice School. He was placed on our training course on December 8, 1941.

Previous to his entrance on our training course, this young man was graduated from the college preparatory course of East Pittsburgh High School, East Pittsburgh, Pennsylvania on June 5, 1941.

While serving his apprenticeship with our Company, he attended our Apprentice School four hours weekly where he received training in related mathematics, machine shop analysis, and blueprint reading. He also correlated this training course by completing several National Defense courses given under the auspices of the University of Pittsburgh, namely: Essentials of Engineering, and Drawing and Drafting.

His shop experience consisted of the operation of a drill press, milling machine, engine lathe, and vertical sidehead boring mill, working on actual production work to blueprint specifications and details.

In both his school and shop work, he was classed as an average student. His honesty, reliability, and character are beyond reproach.

Very truly yours,

S. J. Dexreed, Supervisor
Trades Training Department

D:r

WESTINGHOUSE—THE NAME THAT MEANS EVERYTHING IN ELECTRICITY

As I arrived at the test site, I was very nervous. An Air Corps Captain wearing a pair of silver wings greeted all who were gathered there to take the test. I had no idea how well I did, but I answered most of the questions and finished about three o'clock in the afternoon. My desire to pass was very intense – I wanted a pair of Silver Wings! If I failed, my dreams of flying would be shattered. Before too long I received notification that I had passed the written test and now needed to report for a physical exam, a standard doctor's office physical which checked height, weight, eyes, ears, nose, throat, etc. I passed this exam with flying colors, except that I was overweight by five pounds.

It was football season and so I went down to the Quarry, East Pittsburgh High School's football field, and began working out with the football team. I knew all of the kids from the class behind me, so I just joined them in throwing footballs, running drills, and everything else they were doing to get in shape. It took me about two weeks to get under the weight limit of 180 pounds, and then I qualified for the Aviation Cadet Program. I was going to be part of the Air Corps which meant that I was going to be taking more tests to qualify for flying. My dream was becoming a reality – I was going to *fly!*

At this point, my parents didn't know that I had enlisted. I was waiting until the last possible minute to tell them, but all of my exercising and cutting back on eating was causing a lot of questions. I finally broke the news to them by simply saying, "I'm going into the Air Corps." That was it. I told them that joining the Air Corps was what I really wanted, that the paperwork was completed, that I had been accepted, and that now I was just waiting to be called. I emphasized that there was nothing they could do and that they couldn't apply for another deferment. I don't think they were happy with the whole thing, and they didn't talk about it much. Looking back, I know they felt bad for me and only wanted to protect me. I'm sure it was hard for them to send another son off to war, and I know their prayers helped to bring me back home.

The completion of my apprenticeship program conveniently coincided with my call up to service. I received the notice of acceptance on September 24, 1943, with orders to report on November 2. At home with his family in East Pittsburgh, George was the only one of my older brothers that I could notify that I was going. We hadn't seen Mickey or John since just before they went overseas.

After I informed Westinghouse of my plans, the guys in the shop went out of their way to wish me well, and along with my foreman, had a little party for me. The reality of what I was about to do was beginning to kick in and I was very enthusiastic.

When the time came for me to leave home, I decided it would be better if I said good-bye to my family at home instead of at the train station. So I hugged and kissed my mother, father, sisters Anna and Katherine, younger brothers Eddie and Tommy, said my good-byes and that was it – I was off to war.

Anne and I had been going out together quite a bit at this point, and seeing each other even more often as the time approached for me to go into the service. I shared my excitement with her about wanting to go, and she understood because all of the guys from our circle of friends were either already gone or going soon. I wanted Anne to be the one to take me to the Baltimore and Ohio Rail Road station in Pittsburgh, so her dad let her use their car. My destination was Greensboro, North Carolina, Army Air Corps Base, and I wanted to be alone with my girlfriend before I had to leave. I was 19 years old and Anne was 16. As we said good-bye to each other, I knew that I had to come back.

NOVEMBER 2ᴺᴰ, 1943

FRANK LEAVES HOME TO BEGIN MILITARY TRAINING

Chapter Three

INTO THE WILD BLUE YONDER –
FLIGHT TRAINING

November 2, 1943, was the day I left to begin my training with the United States Army Air Corps. I boarded the Baltimore and Ohio Rail Road train in Pittsburgh, Pennsylvania, and headed for Greensboro, North Carolina. There were servicemen travelling in the car with me who were going to other bases. They were already wearing their Army issued uniforms. I was still in civilian clothes. As we talked, I told them that I was going to Greensboro because I had enlisted in the U.S. Army Air Corps Cadet Program and that was pretty much all the conversation that there was. They wished me good luck.

In Washington, D.C., I changed to the Atlantic Coastline Rail Road. Once aboard, a uniformed porter showed me to a Pullman car and said that he would return to take me to the dining car for dinner. Sure enough, when it came time for dinner, he came to escort me to the dining car. I enjoyed a good meal, and then he took me back to the Pullman car where he had made my bed. Since it was already dark, he showed me how to contact him if I needed anything and then said good night. Pretty snazzy, I thought. I realized I was travelling first class, and I was beginning to like the Army Air Corps. Tired from the emotions and excitement of the day, I was soon asleep and slept well all night.

The next morning, shortly after breakfast, the train pulled into the station at Greensboro, North Carolina. I travelled to the Army Base where I was greeted along with a group of other new recruits. We were told that we were "in the Air Corps now" and were then fitted for our basic training uniforms. We went through orientation and were given our new mailing addresses. There were phones available for all of us to call our families to let them know we had arrived safely.

For the next two months my address was:
PAC (Pre-Aviation Cadet) Frank A. Kravetz
Army Air Corps Base
301ˢᵗ Wing B.T.C. (Basic Training Center)
Greensboro, North Carolina

The Air Corps didn't waste any time getting down to business. Our Basic Pre-Aviation Cadet Training started immediately and consisted of three parts.

Part one was military orientation where we were given a basic introduction to Army life and the Air Corps, including rules and regulations. We learned the reasons for and the methods of discipline, the proper way to salute and stand at attention, and the correct wear and care of our uniforms which included polishing our shoes and shining the brass buttons on our jackets. I was very proud to put on my uniform for the first time and also very glad about my five pound weight loss.

We were also taught to march, and I found that to be really enjoyable. As we marched we sang cadence songs, and I felt like I was part of something – and I was. I fit right in and it felt good. We went on some pretty long marches, but nothing like the infantry guys were required to do.

Then there was my introduction to the rifle range. I liked learning to use a rifle, but, since we would be carrying side arms and firing fifty caliber machine guns and dropping bombs in combat instead of using rifles, we only received basic training on them.

We also had to do guard duty and kitchen patrol. I didn't like guard duty – being out there by myself. At least in the kitchen doing KP there was a chance to get some grub every once in a while – maybe an apple or an orange. As far as any training for situations we might face in the war such as bailing out of a damaged aircraft, the only preparation we received was done by instructors who taught only the basics by showing us films.

Part two was physical fitness which required twice-a-day participation in an intense program of calisthenics, jogging, sports, etc. I was in good shape then. In fact, I was down to 160 pounds. I would even go so far as to say I was in "tip-top" shape.

Part three was the Nashville tests which checked each person to make sure he fulfilled all the requirements necessary to become an air crew member. We were scrutinized physically (eyes – 20/20 vision required and no color blindness allowed, teeth – no cavities allowed, motor skills, endurance, depth perception, etc.); tested in mathematics, geography, and map reading skills; and we were also given psychological tests. I wasn't worried about any of these tests, and I did very well on all of them.

I found everything to be interesting about the training. Learning about what I would be doing was exciting, and the progression of learning, and then building on that learning was very stimulating. Of course, talking about flying was the best.

The only boot camp friend that I recall was another trainee named Sam Kasoy from Philadelphia. There wasn't a lot of time to just hang out, but on the rare occasion when we were given a pass, there were shows to see on the base, or we were allowed to go into town.

Sometimes the wait would be three or four hours to get a phone to call home. There were only so many banks of phones to go around for the many servicemen anxious to make calls. I would go to place a call and see how long the line was. There was often a chalkboard there saying that from this point there would be an hour wait to use the phone. It was a time-consuming process. The best thing to do was to write letters to let everyone know what was happening. There were a lot of people writing to me, and so I wrote a lot of letters back to them. Anne wrote often and so did some of her friends that we pal'ed around with. My brother John, who was already in the Pacific fighting with the Marines, my brother George and his wife, Myra, my brother Mickey, and my sister Katherine wrote to me, but my younger brothers, Eddy and Tommy, didn't write because they were just too young.

There was no graduation ceremony after basic training was over. They just posted announcements on the bulletin board showing the results from all the tests we had taken. Even though we had finished our basic training, they continued to show us more training films. We also kept up our marching and physical training and even played some baseball. All of this was designed to keep us occupied while we were waiting to see where we would be going.

When the time came for the review of my time in basic, it turns out I did so well on all of the training that I was selected to go to Syracuse University in New York to get one more year of college credits. (I was given one year of credits for the University of Pittsburgh Engineering Program and I needed two years of college to join the Cadets.) I passed all of the tests, then waited and waited for the orders to come through. When they finally came, I wasn't on the list to go to Syracuse. Instead, I was on the list to go to Kingman, Arizona, to Aerial Gunnery School. I was very disappointed at that turn of events, but I said to myself, "Well, maybe after I go to gunnery school I can reapply for cadet training where I can go on to be a pilot, bombardier or navigator."

I spent Christmas of 1943 at the base waiting to be sent to Arizona – and that was kind of sad because I was thinking of home a lot. The base provided a good Christmas dinner with turkey and stuffing and all the trimmings and also had chapel services available. Shortly after Christmas in early January, 1944, I left for Kingman, Arizona. I traveled by train from North Carolina to Mobile, Alabama, and then across the lower tier of the United States. The train was what was referred to as a real, old fashioned "troop train," and we were literally jammed into the cars and leaning out of the windows. There was certainly no Pullman sleeping experience on this journey. This time it was just sleeping wherever I could – in my seat, in the aisles – whatever spot was available.

My trip took six or seven days because the train stopped many times in many cities. Travelers on this train were going everywhere, being picked up or dropped off at all kinds of different spots along the way. Every type of soldier, from airmen to tank drivers and everything in between, whose specialty was useful for wartime service was being dispatched at this time and using this train. All of the branches – Army Air Corps,

Army, Marines, and Navy – were represented. Sometimes there would be a whole carload of a particular branch or division of men all going to the same place, and so the train would pull off the main track to add or remove cars.

I remember that as we approached a town we would open the windows. Many people would come to the station to greet us, and we would all wave to the townspeople outside. At every stop we could get off and stretch our legs. There were always people with simple ham, cheese, and mustard sandwiches wrapped in wax paper ready for us. They would also have drinks and sometimes apples, oranges, or other fruit. The USO or other groups would hand out cigarettes, candy bars, donuts, and cookies and we appreciated their generosity.

I hadn't been to the south before, so I didn't have any opinions or thoughts about that part of the country. I remember seeing the cotton fields, and we were told there were a lot of tobacco fields, too. When we got into Oklahoma we started seeing cattle ranches and oil wells, and a lot of us guys thought, "This is the Wild, Wild West!" It sure was the wide open spaces we had heard about – nothing but a clear, flat view for miles and miles. I was happy to be passing through, getting to see more of our country, but we were all anxious to get where we were going, even though we didn't know what it would be like.

When the U.S. declared war on Germany, the B-17 aircraft, along with the rest of the family of war planes, was needed immediately on both war fronts. In May of 1942, the Army Air Corps authorized construction of a gunnery school in Kingman, Arizona, to prepare gunners, pilots, and copilots for battles in the air. By war's end, 35,000 cadets had earned certificates there.

Just prior to the arrival of my cadet class in Kingman, an entire class of new cadets was killed. On January 6, 1944, a bus loaded with gunnery students bound for the base crossed the railroad tracks just north of the entrance. The driver did not see the oncoming train, and when train and bus collided, twenty-eight students died.

Frank proudly wearing his uniform

As our train finally arrived in Kingman, we found the town to be just a whistle-stop out in the desert. That's all it was. There was no big train station, just a little shed. There were some Native Americans around the area, but that was it. It wasn't very populated at all. The military really put us out there for a training spot! But the truth was we needed this type of wide-open area for flying and training purposes.

We were finally at the base, and it was time to get to work. We were there to attend Gunnery School and learn how to operate the .50 caliber machine guns that would be fired from our positions on the B-17. But before getting to the .50 caliber guns, we first had to qualify with smaller weapons like shotguns for skeet, .30 caliber infantry rifles, and .45 caliber pistols.

The skeet shooting was a lot of fun and very challenging. It involved firing shotguns at clay pigeons which had been thrown into the air. Sometimes we would be standing on the ground while we were shooting and sometimes we would be in the back of a moving truck. The clay pigeons would be coming out of hidden areas. They were on the move, and so were we in the back of the truck, making it true moving target practice. We really enjoyed it.

Then I went to the firing range where I got my first opportunity to fire a .50 caliber machine gun. The first time I shot a .50 caliber gun I thought it was a cannon! It was very explosive and strong. We were instructed to shoot little, short bursts of gunfire, "Brrt, brrt." A short burst fired a lot of bullets. The weapon had to be held very securely because it sat on a post that swiveled, and the gun could pivot around and shoot the shooter. In fact, we were required to have somebody with us when we were firing to make sure we didn't have a runaway gun. Sometimes the instructors had to push a guy out of the way for safety. They were always saying, "If you don't have control of it, don't touch the trigger, just drop it!" We had live rounds in the weapons from the very beginning.

The next step after learning to shoot the .50 calibers was learning how to take them apart to clean, repair, and maintain them. We also had aircraft recognition drills, which required us to identify planes by looking at silhouettes of them in the classroom. We had to be able to identify both our aircraft and the enemy's aircraft. In addition, there were classes to learn all about the B-17 aircraft. As I sat in the classroom learning about the Flying Fortress, I became more anxious than ever for my first flight on a B-17.

Before we could actually fly, we had training in decompression chambers to prepare us for flying at high altitudes. In these chambers, the air was slowly decreased to see how long we could be without oxygen at high altitudes before passing out. It was at this time in my training that I first learned about a weird, very painful, cramping, hard-to-describe feeling called 'the bends'. There were always two people in the chamber at a time so if one person got in trouble, the other could grab an oxygen mask and put it on the one in pain.

When I finally saw the B-17, it was love at first sight. I thought it was a huge, majestic, flying machine. It wasn't long before I had my first flight, and it was well worth all the anticipation and waiting. I wasn't disappointed at all. Our training took us up in the Fabulous Flying Fortress, as it was called, going on many different types of flights, some long, some short.

During our time in Kingman, we flew to Las Vegas once, because there was a gunnery school up there, too. But just like Kingman, it was very sparse and barren. We touched down in Las Vegas to refuel and then returned to our base. It's amazing when I think about what Las Vegas is like now versus back then. Then it was a desolate place with a few small casinos and many Native Americans in town. Now Las Vegas is a major resort destination – a booming multi-billion dollar venture.

Morale was always an issue among a large group of young men miles from home, many for the first time, and no place to go with their weekend passes but the tiny desert town of Kingman. Enter Bob Hope and others, such as the Three Stooges and Kay Kaiser with his orchestra, to the rescue. The USO-organized shows certainly went a long way to keep the men relaxed and prepared for the war effort. Bugs Bunny was there, too.

With sanction from Warner Brothers, Bugs was adopted as the official base mascot. The poster of Bugs with a fierce countenance and armed to the teeth for war was displayed in the most prominent location on the base.

Once our training was completed at Kingman, there were ceremonies on base to commemorate the occasion. It was only for us trainees, no family or anyone else in attendance but us guys. The remote location would have made it difficult for families to attend, even if it had been allowed. I don't know the exact day that I received my "wings," but on that day I proudly put on my dress uniform for the awarding of that coveted pin. Part of the ceremony was to walk up on stage and receive a little diploma which featured a cartoon picture of Bugs Bunny in the cockpit flying an airplane. Then wings were pinned on our uniforms. A lot of hard work had gone into earning those wings. I had a right to be proud of my accomplishment. I was very happy that I was now an Airman and very proud that I had earned my wings. Getting our wings also meant that we would be going home for a ten day furlough before we would have to report for our next assignment. The celebration after the ceremony was simple enough. We just all stayed on the base and went to the NCO (Non-Commissioned Officers) club to enjoy a few beers and movies. They brought in bus loads of girls for entertainment and dancing which was a nice way to unwind and celebrate our accomplishments. Kingman was not to be the end of my training and I knew that. But, at the moment, my thoughts were on the furlough ahead. Ten days to be at home.

When I came back home, there weren't very many of my friends around. We were all scattered across the country being

Frank enjoying his time at home on furlough

trained to enter the war effort. I did meet up with some other guys from my hometown who were also home on furlough, and we all went on double dates. I was with Anne and we went to movies, jukebox dances and out to dinner. Anne had been sending me letters, notes, and gift packages which, of course, I enjoyed receiving. She sent cookies from National Biscuit where she was working at the time, and small personal items like toothpaste or gum. I sent her a vanity set with a mirror, brush, comb, and tray. To this day, that set still sits on our bedroom dresser. Anne has cherished it for many years. For me, my relationship with Anne became a driving force in my life. It gave me something, and more importantly, someone to come back to. Anne became my pinup girl and I treasured the beautiful picture of her wearing a sweater that I always kept with me.

I was back home eating home-cooked meals but I didn't request anything in particular – all of the meals were special and delicious! I used the time to catch up on my sleep, and I sure didn't keep up with my physical fitness routine while at home! It was enjoyable having time to just visit with my family, to be home again and enjoy all that goes with that.

Before my furlough ended I received train tickets, travel expenses, and orders to report to MacDill Army Air Force Base in Tampa, Florida. Once again I left Pittsburgh by train, this time taking the Pennsylvania Railroad to Washington, D.C., and from Washington, D.C., I boarded the Southern Railways "Silver Meteor" – a streamlined train. That was something brand new in those days. Not a big iron horse, but rather a sleek, modern, classy design. My travel from Pennsylvania to Florida took a couple of days. Before we actually reached MacDill, they put us up in a stadium at the University of Tampa as our "home away from home." The Cincinnati Reds baseball team held their spring training in this area.

We were on our own here for a while. It was my first trip to Florida, and I quickly discovered that I liked the warm climate and surroundings very much. They had set up portable showers, but essentially, we were living and sleeping under the bleachers of the stadium. I thought that was pretty neat. It was so nice being in Florida in March; the weather was warm and pleasant, and the nights were so balmy I was sleeping in my skivvies – we didn't need air conditioning. I remember thinking, "This is nice down here, and up in Pittsburgh, they're freezing right now." We were wearing our summer khaki uniforms and had plenty of time for leisure activities. There were no worries at this time about marches or classes or anything structured like that. We were all just taking life easy, playing softball, golf, and pretty much doing whatever we wanted. There was a building on the football field that they used to cook and prepare all of the chow we ate while there. We weren't allowed any furloughs or weekend passes during that time, because we were going to be assigned to an aircrew any day. We were in a holding pattern until the assignment took place. Every day I would look at the bulletin board, and the other guys and I would say, "OK, nothin' up there today." If a guy's name was posted for a crew assignment, they would give him time to get his stuff together.

My future crew mate, Bill Rhodes, and his wife, Ruthie, were living in town at the time. They were both golfers and I got together with them to play some golf. We played at a private golf course called Palma Ceia Golf and Country Club. When

Frank with Bill and Ruth Rhodes at the Palma Ceia Country Club

we would arrive at the club, the staff would say to us, "Just go up on the porch and take any bag of clubs you want, get some golf balls, and go out and play golf for free." I had played a little golf before I got to Florida, but not much at all. My brother, Johnny, was a very good golfer, and so was my brother, Mickey. I guess I kind of followed in their footsteps with an interest in golfing. A long time after the war was over, I remember speaking with someone and telling them that while in the service I played at the Palma Ceia country club. He said to me, "You couldn't afford to play at the club today, because the price is $400.00 per round of golf!" It was an opportunity of a lifetime to play there absolutely free, since the club has become quite exclusive in the years since my training.

Soon enough we were on our way from our temporary Florida quarters and on to MacDill Field. MacDill Army Air Base is located eight miles south of downtown Tampa. It was activated in 1941 for the purpose of training World War II airmen on B-17 and B-26 aircraft. Following the Japanese attack on Pearl Harbor, MacDill became a major staging area for Army

Air corps flight crews and aircraft. The number of crew members trained at the base varied from 50,000 to 120,000. MacDill served as a detention center for German prisoners of war in the latter part of 1944-45. At its height, 488 German POWs were interned at MacDill.

When we did arrive at MacDill Field my first impression was that it was huge. There were a lot of planes on the base, most of them B-17s, because that is what we were there for – to train on the B-17. I had flown in B-17s in Gunnery School in Kingman, Arizona so this wasn't my first time around the block with these aircraft.

We were now housed in barracks, not sleeping under the stars this time. Enlisted men stayed together and the officers had their BOQ (Bachelors Officers Quarters) which were a little fancier. They had their own individual rooms and we had a dormitory style arrangement. The married men lived off base in rented houses or apartments. If they did decide to stay on base it would be mostly because they'd have to get up for a really early flight in the morning.

Finally, the day came when I was assigned to a B-17 Flying Fortress Crew. This was when I met the rest of my crew, having already met Staff Sgt. Bill Rhodes; Waist Gunner, while in Tampa. The fellas I met were our Pilot, Lt. Kenneth Guptill; Copilot Lt. George Keller; Navigator, Lt. Edmond McNamara; Top Turret Engineer, Staff Sgt. Harry Connors; Radio Operator, Staff Sgt. Virgil Smallen; Waist Gunner, Staff Sgt. John Simmen; Bombardier, Ball Turret, Staff Sgt. Herb Brayman; and Bombardier, Lt. Thomas Dunn. I rounded out the crew as the Right Waist Gunner and held the rank of Staff Sgt.

Other crews that were being formed were meeting their crew mates for the first time right alongside of us. It was an orientation opportunity for lots of airmen. There was a lot of informal discussion among us asking questions like, "Where are you from?" and "What did you do back home?" and other similar questions to help us get acquainted with each other. And, of course, we discovered that we were all from different places across the country. My crew hailed from as far west as Oregon and as far east as Massachusetts and several states in between. To this day, I can still remember where they were from. In my mind I can go back to that first meeting and hear them tell me about their hometowns.

I would find out later that individual crew members were purposely selected from cities and towns all across the country for a reason. It was to prevent the inevitable heartache of having too many young men from one location being on a downed aircraft together – they knew many young men would be killed or missing in action.

Three of the guys, Kenneth Guptill, Herb Brayman and Bill Rhodes were there with their wives. The camaraderie among the crew was great. We all got along really well, and I felt really good about being part of a crew.

Then it was time for more classroom work. I had to accompany the flight engineer to all of his classes learning all about the B-17. I was essentially the assistant flight engineer. This was in addition to my waist gunner assignment. I was really into it – all of the training and being on a crew. I felt important and felt proud of what I was doing. Our crew was real compatible and competent.

Every day was busy, filled with different requirements for the crew. There was no time for anything else except getting down to business. We learned all about flying. Once we started to actually fly together as a crew, we all had our duties to perform and we were reenacting different scenarios that we might encounter. We also continued our gunnery training at this time, and we were provided updates about the status of the war effort. We also had access to newspapers on the base and other news sources.

I was anxious, we all were, to get "over there" – overseas, to get going and be a part of the war effort, even though we weren't sure what "getting over there" really meant yet. We knew that after we were qualified we'd be shipped out. I never thought about a time frame, it would happen when it happened. The truth is that we were just so busy with every phase of training that we didn't have time to think about the day we'd actually go.

Part of our training was to do simulated bombing runs. For example, taking off from Florida and flying up to Omaha, Nebraska and back again. We flew around the clock, from early morning until the afternoon, then early afternoon to dusk, then dusk to evening and finally, night flying. We covered all three shifts, because we had to be trained to fly and perform whenever we were needed. There weren't that many planes, so we had to juggle schedules to get our flying time in to get trained to do all of the things for which each crew member was responsible. We would then switch positions during these flights so we could learn about each other's duties. Flying at night time was something I really enjoyed. I could look down and see so much down below because we weren't flying that high at the time. Then we started getting used to being on oxygen. To do that, we would take longer, higher altitude trips. A far trip would be considered one that took us to Nebraska, or somewhere out west like Texas, or we would head up to the northeast, then turn around and come back. Most of these flights were five to eight hour flights, giving the pilots and the navigator time to sharpen their skills.

Frank (right) with USA Singing Sergeants

As far as some R&R (Rest and Relaxation), one of the things I did was volunteer to sing with the Air Corps Chorus. After all, this was much better than having to participate in barracks inspections and parades. I was part of the Air Corps Enter-tainment Group. Sometimes it was every weekend and I had the opportunity to sing quite a few times. On Fridays we would go to other airbases and we would sing with the USO shows. They introduced us as the "Singing Sergeants." We would sing some opening songs with a band and entertain the troops until the main acts would come on stage. There would be comedians, movie stars, dancers, singers, and big show headliners. We were able to see the whole show. We then closed the show by singing patriotic songs. The time with the USO was very enjoyable.

We all liked going to the beaches in Florida during our training. In St. Petersburg there was dancing on the pier. The Air Corps bus would take us down and bring us back to the base. I wasn't much into going out and doing a lot of drinking like some of the other guys. That wasn't my type of fun on the weekends. I'm not saying I didn't participate, but that wasn't my bag. I'd rather go to a restaurant and get something good to eat. If I did stay overnight somewhere, I'd get a decent room to stay in.

An interesting thing happened to me while I was down in Florida. One of our next door neighbors from Bessemer Terrace in East Pittsburgh was the Boback family. They were elderly, with two daughters and one son, Robert, who was in the service, plus two older brothers who were married and away from home with families of their own. Mr. Boback, Sr., the father, had died and eventually they sold the house. One of the two daughters had moved to Florida, so when Mr. Boback died, his wife went to live with her daughter in Florida. While I was in Florida, I looked this family up, found them and went to their house for a visit. They were glad to see this young man from East Pittsburgh – from home. They lived right on the beach, so they took me out for a swim and then provided a real nice dinner for me. I had gotten the address for them from either my brother Mike or John, who knew the older brother. I surprised them – didn't tell them I was coming and just showed up on their doorstep. They knew me growing up as a kid because we lived right next door to each other, and they were glad to see me. Mrs. Boback, their mother, was a real nice person, as I remember. That's a story from my life that I enjoy remembering – it was just a pleasant day spending time with my next door neighbors from back home. A little slice of home-for-the-day for an airman in training far from home.

While in Florida, I invited Anne to come down and visit with me but it didn't work out. In fact, I wanted her to come down and marry me! (She may not even remember.) I'm fairly certain that my seeing the other guys on the base with their wives with them made an impact on me. I thought, "If everybody else is doing it, why can't I?" I told Anne, "My buddy down here got married," hinting that I would have liked her to come to Florida so we could get married. Deep down, I knew her parents wouldn't let her go; she was only 17 at the time. But there was always that thought in the back of every service man's mind that you might not come back, and you wanted to live as much of life as you could while you still had time.

After completing five months of intensive training as a combat crew of a B-17 Flying Fortress, we received orders to report to Hunter Field in Savannah, Georgia. We flew from MacDill Field in Tampa, Florida to Savannah, Georgia. Once we arrived at Hunter Field we were assigned to a brand new, shiny, silver B-17G that had just come right off of the assembly line. There were a few days of indoctrination and flight plans to review, and then we spent a few days checking the plane over making sure everything was functioning properly. Once we checked it out as a crew, then another team gave it the final inspection, gave us our flight plans and said, "OK, you guys are ready to jaunt over the ocean." That's when we knew we would be leaving to fly overseas. We were ready to take off for England.

Chapter Four

ORDERED OVERSEAS –
457TH BOMB GROUP

We left Hunter Field, Georgia in September of 1944 in a brand new B-17 Flying Fortress. It was very exciting for me to be aboard this magnificent aircraft that had entered the service with the Eighth and Fifteenth Air Corps in late 1943. Even though I had trained on a B-17, this was the 'real thing' – I felt like a teenager getting behind the wheel of a car to drive for the very first time. As we flew up the East Coast, we were low enough to recognize points of interest such as Washington, DC. As we passed New York City we said, "So long!" to Lady Liberty. This was a very exhilarating time for me – all the anticipation of what was awaiting me in this adventure was finally taking place.

Our first stop was Grenier Field in Manchester, New Hampshire, an Air Transport Command (ATC) base, until we received orders to continue our journey overseas. We were provided with meals and housing which resembled a barracks-type formation. When we had free evenings we ventured into the town of Manchester, which was known for its shoemaking factories. It was the first time that the flight crew was simply hanging out together, and I was with my fellow crew members, Bill Rhodes and Harry Connors. We were issued 24-hour passes and were instructed to be back at the base on time to be ready to takeoff on a moment's notice. Our time was spent seeing the sights around town, visiting a local USO and eating dinner at a local restaurant. It was a nice break for all of us.

The rest of the time at Grenier Field was all business for our crew. While on base, and at all future stops, our crew was responsible for guarding the plane. During this time absolutely no one was permitted on the plane for any reason. There was always a concern that someone could sabotage the plane. Two crew members would rotate guard duty – four hours on, four hours off. I remember working the guard duty with Bill Rhodes. We only had our .45 caliber pistols, no rifles. There were no bombs on the plane. Instead, our bomb bay was filled with sports equipment; baseballs, baseball bats, footballs, books, movie films, record players, records of the latest popular songs of the day, card tables and dart boards to take to the boys already overseas. We would get our payload when we arrived. While on duty, we watched while the mechanic crews carefully inspected our plane. Since the plane was brand new anything on the plane that needed attention was reported right away so repairs could be made quickly, making it ready to continue on our journey overseas. We knew there would be more training once we got to Europe, but for now, we waited.

When we were finally given orders to leave Grenier Field, our next stop was Goosebay, Labrador, Canada. This leg of the trip took us over some very desolate parts of the country including a lot of water below and not much to see. Goosebay

Our North Atlantic Flight Overseas

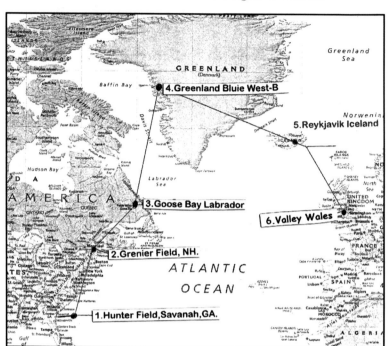

was another Air Transport Command Base for ferrying planes to England. The base served as a stopover for refueling, rest and inspections. We were given accommodations and told there was a movie house on base. Going to see some of the latest movies was a great way to relax. The planes couldn't take off in bad weather, so we passed the time by reading, playing cards and exercising to stay in shape.

The next leg of our journey took us to Greenland. When we landed there I couldn't help but notice that it, too, was a desolate country with no vegetation, only rocks and water. After a brief stay in Greenland we were off to Reykjavik, Iceland, another stop on our journey to England. The weather was also bad in Iceland – cold and rainy with snow flurries again. We had to wait out the bad weather for a few days until we were cleared to fly again. There were other planes and crews on base, so when the weather cleared and the sun came out, we had a little free time to get together and play catch with the baseballs and gloves we were transporting on the plane.

With the weather finally good enough for flying again, we flew to our last stop, which was Valley Wales. We had to say good-bye to our plane as it was being taken to a replacement depot to be fitted for combat. New planes were assigned to other groups whose planes had been shot down, or crashed. It was the beginning of September and it took us almost two weeks to get overseas due to bad weather and some engine trouble.

I enjoyed the whole trip over in the new plane we had. We were just ferrying it over – but I can tell you it was a much better way for us to get overseas than going by boat! We talked and played music on the intercom. We would stand behind the pilot taking turns seeing the sights from up in front of the plane. It was a great new experience to cross the ocean. Making all of the stops was a good geography lesson for me, as we hop-scotched across ocean and land. This flying time gave our pilot and navigator – all of us – experience being aboard the plane that we would be manning in combat.

After finishing up all of our business in Valley Wales, we left the B-17 and we boarded a train headed for Glatton, England, location of the 457th Bomb Group Base. We were taken to a part of England called "The Wash," an indentation in the King's Channel side of England. The "Wash" was a replacement depot where instructors indoctrinated us to get accustomed to English ways. We learned where we would be stationed, the history and geography of England, means of transportation, and what type of currency they used. We also were given instruction on how to behave ourselves, act respectfully, and to obey the laws of the land. Once the indoctrination process was over, we travelled by bus to Peterborough which was near Glatton.

After all of my training in the Army Air Base in North Carolina, Arizona Air Corps Gunnery School, Crew training at MacDill Field in Tampa, Florida, I finally arrived at the 8th Air Corps Bomb Group base in the town of Glatton, England near the town of Peterborough in September, 1944. This was the last stop of my journey overseas.

As I got off the bus, I looked around and saw streets lined with local pubs and people riding bicycles. It was interesting getting used to hearing the "Limey" accent of the Englanders and just to take it all in as I walked around this town so far away from home. In the local pubs, they served two kinds of ale – bitter and mild. Bitter was a mid-brown heavier brew while mild was a lighter-bodied, but dark-colored beer. At one of the local pubs I and my crew mates sat around robustly singing songs like, "Beer Barrel Polka," "Deep in the Heart of Texas" and "Praise the Lord and Pass the Ammunition." We all were really enjoying a wonderful time of camaraderie and just hanging out together experiencing some of life's simple pleasures before heading off to the real danger of fighting a war. I buddied around with Bill Rhodes as he and I had a lot in common – we were both physical fitness buffs who enjoyed going to the gym and working out.

Soon it was time to board a bus and head to our air base where we'd be stationed for our combat missions. The first thing I noticed when I stepped off of the bus was an odd-shaped building that in some ways looked like an aluminum tent. It was a Quonset hut and it was to be home for all of us while on base. As I approached, it looked like a small cave. It had a cylinder shape and was made of metal and was to serve as our barracks. Lots of these prefabricated structures were built especially for the US military.

Once inside, the hut was dark, gloomy and cold. There were small windows that were covered by thick black curtains, with two light bulbs hanging from the ceiling that did not provide much light. The potbelly stove in the middle of the hut didn't provide all that much heat, either. My first thought was that there wasn't much about this place that was inviting. It always felt damp inside. I would soon learn that there wasn't very much coal available to put in that potbelly stove, hence, the dampness and cold.

The little hut held 12 enlisted men with six double bunks for two crews of six men each, which made it very crowded. The crowded conditions and the scarcity of coal were pretty good reasons to avoid the hut. As a result, the time spent in the hut was mostly for sleeping.

When we were off-duty we would go to the NCO club on base. The club had a bar, pool table, card tables, dart boards, checkers, puzzles and plenty of books to read. Plus, the added bonus was that it was so much warmer in there.

Shortly after our arrival on base, we started our overseas training for bombing missions. Every day we would fly and simulate bombing runs until we were classified as prepared to go on bombing missions, finally getting to be part of the war effort. We did practice missions to be combat-ready, wearing our combat gear and holding our positions.

During these training sessions is when we thoroughly reviewed all phases of 'formation flying' with four squadrons of nine planes per group, where the more experienced crews were in the lead box, navigating our course. They would radio back to the rest of the group where to stay in the formation and what to look out for from the enemy. These tight-flying formations provided the best defense because it allowed all the guns of many planes to fire upon enemy fighters.

The plane we flew was a B-17G and had the defensive firepower of thirteen Browning .50 caliber machine guns. The machine guns were positioned to cover all directions, providing protection from enemy fighters during missions. The pilot and the copilot had no guns – they had enough responsibilities piloting the aircraft.

As part of a bomber crew we all learned in training that at high altitudes (above 30,000 feet) temperatures would be below freezing, often as much as 50 degrees below zero. Any exposed flesh would freeze to metal in an instant. Because of this, getting dressed into combat flying gear was no small task. The layering began with putting on long underwear, then an electrically heated flying suit. I first slipped the pants on which had heated nichrome wire coils sewn inside the pant legs, with cuffs that snapped into clasps on my combat boots. After this I put on a regular army tee-shirt, either long or short sleeved followed by a buttoned shirt. The last piece of outer clothing was the flying suit jacket with heated wire coils woven into the jacket. This jacket resembled the popular waist length Eisenhower jacket. Every piece of the flight suit snapped closed and once all of the combat clothing was on and snapped into place, the final step was 'plugging in' to an electrical outlet on the plane. Flak jackets were worn over top of our flight suit and they were designed to provide some protection from the flying shrapnel encountered in combat. They were heavy to pick up and put on.

Our flight training took all day. Mixed in with actual flying was classroom training. In the classroom we learned the finer points of what to expect in combat and how to take care of ourselves at high altitudes. The inside of the B-17 wasn't pressurized, so we were all required to wear an oxygen mask at altitudes above 10,000 feet. Most of this was a refresher course to hone our skills and prepare us for combat flying.

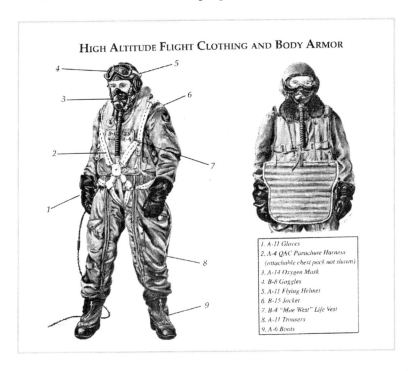

HIGH ALTITUDE FLIGHT CLOTHING AND BODY ARMOR

1. A-11 Gloves
2. A-4 QAC Parachute Harness
   (attachable chest pack not shown)
3. A-14 Oxygen Mask
4. B-8 Goggles
5. A-11 Flying Helmet
6. B-15 Jacket
7. B-4 "Mae West" Life Vest
8. A-11 Trousers
9. A-6 Boots

We were going to put on the nose of our ship (B-17s were commonly referred to as ships), 'Guptill's Flying Bastard's' – envisioning some artwork that would accompany our pilot's name. But once we were overseas we had different thoughts about all of that. We soon learned that you didn't keep your planes all that long. In the early part of the war, as with the *Memphis Belle*, crews could have their planes with them for 25 missions or so, long enough to make it *their* plane. However, the war was at fever pitch when we entered into battle. Planes were being lost all the time and crews took replacement planes to get right back in the action, so we ditched the thought of naming our B-17 after we flew our first combat mission.

Every day crews would look at the bulletin boards outside of their barracks to check a list to see who was scheduled to fly the next day, that's how we would know when we'd be flying. They would put us on alert and eventually you'd hear the words, "You're flying tomorrow." I really didn't think much about flying my first mission; it was just something I had to do. I was prepared, personally, and we were all anxious to go, to get started and do what we had all trained and worked so hard for.

Then the day came when our Pilot, Second Lieutenant Kenneth Guptill was alerted by the base commanders that we were scheduled to go up, and he said to us, "We're going to go on our first mission tomorrow." The date was September 30, 1944. I went through the words in my mind that tomorrow for me and my crew would be our first combat mission over German territory.

Tomorrow I was headed to war.

Chapter Five

FIGHTING A WAR FROM THE AIR

On the morning of September 30, 1944, my crew mates and I were awakened at three a.m. for our entry into air battle. After grabbing some breakfast chow, we all headed for the briefing room.

Getting ready to fly into combat was the realization of a goal for me. I had an enormous love of flying and a determination to serve my country in this war. It took a lot of work to get ready for our bomber runs. There was so much that had to happen before we ever got in the planes. And if it wasn't done right, it could have resulted in something as bad as getting shot at by the Germans on the actual mission. The altitudes, timing and rendezvous points had to be precise – everything was planned to the nth degree – and we had to understand and follow those directions or risk a midair collision with our own guys.

The planning that went into a mission was amazing. All the planes for that mission would be parked near the runway that we were going to use for takeoff the next morning. When we were all in place and ready to fly, the guys managing this huge armada would set off a green flare, and the first plane would roll out. Then every thirty seconds or so, the next plane would take off.

The planes would take off in groups, for example, first the planes that would run high in the squadron would take off, then the lead planes, and finally the squadron that would be flying low. We all kept in touch with each other using low frequency radio signals. The groups flew in different patterns like circles or triangles or rectangles and each group fit into the other like they had been cut from a jigsaw – and each pilot had to know exactly where he was supposed to be in the lineup. Let me tell you, there were always a few close calls as we got the planes up into the air and settled into their flying patterns.

There were no GPS's available to us in those days – the way we kept an eye on our lead plane was to watch for a colored flare that the lead plane would fire about every thirty seconds. That flash of a particular color would tell the lead plane's squadrons where he was, and allow us to line up in our pattern and keep the lead plane in our sight. Then, when each plane got into the proper position, the lead plane would fire a flare to signal all was well. It made for quite a fireworks display in the early morning as we took off on our missions!

And we're not talking just a few planes here. When all the fighters and bombers on a particular mission were in the air and assembled, the number could be as high as 2,000 aircraft at a time. One wrong move and you were in the cockpit of the plane next to you.

Even with all the shock-and-awe tactics of today's military campaigns, I doubt they will ever match the sheer numbers and firepower that we assembled in our day. We were "The Mighty Eighth" – and proud of it.[1]

More specifically, our crew was a proud part of The Mighty Eighth Air Force, the 457th Bomb Group, 750th Squadron. The insignia consisted of a shield with a scroll and the words "FAIT ACCOMPLI" below it, which was French for 'an accomplished fact.' The shield itself is divided into four sections, each of which represented a station through which the Group had passed in coming overseas. The outline of a B-17, leaving a flaming red trail, was shown passing through each quarter until it reached the skies of combat in the upper left portion of the shield. It was this B-17 with its fireball trail that gave the 457th its popular name, *The Fireball Outfit*.

Our unit was recognized by the huge black triangle with a 'U' on every plane in the group, and is affectionately referred to as 'Triangle U'.

At the briefings we attended we were reminded of what to do if we had to bail out, and not to get our harnesses stuck if we had to salvo the doors. In the event of having to bail out, the small plane doors were jettisoned from the plane – they 'go to the winds' and then it was time to jump. We were given escape kits consisting of some candy bars, first aid kit with morphine, sulfa powder, and bandages, a silk map of Europe, some escape money, a pocket knife, compass and passport picture taken of us in civilian clothes.

We already had our flight suits on as we got dressed at our quarters after breakfast. We picked up our parachutes, extra flak suits, grabbed our thermoses and were ready to go. Finally, we jumped onto the back of trucks and were driven out to the

---

[1] For a more detailed account, see the Voice of the Mighty Eighth article entitled "Assembling the Eighth."

tarmac. Once at the tarmac, I stepped aboard the B-17 we had been assigned to for our first combat mission over the skies of Germany. I was part of a unit that was about to embark on missions that would alter history. I was proud and I was ready. Once onboard our B-17, we put on our very heavy 30 pound flak suits and steel helmets, then went to our positions. This first combat mission was to be part of an all out effort to bomb the vital railroad junction at Munster, Germany. The distinctive hum of the B-17 lifted us above the clouds and on our way.

We could all pretty much take it easy as we flew out of England and into France. I sat on the floor atop some stacked up flak suits near my right waist gun position located directly behind the right wing, sipped some coffee and tried to relax. When we reached 10,000 feet we went on oxygen. The cold was something to contend with because you just didn't have the freedom to move around the plane. If you wanted to walk to another part of the plane, you'd have to use a small 'walk around' oxygen unit that you put over your shoulder. Once at your position, you'd plug into the ship's supply of oxygen. Even our chocolate bars would freeze at these temperatures. We'd pull our leather caps down over our foreheads. The caps even covered our upper cheeks a little for added warmth. Once you put your oxygen mask on it covered your nose and face for even more warmth, but it was still cold, for sure. We didn't plug into the heat until we climbed a little bit higher, as we didn't want to be sweating before we got ready for combat.

Once over German territory, we took our ready positions on the plane – mine was at the open window on the right side of the plane, manning the .50 caliber machine gun. I had done this many times before – but now it was the real thing. We were in a formation flying pattern where we created a kind of three-dimensional pattern – the 'boxes' of aircraft were stacked one above the other to take advantage of the combined defensive firepower the B-17 provided. At this point, I started to scan the skies for enemy fighters through the post and circle mount, using the cross hairs that sat at the end of the gun barrel. Every crew member was now doing the same thing – we were on the lookout for any signs of enemy aircraft in the area. My job was pretty simple, shoot down enemy planes.

We were all listening on the intercom to the instructions of the pilots and navigator relaying information from our lead plane, including the constant reminder to "be on the lookout for enemy fighter planes and flak from enemy antiaircraft fire." The mission was pretty much uneventful, but the closer we approached our target, the more we started to see puffs of black smoke in the distance – the sighting of flak. A short time later we were in the thick of it as flak was flying everywhere around us. Flak is an acronym from a long German word describing a cannon shooting at fliers – Flugabwehrkanone. Flak was from bomb bursts, and it produced shrapnel – junk metal. Antiaircraft would send it up. Sometimes the Germans fired up metal containers with timed fuses on them, so that exploding shells would randomly burst, spewing out various sizes of sharp, penetrating metal of all kinds.

In spite of the flak, we were able to reach our target. Our navigator identified the IP (Initial Point), which is an identifiable landmark near the target. Once there, the bomb doors opened and the bombardier dropped the bombs. As soon as the bombs left the bay, there was a sudden surge that we all felt in the plane – a kind of a jolt. The huge bomb load was heavy and now that it was gone, the weight of the plane shifted and us with it! The pilot had to compensate for the fact that the plane got significantly lighter all at one time, and proceeded to make adjustments. Once the bombs were dropped we headed back, safely making it back to base. We did what we came to do and we got back to the base.

We did get some holes in the plane from flak. When we got back to base, if we thought we took flak, the ground crew would hand us a yellow crayon and ask us to circle the 'flak hits' on the plane. Someone would count them off as they were being circled, "circle one, circle two, circle three" and that's how they knew how many holes we had in our plane from the mission. On that first mission we circled about a dozen or so holes. The ground crew would assess the damage and determine if they could repair the plane overnight. If they could repair it, then the plane could go up the next day. If not, the mechanics always had other planes that were ready to go. Even if there was engine damage, they had spare engines at the ready, as well.

Once back from a bombing run, we all returned to the briefing room, where there were several large tables set up. Someone would greet us at the door and direct the whole crew to a table. Every crew from a particular run was returning at approximately the same time, so someone would shout out, "Guptill's crew report to table five, Smith's crew report to table nine." The procedure then was that each crew member was briefed by the officers to retell the events of the missions from their position on the plane. We would report what we knew, such as if we saw another plane go down, and off of which wing it happened, and if we saw fighter planes, where they were seen… things like that. As I reported, I didn't see any fighter planes on that first mission, just a lot of flak.

Once the post mission briefing was complete, we were given chits. Chits were tickets that were used to buy whiskey, beer and chow. After 10 or 12 hours in the air, everybody got something to eat and drink, and then we hit the sack for some much-needed sleep. If we had a mission the next day, we were expected at roll call to do it all over again. If we weren't flying there were classes to attend, then after class, we were pretty much free for the day.

September was a bad month for the 457th Bomb Group. Thirteen missions were flown and 16 planes were lost.

During some of these missions, it was our turn to toss out US 'anti-German propaganda' leaflets over occupied territory that the Allied troops had taken over. We opened the side door of the plane, throwing them into the wind as thousands upon thousands of pieces of paper drifted down like snowflakes. The leaflets were designed to tell the Germans our side of the war effort, letting them know we were winning and advising surrender or we would continue bombing, things like that. They warned the German civilians to not listen to the propaganda the Nazi's were still telling them, and they included messages to German soldiers to give up because their cause was lost.

October was almost as bad a month as September, as 11 planes were lost. In spite of that, our crew flew three more missions: October 7th to Politz, October 15th to Cologne and October 17th back to Cologne. We didn't know about these losses at the time, as we hadn't seen the statistics or results from previous crews' missions – these were reported later. We were pretty much rookies and hadn't had to face any of the terrible times that other guys had gone through yet. Our crew didn't talk about it, either. We faced our missions with an "it's not going to happen to me" attitude. We tried not to think about casualties, loss, or what might happen to us.

At this time of the war, there were so many losses in air battles that the base was waiting for new replacements of both men and planes. There wasn't enough time to get the replacements to the base fast enough or to repair planes to prepare for more missions. So, what to do with us in the meantime? Instead of just having us wait around, maybe getting nervous and apprehensive during the down time, it was decided it would be better to just get us away to forget about it all for awhile. Because of this decision, six days after our crew flew our fourth mission we were given a five-day furlough to London, England. On October 23rd, we left by train from Glatton to London, England. Once in London, we took double-decker busses and headed for the famous USO Rainbow Corners. During the war, this American-run USO was open 24 hours a day, serving food, as well as sponsoring dances and live entertainment. American servicemen flocked to it, and we were among the many who did.

At the USO, we asked about sight-seeing tours, entertainment and what else we could cram into our five-day stay. At some point, I mentioned that I would be celebrating my 21st birthday on October 25th while in London. I couldn't believe what happened next. The USO staff said that because I would be spending my 21st birthday in London, they wanted to do something memorable for me and give me a special gift for the occasion. They arranged for me to stay at the Grand Hotel in London, a first class hotel at their expense – to include breakfast in bed. Talk about a surprise birthday present! They also gave me tickets to attend the London Opera. It was a pretty exciting time for this young Army airman from East Pittsburgh, Pennsylvania.

Our crew doubled up with each other and Bill Rhodes was the benefactor by way of getting to stay in the ritzy hotel with me. When I got to the hotel and checked in, I really felt big time. It was one of the finer places to stay, with a spacious room and best of all – a great big, fluffy, soft, comfortable bed. Once, while standing in the lobby of the Grand Hotel, I saw Bob Hope and Bing Crosby pass through the doors. There were so many entertainers around that were brought in to perform for the USO and I got to get a glimpse of two of the biggest in all of show business at the time.

Sight-seeing at some of the more famous places was on the top of the list of things to do. We saw Buckingham Palace, Westminster Abbey, Big Ben, and St. Paul's Cathedral. Everything was so impressive, ornate and interesting and I learned a lot about the historical significance of all of these places. As I strolled through town taking in all of the sights, I couldn't help but notice the bombed-out buildings and how much destruction the city endured from the German bombings.

Eventually I used my ticket to go the London Opera House and saw *The Merry Widow*. I had two tickets, but none of my other crew mates wanted to go, so I went by myself. Not being a student of opera at all, but a big fan of music, dancing and theatre, I thoroughly enjoyed the beautiful music and acting.

At night, London came alive as electric signs and billboards glowed with life and adventure, just inviting us to take part. The hustle and bustle was everywhere – what a fun time for us all. We stopped into pubs and, to paraphrase, "when in Rome did as the Romans did." Well, being in England in a pub, what else was there to do but drink beer and sing songs around a piano? We had a great time doing so.

We went to some terrific restaurants, attended dances at the USO and enjoyed strolling down the streets of London, decked out in our Army Air Corps dress uniforms. There were so many servicemen in town – many just like us – given furloughs to get away from all the stress of combat and the war. The streets were packed with us 'Yanks'.

The one place that didn't hold any appeal at all for me was our visit to the famous Piccadilly Circus – famous for its prostitution, that is. Before we left base, the base commanders dished out dire warnings about Piccadilly Circus; how it was a seedier side of town and how prostitutes would proposition us. They even passed out condoms and information on how not to contract venereal disease. The hookers were beckoning, but I wasn't having anything to do with their ploys. Piccadilly Circus had some high class places, but some low-life goings-on. I was approached by 'ladies of the night', but I wasn't well-versed in any of that, and wanted no part of it. My visit to Piccadilly Circus was a quick look-see and then I got out of there. That wasn't for me.

Back at the USO is where we did our hanging out with the opposite sex. The place was so big that there was more than one dance floor. We had such fun listening to the sounds of the Big Bands, making friends, dancing, and hanging out. Lots of the couples that met at those dances stayed together and many of the English girls eventually became British war brides.

London, at the time, was known for the many 'Flak Houses' in the area. Those houses were usually on someone's estate, castle, or out in the countryside. They were really combat rest homes, operated by the Army with help from the Red Cross. They provided sporting and recreational activities to stressed-out airmen. When crews flew a lot of missions they experienced tremendous battle fatigue. Their nerves were shot, and some guys had experienced so much tragedy they couldn't get over their fear of dying. The flak houses gave air crewman a break from the action in a civilian setting, where they could wear civilian clothes and get some much needed R&R to help them recharge their batteries.

As for us, our five-day furlough was coming to an end, having passed by much too quickly. So, after spending a memorable 21st birthday in London with my crew, it was back to our Air Base on October 28th, 1944.

I wrote to my parents and to Anne to share with them how exciting it was to go on furlough to London, and to tell them about all I had seen and experienced. Letters that were written from the base had to be censored by a US commissioned officer. They didn't want anyone to reveal any references to names of towns that were nearby, as they didn't want to jeopardize revealing our location. As a result, my letters were fairly generic. I wrote things like, "I'm fine, don't worry" without ever mentioning anything about missions or how the war was going. In spite of this, most letters we wrote were confiscated for security purposes. Much later I found out no one ever received my letters talking about my London trip and my 21st birthday celebration.

The realities of being at war set back in quickly as we assembled for our fifth mission which took us back to Munster. On this flight, as with all the others before, we did encounter flak but completed our mission and came back to base.

We didn't fly on November 1st due to bad weather; instead I was able to attend Mass on base as it was The Feast of All Saints – a Catholic Holy Day of Obligation. We attended classes for part of the day and also caught up on sleep. In the evening they showed the film, 'Marriage is Private Affair' starring Lana Turner. She was my favorite movie star of the time and I enthusiastically was in attendance.

With the new month of November ushered in, our next mission, scheduled for November 2nd, would be to a small town in Central Germany about 20 miles west of Leipzig. Little did I know how that mission would change my life.

November 2ND, 1944

The Mission

Chapter Six

MISSION NUMBER SIX

The date was November 2, 1944 and we were scheduled to fly, so we received our usual early three a.m. wake up call. After making the trip to the mess hall for breakfast, we reported to the large Nissen hut where the briefing room was. This served as the big war room where crews who were going to be on a particular mission for the day assembled.

The commanding officers in charge pulled the curtain back to show a big map of Germany and pointed out the target for the day. As they pushed the sticks around they moved planes into different locations pinpointed on the map. I watched intently and vividly remember seeing a target that was highlighted for this morning's mission.

The target was Merseberg, Germany.

More specifically we were heading to the Leuna synthetic oil refinery near town, a large production plant for Germany's war efforts which made oils, plastics and fertilizer. After this was announced the room filled with airman's responses of "ooh's and ahh's" – a recognition by everyone that this would be a tough target. We all knew that this would be a very dangerous mission and slowly adjusted to hearing the announcement. It was common knowledge that Merseberg was very heavily defended by hundreds of antiaircraft batteries and that made it a very unsafe target. Other crews had been there before and got clobbered – and everyone was aware of that fact.

The briefing continued, with explanations given that our main objective was to bomb and wipe out the synthetic oil refineries and that this, in turn, would destroy Germany's capability to fuel their fighting machines as well as the many other needs the refineries fulfilled and the war demanded. They said we were sending over 1,000 bombers, so it was a big deal.

We were given last minute reports about the weather, bombing altitudes, possible flak alleys, and antiaircraft activity. Lastly, they told us, "You may see fighters, so be alert." Followed by commands of, "Scramble," "Get up there, guys," and "Go get 'em!" We were left on our own to think about what was ahead.

By now we all knew that Merseberg was a bad target and that we would have a lot of opposition, but were weren't expecting fighter planes. It turned out that the Germans knew they really needed to defend this area and they reserved the bulk of their fire power for the defense of Merseberg. History would record that this mission would be the biggest air battle of the war, involving over 500 of our 8th Air Corps heavy bombers, with an escort of 900 fighter planes. Each plane was carrying eighteen 250 pound general purpose bombs. We hadn't heard at this point that the Luftwaffe had been conserving its fighter strength to defend against this mission. The Germans knew what strategy they needed to employ, and they did. We were later informed that on this date, the Luftwaffe had put up over 400 fighters in defense of this target.

When referring to this mission mostly everybody just refers to it as 'November 2nd'. Our tail gunner, John Simmen, was out on sick call, so I said I would take his place and fly the tail on this day. Bad colds and flu-like symptoms could keep you off of a flight, because of the close quarters in the plane coughing and breathing difficulties could cause a lot of problems especially with oxygen masks. I had never flown the tail before on a mission, but I never had any second thoughts about it at all. It was an opportunity to fly in an important mission and that's what I wanted to do.

Our entire crew practiced changing positions on the planes, getting experience in other roles and learning other crew members' duty station responsibilities. So when I volunteered to go into the tail I had some knowledge of what to do while in flight. In exchange for me moving to the tail, we took on a crew member from another plane, Stephen Marklin, and he took my position on the waist.

Our flight crew for the day was: Pilot, Kenneth E. Guptill; Copilot, George H. Keller; Navigator, Edmond C. McNamara; Engineer, Harry J. Connors; Radio Operator, Virgil H. Smallen; Ball Turret, Herbert Brayman; Waist Gunner, William Rhodes; Tail Gunner, Frank A. Kravetz; and Waist Gunner – Stephen Marklin. Crew not flying mission: Bombardier, Thomas Dunn; Tail Gunner, John Simmens.

Once I crawled into the tail, I had some wiggle room for my shoulders and could move just a little bit, but I really was crammed in there – it was a confining space. The best way to describe it was that I sat in a little motorcycle type seat.

I manned a twin .50 caliber machine gun as the tail gunner and I was responsible for the primary defense against enemy fighters attacking from the rear. I was always to be on the lookout for what was happening behind the plane and reporting it to our pilot as well as the results of our bombing runs.

I couldn't fit into the turret with the flak suit, so I put my suit on the bottom of the tail section. It was flexible, worn like a sandwich board, with a shield for front and back. It was essentially a big bulletproof vest. The flak suits were so heavy that you had to kneel down to put them on and if you tried to stand up the weight of them would drop you to your knees. I also took extra flak suits into the tail section, placing them under my feet and all around, leaning them up from the bottom against the inside wall of the tail, creating a cocoon of extra protection to surround me. I did not take my parachute into the tail section, leaving more room for the flak suits. My thought process was that, hopefully, if enemy fire was coming up, the extra flak suits would protect me. I didn't plan on needing to use a parachute.

Positioned in the tail, I could see where we came from, but couldn't see where we were going. I had to rely on the intercom and radio to know where we were at all times. The takeoff for this operation began at around 8:30 a.m. and soon we were airborne heading to Merseberg. Everything appeared to be routine during the flight. We were on time and on course. Our 750th Squadron made up the nine planes that flew in the lower box.

Once over our target we dropped our bombs, everything went well, so we turned around and started back for base. Not ten minutes after dropping our bombs and heading for home, we were attacked by enemy planes approaching from the rear

– they seemed to come out of nowhere. The attack came in waves, part of over 400 German fighters sent to do battle in the sky with us.

Our engineer, Harry Connors, recalls this part of the flight, "We were hit in our #1 engine and it caught fire, we turned, lost some altitude and the fighters hit us again. This attack knocked out #2 and #3 engines, our intercom, severed the control cables and made a lot of 20 mm holes. The fighters again started attacking from the bottom. We dropped out of formation on a northern heading."

Radio operator Virgil Smallen remembers, "We were returning from a bombing run over Germany when a formation of enemy fighters swooped in from behind and shot our plane down. The plane was buffeted not only by machine gun fire from the fighters, but by flak from the ground. The Germans could put the flak up so that it looked like you could put out a carpet and walk on it. They left our plane full of holes."

The attack came in waves and they concentrated on our group, coming in directly at the tail level. Our plane was hit by 20 mm fire from the enemy aircraft in the outer wing near #1 engine causing the engine to start to burn. I heard the shots and saw the FW 190s – they were firing and shooting right at me!

The first three that came at me were shooting at me – I could see fire come exploding out of the wing. I was firing back at them, giving it all I could. (An estimated 40 Focke-Wulf FW-190s concentrated their attack on the low box. I was in this low box.) The fire fight was intense and then I saw a second wave of three FW–190s that came in directly behind the tail shooting with rapid fire. There was an explosion in the tail section of the plane and it filled up with smoke. I realized that I took a direct hit.

I pressed my throat mike and urgently yelled, "I'm hit, I'm hit, I'm hit!"

Chapter Seven

SHOT OUT OF THE SKY

I kept pressing my throat microphone, shouting, "Tail gunner to crew, tail gunner to crew, I'm hit, I'm hit!" I heard nothing in response – no one answered my call. I found out later that our intercom system had been knocked out by fire from the FW-190s, which is why my crew never heard my cries for help over the radio. The tail section was filling with smoke from the direct hit received from the enemy fighters. I had no idea how badly I was injured and shortly after my repeated attempts on the radio to reach a crew mate, everything went black and I passed out.

When I came to, my leg felt like someone had shoved a hot poker into my thigh. The heat and burning in my leg was unbearable. I was feeling the effects of shrapnel that had torn into my legs from the hit delivered by FW-190 fighter's 20 mm cannon fire. Blood was splattered everywhere, the sides of the tail section of the plane and my uniform were now bright red. I was in shock and drifting in and out of consciousness due to losing quite a bit of blood.

It wasn't until our plane left formation from our squadron because our engines were damaged and we were losing altitude that my crew members realized I had been injured. I came to in time to see my crew mates coming back to the tail section. I thought to myself, "My buddies are coming to help me" – I was so thankful and relieved. Waist Gunner Bill Rhodes and Navigator Ed McNamara came back and rescued me from the tail section into which I was crammed. They began to pull me out from behind the machine guns and tail wheel... trying to get my body turned around in that small tail section that was barely big enough for me to fit in. It must have been a terribly difficult job for them to do in those close quarters.

My crew mate Ed McNamara recalls the event, "As I and the crew were stripping the plane of gun barrels, ball turret, anything we could throw out to keep the plane lighter, I reached the tail of the aircraft and saw Frank wedged in by the tail wheel, which was retracted. He had been very severely wounded."

Once again I was slipping in and out of consciousness, but I knew that I was being pulled out and away from my entrapment. I put my arms around their necks as they dragged me out of the tail section, along the floor into the radio room; where there would be more room to move around. This section of the plane is where Virgil Smallen (our Radioman) sat. It was situated further ahead of the waist gunner position and right above the ball turret.

Herb Brayman was the first to begin giving me medical attention, quickly joined by the others. They turned their attention toward me and began giving me first aid, but I still had no idea how badly I was injured. As they worked on me, I saw my bloodied flight suit, which was wet from the soaking of my own blood, and I was in tremendous pain. I knew then I had been hit and dealt a severe blow. The guys took the time to put sulfa powder to my wound, and then applied heavy compresses – eventually wrapping up the wound with bandages. At this point, they managed to get the bleeding to stop. Lastly, they gave me a shot of morphine.

Our Radioman, Virgil Smallen, recounts the event, "The tail rudder was damaged, leaving the pilots unable to navigate the plane. The plane was losing power and altitude."

Flight Engineer Harry Connors account, "Suddenly everything was quiet and a quick look around showed only #4 engine was running, the fire in #1 had gone out and #2 and 3 were streaming oil in a long stream behind us. We were lucky to be headed toward England but in a slow, steady descent. After checking with the pilots, I found that we had no directional control of the plane and no control of the remaining #4 engine. Lt. Guptill asked me to go aft and check on the crew and to see if there was any hope of getting any control of the elevator and the rudder. As I climbed through the bomb bay, I wondered how we were still in the air as there were large holes everywhere and the radio room was even worse. There was no hope of repairing the control cables."

My crew was comforting me, assuring me that I would be OK as they began throwing things out of the plane while I was lying there on the bomb hatch floor. I watched the flurry of intense activity all around me as they worked feverishly, chopping the ball turret out, letting it drop from the plane. Next they tossed out the guns, ammunition, and armor – anything that could be moved to lighten the load.

The guys were working so hard to help our crippled plane and increase our chance for survival. I was so proud to be part of this crew as they unselfishly worked together as a team in a horrible situation, one truly of life and death proportions. Crew mate Harry Connors said, "It was unbelievable that there weren't more injuries than Frank."

Our entire crew had trained for these types of moments, hoping they would never come. But come it did. Now we were in a real emergency as the plane limped along at an altitude of between 5,000 and 6,000 feet. Enemy gunners zeroed in on our crippled plane and we were sitting ducks at this time. Antiaircraft fire was being thrown up at us from the enemy below when our Pilot, Lt. Ken Guptill rang the bell for everyone to bail out, to abandon ship. We only had one engine left and were losing altitude rapidly. The crew was able to keep the plane in the air long enough for everyone to bail out.

Training kicked in and soon the plane's door was kicked out, parachutes were being grabbed, and the crew was in constant motion all around me, but I couldn't do anything to help because I was lying on the floor in a pool of my own blood. Immediately upon hearing the pilot's announcement, the crew began scurrying around, executing plans for exiting the plane. We only had one engine left; two of our engines were knocked out. I believe that I was hit at the same time our engines were hit. We were unable to keep up with the rest of the formation. There was no protection. We were alone and vulnerable.

I heard the bell ring. Now everyone was desperately yelling to each other so that the message got to each person, "Bail out!" "Bail out, now!" "Everybody bail out!" After the call to bail out was sounded, my crew members came back and checked on me.

Harry Connors recalls, "We normally took a V4 bag, a chest pack, an oxygen mask in case somebody went out – there were extras. But when we had to empty the plane, all of that extra stuff had been tossed out. And we never flew the same plane, which was another problem. A lot of stuff just wasn't in the plane that day. Typically most of the fire equipment was located in the center next to the radio room. On this day there wasn't anything there. Looking back, I know that Bill Rhodes and I were mostly interested in more ammunition and flak suits. Those flak suits we used for extra protection, so when loading the plane we grabbed extras of those."

McNamara added, "We knew we would have to parachute to safety, but that left us with one dilemma. Frank Kravetz, the tail gunner, had been injured in the attack. Because the tail gunner's turret was so small, he had left his parachute lying on the floor of the plane when he climbed inside the tail. In attempting to get a parachute on Frank, the only one available had already been opened as far as the outer covering, so we put the opened chute on Frank."

Bill Rhodes and Virgil Smallen began to place a parachute harness on me, preparing me for the bail out. As they reached to get a parachute to give me, the chute opened in the plane.

(The following accounts are as told from crew members.) "I was having trouble getting the chute over Frank's shoulders, as we struggled to pull it in, the chute opened behind me. We were dumbfounded." Each plane was supposed to have extra parachutes that were available to pick up and take onto the plane at the start of the mission. There were no extras on this flight. All we could do was fold the chute and tell Kravetz to hold it in his arms as he jumped from the plane. As long as the cords weren't crossed, we reasoned, the chute could still open.

We helped him to the door, threw him out and watched as he made his descent."

With no other recourse, they rolled the cloth chute into a ball, placed it in my arms, folded on my stomach, and with one grabbing my legs and the other my arms, they tossed me out of the plane.

"His chute opened."

It was now out of my hands, and theirs... whatever happened, happened.

Chapter Eight

Freedom Lost –
A Prisoner of War

I was conscious as I dropped from the waist section of the plane, feeling the parachute unravel almost immediately and open above me at 5,000 to 6,000 feet. As I hung suspended, floating under the canopy of the parachute it was eerie, yet peaceful – drifting down through the sky in the middle of war. This midair plight I was experiencing was uncanny and surreal, mysterious really.

Surrounding me now was such a calm serenity compared to all of the confusion and rapid activity of combat fighting that had just taken place. Moments before, the noise was loud as the formations of B-17s hummed above us, droning in the sky. The deafening noise of the machine gun blasts being shot at a rapid fire pace rang in my ears. The clanging of the brass shells from the bullets of the .50 caliber machine guns being fired were dropping and banging on the metal floor. Crew mates were yelling and screaming to each other on their radio headsets with frantic attempts to relay messages. Smoke filled the plane from the crippled engines and electrical equipment that screamed and hissed as power was lost and confusion reigned. But in an instant, that was over. Now there was no noise, not a sound, I heard nothing but silence as my body now quietly sliced through the clouds. Everybody who has been through this experience will tell you the same thing.

I quickly glanced at my watch and noticed that it was 2:10 in the afternoon.

As my fall continued, I looked down and saw that one of my flight boots fell off – one of those heavy boots. So here I was with one bare foot dangling and the other foot with a boot on. I stole a quick look and saw my torn uniform pants with blood splattered on my flight suit and I really couldn't comprehend it all. As out of the ordinary and unbelievable as this falling through the sky was, it still is a most vivid experience to this day. I remained conscious throughout my free fall.

All I can say is that angels must have been right there beside me, providing divine intervention for sure and someone 'up there' liked me. My descent took me across a country road as I barely cleared the draping electrical wires. I was trying to take in all that was happening to me, and all of a sudden as I looked down the ground was rising rapidly to meet me. I could see farms below me as I floated down from the sky, and the farms were getting closer and closer and then, all of a sudden, *zwomp* – it goes like that – *BOOM!* – I was down on the ground. My peaceful ride through the sky had come to an abrupt end.

My time in the parachute was not very long and now my air ride was over. I remember saying to myself, "I'd like to stay up here for a while" – to be able to reflect on all that was happening, to slow it down, to take it in. Instead, I landed on a somewhat soft and muddy surface in an open field. (*National Archives Report indicates the field that I landed in as an area of Ostermunzel near Dedenson, where the plane crashed 15 km west of Hanover.)

REPORT ON CAPTURE OF MEMBERS OF ENEMY AIR FORCES

POST: Air-Field HQ A(e) 23/XI

PLACE: DUNSTORF

DATE: 18 Nov 1944

REGARDING:

CRASH: (DOWNED) OF. Fortress

EN. LANDING: AT: DEDENSEN, 15 km west of HANNOVER

NAME: (LAST OR SURNAME) KRAYETZ

FIRST NAME. FRANK A.

SERIAL NUMBER: (USA) 337*61447

RESULT: (DEAD OR CAPTURED) Captured , Wounded

PLACE AND TIME OF CAPTURE: Field-Area of OSTERMUNZEL (near Place of Crash) 2 Nov 1944.

NAME OF HOSPITAL: Military Hospital IV HANNOVER, BISMARKSCHOOL.

PLACE, DATE AND TIME OF INTERMENT:

GUTSCHE

Lt. CO. and Staff-Officer.

Report indicates where Frank landed after bailing out.

As soon as my body hit the ground, I tumbled like a jack-rabbit hit by rifle shot. Immediately my body automatically moved forward with the force of the wind propelling me and my parachute until I eventually came to a stop. To my surprise and relief, the landing didn't hurt at all. Everything was just happening so fast that I still couldn't believe it. Yet, here I was in the middle of my own drama.

I needed to rid myself of my parachute and the restrictions of movement it caused now that I was on the ground. I unbuckled the parachute from my harness and was wriggling out of the cumbersome contraption as quickly as I could. While trying to get rid of the chute, the wind took hold of it, and the chute immediately blew a short distance into a small nearby wooded area, wrapping itself around a tree. I was now clear and free from my restraint, lying on the ground and about to encounter my next challenge. As I attempted to get up I was surprised to discover that I could not walk. Realizing the predicament I was in, I decided I had to get to a place to rest and take inventory of just how badly I was injured and collect my thoughts.

As I looked around the area, I could see that there was in an open field – a cabbage patch that had been picked already because there were remains of cabbages strewn about even though it was November. I began crawling on my butt with my hands moving me forward about 20 feet to a mound of dirt I spotted in the near distance. The area was mucky and soft and I saw this pile of sticks that I used as a crude lean-to on a little grade. I crawled up to those branches of wood and moved my body to be propped up in a sitting position, and this worked for me also serving as a back rest. I was now ready to assess the situation, and come up with a plan.

My immediate attention turned to my wounds. I noticed that the bandages that my crew members treated my leg with on the plane had become dirty from the soft dirt I tumbled onto upon landing. By now I was in pain, and I found the morphine from my flight kit and gave myself a shot right above the wound. A short time later, I heard some voices in the distance over the rise. Some of the local townsfolk had seen the parachute in the sky, followed its path of descent and now were on their way to the landing spot. I could see three or four people making their way toward me and a vehicle moving down a blacktop road that was maybe 100 yards away. The car stopped on the road near me and two German soldiers got out of the car and began running toward me carrying rifles. One of them fired a shot from his rifle into the air to ward off the civilian farmers who were running toward me and who more than likely would have beaten me up. Local folks displayed much hostility toward downed airmen who had been dropping bombs on their towns, and there were often mobs set on retribution. Seeing the soldiers fire the warning rifle shot to the civilians who were headed toward me was such a relief. I was glad for the German soldiers' intervention, which gave me protection from the angry civilians. I was in no condition to offer any resistance, I wasn't going anywhere, and I wasn't going to be moving on my own for a long time. What I really needed was a *lot* of help.

I didn't want the soldiers to think I was reaching for my gun to shoot at them so as the soldiers approached I reached for my weapon ahead of time, pulling the .45 caliber pistol out from its holster. As the soldiers drew near, I immediately laid it in the palms of my outstretched hands in a nonthreatening manner and offered it to them in a surrendering gesture. The German soldiers had drawn rifles aimed at me, but after seeing that I was wounded they put their rifles over their shoulders and took my pistol from me. This, too, was a relief. They frisked me and took my wristwatch, high school graduation ring, wallet and a few personal photos of Anne and my family from me. They also took my 'escape photo' which was a false ID issued to us and to be used like a passport in the event we were somehow able to escape from our captors. The process of creating the photo ID was interesting. They had us put our arms through just the sleeves of a shirt, then we walked into a suit coat front where the back of the coat was open, but pinned together for fit, and the tie was also pinned to the front of the shirt collar. At this point I wouldn't need my escape photo, so I did not resist when they took the items.

Events up to this point were happening so fast it was hard to wrap my mind around everything. The German guards could see I needed medical care, and sent some of the civilians who were nearby to get help for me. It wasn't long after that the farmers had found a part of a picket fence to use as a stretcher, and returned to where I was lying. Picking me up from the ground, I was placed on this piece of fence to carry me from the cabbage patch to the road. Shortly after, more help arrived in the form of a cart with two big wheels. The farmers placed that section of fence, with me on it, across the opening of the cart and began wheeling me down the road. The two guards that captured me got in their vehicle and drove alongside my homemade stretcher to escort me somewhere other than the field.

While on this journey, we came to a crossroads and they stopped pushing the cart. Another downed American airman, captured and guarded was coming our way. As they drew closer, I could see that it was my good friend right waist gunner and crew mate, Bill Rhodes. Bill was walking toward me with his hands clasped behind his head in a surrendered posture with two German guards following closely behind him. As Bill came closer to me, I saw that his face was all battered and bloody. The Germans let us exchange greetings and talk to each other.

The Germans could speak or understand very little English, so Bill and I just started talking, taking advantage of the moment. Bill leaned over the cart and asked me, "How ya' doin' Frank?"

I said, "I'm OK, but I've been hurt pretty bad." He could see that just by looking at me. I then asked him, "What happened to you?"

Bill explained to me that when he tried to get away, the Germans beat the hell out of him. He wasn't wounded, but when they captured him he had made an attempt to escape. It seemed if you were wounded, the Germans had sympathy toward you, as was my case, otherwise they dished out a pretty severe beating.

I said, "I'll see you somewhere in prison camp" or something like that. After this brief exchange he knew that I was OK, and I knew that he was OK. We only had a few minutes together, but I still remember our meeting. And even with the uncertainty surrounding us we took comfort in seeing each other survive after all that took place on this day. Bill was the only member of our crew that I saw after our ordeal of bailing out of our plane. I found out later that Bill was taken to the town jail.

After this brief but moving encounter with my crew mate, my German guards continued to transport me down the road and about a mile or so later we arrived at a farm house and barn. By this time it was late afternoon and they took me into the barn. Once inside the barn the soldiers left – assigning the task and responsibility of guarding me to a group of Hitler youth.

They began to ask me some questions, speaking very little English. I answered their questions the best I could from what very little I understood of what they were asking me. These youngsters, somewhere between the ages of 12 to 15 years old, were part of Hitler's program to train young German boys in Nazi ideology and practices. Toward the end of the war, with Germany's loss of manpower, these youths were called upon to contribute more and more in the war effort. They weren't mean to me and did not mistreat me or anything like that. I'm sure it was their duty to just take care of me. They knew what I was requesting when I asked for water and they bought me water in a bucket (the same one the cows were drinking from!) They also brought me some apples and pears to eat. I was moved to a little corner of the barn, and placed in a seated upright position, and that's how I stayed with my company of the barn animals – cows and pigs.

The pain in my leg was getting stronger, so I put more sulfa powder on my wound and gave myself another shot of morphine. I felt I was out of danger for the time being, but the uncertainty of what would happen next began to invade my mind, accompanied by a certain amount of fear. Thoughts came to me like, "Just how seriously injured am I?" "Will I live or die?" "Am I out of harm's way?" "Will I be taken to a prison camp?" At the time, I had no idea; I needed help, that's all.

I remained in the barn as daytime passed into night, trying to get comfortable enough to catch some sleep. In the darkness I heard a vehicle approaching the farm house. German soldiers entered the barn, picked me up and carried me out to the vehicle, which looked like an ambulance-type panel truck. During the ride I was in and out of consciousness, going back and forth between periods of sleeping and being awake. I was in shock and pretty much out of it, having lost an awful lot of blood. I was only vaguely aware of what was taking place, but I do recall my body sliding side-to-side in this truck, and I was in a lot of pain.

Since I had no idea where we were at the point my crew mates literally threw me out of the plane, and I didn't know where I landed upon capture, I'm not sure where my ride from the cabbage patch field was taking me. As I remember, it wasn't a very long ride, maybe less than half an hour. Eventually the truck arrived at a building in Hanover, Germany.

Wounded, weary, and concerned, I could only think about what would happen next. One thing I knew for sure, this day, filled with unimaginable drama and terror, was ending.

Chapter Nine

WAR WOUNDED AND MORE

The guards carried me into the building and up two flights of stairs into a big open area, placing my stretcher on the floor. With a quick glance around, I saw several beds in the room and nothing else. I didn't know for sure what this place was, because I was always being moved and transported on a litter and couldn't see a lot from that position. I could see that the place didn't look like a hospital and it wasn't set up like a hospital. It seemed to be an emergency setting, the type of place that was converted to handle the many casualties of war. The official listing from the National Archives Records indicates it was Military Hospital IV, Bismarck School, Hanover. If a wounded airman was captured in the area around Hanover, Germany, this is the place they were taken.

After my crew's bombing run to Merseberg, and with the devastating hits our plane took from enemy fire, our pilots were desperately attempting to get our crippled ship back to base in Glatton. In order to do so, you had to fly over Hanover so, consequently, when our crew bailed out we were in this area.

I was just another one of the many wounded fighting men that was thrown into the mix of those desperately needing medical attention. As the other patients in the beds spoke, I became aware of the many different languages being used to communicate in this place. I was in real bad shape physically – drifting in and out of consciousness, so even though I briefly recall this taking place, it's very dreamlike to me. As the conversations took place around me, I recognized a few words of the French and German language and even heard some Russian being spoken. While I also heard the very distinctive British accent, I was almost certain that I was the only American among this melting pot of Allied wounded warriors being taken care of at this time.

Since I could understand the British fellows, I listened to some of their accounts of being wounded and captured. I tried to catch information of how the war was going. But again, my hazy state of mind wouldn't allow me to retain much of anything.

Shortly after my brief evaluation of the situation I now found myself in, two attendants came, picked my stretcher up off the floor, and carried me to another location in the building.

Communication at this point was the toughest part. There were German soldiers and staff speaking German to each other, and I couldn't understand them. I didn't know what they were going to do *for* me or *to* me. The attendants brought me into another room, and then transferred me from my stretcher to a hospital bed which was located in what looked somewhat like an operating room. There was one doctor and one nun in the room, no one else. Neither of these two spoke any English. It was a confusing time, especially as they began talking about what they were planning for my medical care. There seemed to be a sense of urgency now, as well as a quickness to the pace of all that was happening.

From what little information I could piece together, my wounds were very bad. My leg was turning black and they needed to get me into surgery right away. As I was wheeled into the operating room, which was about ten ft. by five ft. in size, I glanced around and saw, to my dismay, that this was much less than a sterile environment. In fact, it was far from it; the setting was almost primitive. There were a few light bulbs hanging from cords in the ceiling overhead, which provided some very dim lighting. The room was bare and cold; a quick chill of nervous apprehension gripped me as I embraced the reality of what would take place next.

What I remember is that I was lying on the operating table and there was a nun above me, peering down. The best way to describe her was that she looked like "The Flying Nun" from the TV show of the same name. Her starched, white habit covered all sides of her face and forehead.

Knowing that I would soon be undergoing an operation, I motioned to her with my hand, making a gesture across the top of my thigh with a sawing motion back and forth. I was desperately trying to convey that I wanted to know if they were going to amputate my leg. With rising trepidation, I watched her face, my eyes staring into her eyes to make sure she understood my question. To my great relief, the nun said, "Nein, nein" (no, no) – they were not going to cut off my leg in surgery.

By this time I really needed a little peace of mind before going under for the surgery which is why I so frantically sought information from the nun. I was somewhat comforted by the knowledge that amputation was not to be a part of the operation, but I still wasn't completely convinced, because my leg was turning black and the injury just seemed so bad. My understanding of what was going to happen was that the doctors would remove the many pieces of shrapnel deeply embedded in my thigh and foot, cut away a lot of dead flesh and clean out the damaged, rotting skin. The tandem of Doctor and Nun prepared me for surgery. There now was nothing I could do or say, so with quiet resolve, I made the sign of the cross, folded my hands, and prayed silently, "Lord, do with me what Thou wilt." It was now up to God.

It was time for the anesthesia to be given, and the anesthetic of the day was chloroform. The doctor had a strainer with cotton soaked in the chloroform. He put it over my mouth and I guessed that he was asking me to begin, counting backwards, "100, 99, 98..." and I counted way down into the 20s until I finally went out. I had no idea of the time frame from the operation until the time I woke up after surgery – whether it was that same day or the next day. It turns out I was out for about eight or nine hours. I do remember that when I did wake up I was so, so sick. I vomited and vomited and vomited some more. I had been given nothing to eat, which just made it worse, I was dry heaving and vomiting up my own bile, unable to stop. A lot of my experience up until now had been bad, but this was one of the worst parts. Between my horrible nausea, sickness, sedation wearing off, and being in intense pain, I was really miserable.

I was finally awake, and I knew immediately what I needed to do. I slowly glided my hand downward, reaching to see if my leg was still there. It was a terrifying moment, and then my hand felt the mass of bandages wrapped around flesh, not a stump. I was elated to feel the bandages and my leg beneath the wrappings! I immediately wiggled my toes and said triumphantly to myself, "Boy, I got my legs yet!" Words can't describe the relief and joy I felt in spite of the circumstances in which I found myself.

Losing my leg was such a real, raw fear because in the back of my mind I thought, "German doctors… they are going to do what is fastest for them…surely the first thing they're going to do is amputate my leg." I knew that my injury was very bad, and we had all heard about bad leg wounds other fellas had suffered – we also knew a lot of them lost their legs. I couldn't shake that fear. Not losing my leg gave me the strength to face whatever was coming my way next. I truly felt God had answered my prayers in keeping my body whole. After the operation, I was moved to a room that was bare and empty, no tables, chairs, or anything. As I lay in this hospital bed recovering from surgery, I noticed the room I was in had real high arching tops to the windows. There were no blinds or drapes on the windows and I could see the sky through the arches.

Allied bombing raids were taking place over Hanover during this time both day and night, as American and British planes were targeting the rail yards and train station in Hanover. When these bombing raids began, the staff immediately began moving other patients down to the basement, to an area that would serve as a bomb shelter. There was much confusion – and as I watched helplessly from my bed, someone approached my bed, preparing to move me. At that moment, someone else yelled, "Nein, Nein!" "Terrorflieger, Terrorflieger!" ("No, No! Don't take the Terror Flyer!") The decision was made to not move me to the basement bomb shelter.

They knew I was an American airman, and they didn't think it was very nice of me to have played a part in the bombings they had experienced on their town, so they made the decision to leave me there alone to face the oncoming destruction of the bombs. I remember watching this all take place, the other patients being moved to the air raid shelter downstairs, the hustle and bustle of accomplishing this task, yet what I fixated on was a sign near the stairway pointing downstairs to the basement. The sign had three words on it, GAS, LICT, VASSER, which I translated 'gas, light, water'– a reminder that all three were to be shut off during bombing raids. I don't know why I fixated on that sign, maybe I was trying to take my mind off of the fact that I was being left there by myself with no one to communicate with.

Soon everyone except me was downstairs and I could see the flashes of light through the high, arched windows as the bombs exploded and lit the sky. It was the most frightening time I had since being captured. In fact, it was downright terrifying. As the blockbuster, high explosive bombs continued to drop and detonate, moving my bed across the floor; the tremendous force literally shook the entire building. The sound of glass windows breaking throughout the building, as well as the deafening, thunderous roar of the planes and the bombs hitting their targets was maddening. I tried to cover my head and face to shut it all out, my hands tightly pressed against my ears to block out the earth-shattering noise all around. I was utterly abandoned, in a completely foreign environment, frightened beyond belief, and my body trembled with each sound I heard and each flash of light I saw above.

The nighttime raids in the dark were the most frightening. I had lived through the hell of combat, through being shot, thrown out of my plane, taken captive, and now, alone in my hospital bed, the very real thought that I might be killed by an allied bomb was unthinkable. It is hard to describe the dark time that this was for me. It was a horrible time to be alone.

Lying in bed I was totally helpless. The only thing I could do was pray. I grabbed both sides of the mattress as tight as I could. As I did, I discovered that the mattress had some loose string hanging from the side. As I kept tugging at it, a piece about 20 inches long broke away. I then tied the string into ten little knots, forming them into a circle. This was now my rosary that I used to ask the Lord to help me – and He did. Eventually my bed stopped shaking, the light show in the sky ended, the bombing run was over, and my anxiety lifted. I was shaken and traumatized, yet thankful that I had survived.

I wasn't in the Hanover hospital very long – just a few days of postoperative recovery. The staff moved patients in and out very quickly because every day new casualties were arriving and they needed every precious bed that was available.

I discovered that next I would be sent to an interrogation center. I had no idea what being sent there would mean for me, but I had a sense of relief, knowing that I would be leaving this place that I would never be able to forget.

Chapter Ten

ENEMY INTERROGATION

I was told that I would be transported by train to Frankfurt am Main, Germany, and the Dulag Luft Interrogation Center for downed Airmen, located in Oberursel. No other information was given to me so I wasn't sure what would happen once I arrived at the center. I think the not knowing at each step of the process was one of the hardest parts – my mind would imagine the worst case scenarios and I would have to calm myself down to be able to mentally prepare for the next phase of the journey.

The date was November 11, 1944. I was carried by stretcher out of the hospital by two German military guards who were accompanied by a German shepherd police dog and taken to the train station in Hanover. Upon arrival, the guards laid my stretcher on the floor of the train station. The train station had been heavily damaged by the bombing runs made by the Allied Forces, and I could see the sky through the broken glass of the rotunda above me. I was so glad to be getting out of Hanover because they were bombing the hell out of it every day – it was nerve-wracking and not a very safe place to be.

As I lay on the floor of the train station, people were gawking at me as they passed by. This made me uncomfortable and I didn't want anyone to know that I was an American prisoner of war. I pulled the blanket up over me, making sure I was completely covered to my face. This decision along with being guarded by the German soldiers and dog helped me to feel a little safer.

While I was waiting for the train to arrive, I had a memorable experience. I had to urinate very badly and, of course, was in no position to just stand up and relieve myself. The first thing I tried was to get the guards' attention by speaking a little English to them, communicating that I needed their help. This did not work, as they didn't understand what I was saying to them and I, in return, didn't understand the German language they were speaking back to me. I really needed relief, so I used the next best method of communication available to me, which was my own version of sign language. I put my hands between my legs and held them over my crotch. One of the guards spoke up and said, "Pishen?" I immediately replied in my limited German, "Ja, Ja!" One of the guards left and came back with what looked like an empty two-liter soda bottle. I put the bottle under the blanket between my legs. This was the first time I ever attempted to relieve myself by trying to urinate into a bottle that had a one inch opening. I did manage to get some in that narrow bottle corridor but, needless to say, not everything made its way into the bottle. I breathed a sigh of relief and handed the bottle back to the guard. It took awhile before I was comfortable again. When I tell of this experience now it seems very comical to me, considering the predicament I was in.

Soon after, I began the train ride to Frankfurt am Main which took about five to six hours, approximately 125 miles. Dulag Luft, Luftwaffe Aircrew Interrogation Center (located near Frankfurt am Main) was the first step for most United States Army Air Corps personnel captured in German-occupied Europe. Newly arrived POWs were usually told, "Vas du das krieg est uber." – "For you the war is over." There, each new prisoner, while trying to recover from the recent trauma of his shoot-down and capture, was skillfully interrogated for military information of value to the Germans. New prisoners were kept in solitary confinement while under interrogation and then moved into a collecting camp. Each prisoner was held in solitary confinement for a limited period of time – usually four or five days. The interrogators used various methods in an effort to obtain operational information from the captured airmen. Most POWs gave only the information required by the Geneva Convention – name, rank and serial number. Upon my arrival to the Dulag Luft Interrogation Center I was carried on my stretcher to a room that was to be solitary confinement for me.

Wounded, recovering and hurting from the recent traumatic surgery, the guards laid me on the floor and left the room, allowing me to survey my new location. My first impression was that the place was dingy and confining. It was unsettling to have solitary confinement be the first thing to which I was subjected. The room was long and narrow, maybe three to four ft. wide, 10 to 12 ft. long, with a really high ceiling. In the ceiling was a little opening through which I could see a small patch of sunlight. I noticed a small pot in the room that was to serve as my bathroom facilities during my stay. Other than me, that was all that was in this cold, empty, concrete floor room. The drawing on the next page shows the room; however the bed and table were removed, as I wouldn't need them since I was on a stretcher.

Dulag Luft interrogation room

I was helpless and anxious to say the least, and had no idea what to expect. Questions began to surface in my mind, "Are they going to do something to me medically?" "How long will I be confined to this cell?" "What else could they be planning for me?" My questions were interrupted by a sound at the door of my room. I watched the door apprehensively, but it never opened; instead, a set of hands pushed a small bowl of soup under the door and into the room. There was really no way of feeding myself as I lay flat on my back on my stretcher, so I just slopped the soup from the bowl, cupping my two hands together to drink the liquid from my hands almost like an animal. After managing to get some soup in me, I once again began to think about my circumstances. I remembered that during my training I was told that if I ever got captured, I might get interrogated by the enemy. A flood of thoughts entered my mind about the training we received on how to respond and what to expect if we found ourselves in this type of situation. In training we were taught that the Germans would use scare tactics, or rough us up physically to try and intimidate us into revealing information to them that could help their cause. I took some solace in the thought that being wounded, perhaps they wouldn't go to any extremes, physically at least, to try and extract information from me.

Somehow, in spite of the conditions I found myself in, and the fact that my mind was working overtime, my wounded body's need for rest won out and I drifted into a restless sleep that night. At some point the next day, my door finally opened and two guards entered my room. They picked up the stretcher I was on and began carrying me to a different location. We entered another room and, once again, I was placed on the floor. While I was lying on the floor, with my head naturally at rest, into the room walked a German soldier in full uniform. He leaned over the edge of the table and looked down at me on the stretcher. He was German, but began to speak to me in broken English. Most of the German interrogators had been schooled in the English language and were familiar with our American way of life. Military protocol established that you were interviewed by an enemy soldier of the same or equal rank. In my case, a German sergeant interviewed me. The idea was to establish a system that was somewhat fair and allowed for military courtesy, recognizing your status within the ranks. For instance, by comparison, a colonel might be asked a different set of questions by another colonel, attempting to get information that a private would not be privy to.

The sergeant began asking me questions. As he asked each question I responded, "I can't answer that." (The Geneva Convention dictated that we only had to supply name, rank and serial number.) The German interrogator then said to me, "We know all about your outfit, when you got shot down, we know everything." He proceeded to recite all of the names of the guys on our crew and asked me a question about our crew, to which I replied, "You know I can't answer that." He then asked questions about our target for bombing, strategies of our bomb group and, again, I answered, "You know I can't answer that." I was steadfast in not giving him any details whatsoever. He was essentially filling out a form he had, asking me questions and completing the form as he went along, and I continued to not answer any of the questions in his lineup.

I did tell the interrogator that I was a student and that I had been studying engineering. I had to be real careful at this point not to make any connection between myself and Westinghouse. The fact that Westinghouse was playing such a huge role in the US war effort with their manufacturing of goods and supplies was something I did not want the enemy to know I was associated with. And I certainly didn't want the Germans to gain any knowledge or information about the whereabouts of any Westinghouse plants. We had been taught to not reveal this type of information during our training for combat. I recall thinking to myself that, contrary to what I had been warned about, this guy wasn't a tough guy at all. He made a few more attempts at asking me various questions, all the while smoking a cigarette. I hadn't had a cigarette since November the 2nd, and here he was smoking the whole time; the smoke was just swirling around me where I could get a good whiff. At that moment I could have died for a cigarette, and I wanted to ask him for one, but didn't.

The interrogation came to an end, probably only lasting ten minutes or so. It turned out there was still one more piece of business to complete. After a few minutes another man entered the room carrying a camera. They were obviously going to take a picture of me, and to prepare me for the photo, I was propped up with something behind my back to pose me in a sitting position instead of my usual stance, which was lying flat on my back. Needless to say, I did not smile for the camera. The date of the interrogation and photograph was 11-20-1944. I was also assigned my prisoner of war number, which was 53620. I find it significant that I still know that number by memory to this day.

As the interrogation ended, I was relieved that I didn't experience any of the rough treatment I had been forewarned about and that the fear factor was gone. I suppose I received a little sympathy because I was so badly wounded. As I was taken from this room, I could see that there were other airmen in other rooms in this building, also being interrogated; and waiting, like me, to find out what prison camp or hospital they would be sent to after interrogation. With my own interrogation and photo session completed, I was

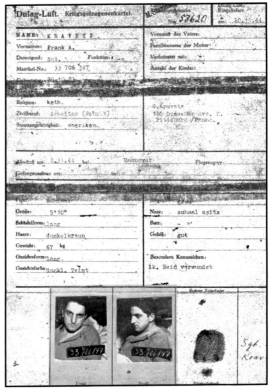

My Dulag Luft POW record

carried back to my solitary confinement room. I was glad the enemy questioning was over, satisfied that I did not break any confidences, and remained strong and loyal throughout the interrogation.

Just a short time later, guards entered my room and said, "You are being transferred to another hospital," but they did not tell me where. In my mind, I thought, "They have to get me to a hospital because I need more medical attention. I still can't walk and have to be carried on a stretcher everywhere I go." I knew I'd be bedridden for a long time no matter where I was going; that was my fate – I knew it and I had to accept it. I was only 21 years old and growing up faster than I could ever have imagined.

Chapter Eleven

THE LONG RECOVERY –
OBERMASSFELD POW HOSPITAL,
GERMANY

Wounded, weak and still unable to walk, German guards carried me by stretcher onto the train, placing me in the back section. They straddled the stretcher across the seats with my feet facing the front of the train, the guards sitting on the sides. From this position, I was able to see out the train window and view a most beautiful scenic ride through some lovely countryside. It was November and the trees were so pretty – all covered with white snow – creating a fresh and invigorating sight for me to take in. I still didn't know where I was being transported to, but with this delightful diversion, it was as though the whole world was at peace and it made the entire trip very enjoyable. The train pulled into several different stations along the way and each time the train stopped the guards would open the window for me to look outside at all the activity. At some of the stops, German Red Cross girls would be on the platform handing out coffee, cookies, and fruit to us through the windows. At each stop, there were people hustling and bustling, getting on and off the train, creating a flurry of activity. I was on the train for about six hours when we arrived at what was to be my final stop on this journey. I had no idea where I was, but I was grateful for the opportunity to be at rest and to have travelled across a scenic part of Germany.

As the train pulled into the station, I noticed it was just a little whistle-stop – no station, just a place where someone could get on or off the train. The guards carried me off the train and placed the stretcher on the wet, wooden platform. A light snow was falling and I said to myself, "Boy, it's snowing out!" with all the excitement of a young boy. The snowfall felt so nice and fresh; it was a pleasant, wonderful surprise that I appreciated very much. I didn't have long to enjoy the snow falling on me, as just a short time later an unmarked vehicle pulled in close to the train platform. The same guards that accompanied me on the journey picked up my stretcher and loaded me onto the panel-type truck. During this ride, the guards produced papers that indicated our destination was Reserve Lazarett, Obermassfeld – a hospital located in Thuringia, Germany. (Lazarett means Hospital in German.)

The location of the building was in a small village setting with a bridge that crossed over a stream that ran through the town. Across the bridge stood a large building that sat in front of a mountain-ridged background, which framed the rather large structure. As the guards carried me to the building, it did not look at all like a hospital. As it turns out, the hospital was actually an old school house that had been converted to a hospital for Allied prisoners of war. Interestingly, during the war the Nazis also used it as a training and shooting school for Hitler Youth Groups.

The ward I was on, on the second floor of the hospital, was set up with 20 beds, ten down each side of the room. I was given an upper bunk – a location that would be mine for approximately three-and-one-half months as I received badly needed medical attention. This is the reason I was given an upper bunk – they knew I wasn't going to be going anywhere for a long time and would remain bedridden as I recovered from my serious shrapnel wounds and burns. The lower bunks were used for the rotation of patients with less severe injuries.

Some of the arriving patients had received flesh wounds and they wound up being treated and released. But most of the patients were seriously wounded with amputations or gunfire wounds and came to the hospital directly from air or ground combat.

Obermassfeld was supervised by German doctors and officers but staffed by captured Allied doctors; British, Australian and Canadian. I learned quickly that my daily routine would be 24 hours a day of lying flat on my back, looking at the ceiling, without even having the ability to turn over. I never got out of that bed. I was bathed and fed from this lying down position. I didn't have any idea early on in my hospital stay how long it would be before I would be able to get up, if ever.

The bed that became my wounded body's home for the next several months had no springs and consisted of a layer of boards. The sheets were only laundered about every six weeks. There were never any spare bed linens available, and if the sheets became soiled with blood and other fluids they were only rinsed out and put right back on the bed.

Obermassfeld Allied Prisoner of War Hospital

Upon arrival to Obermassfeld, I was a real, sick boy; there is no other way to describe my condition. My discomfort level was exacerbated by the fact that I had not gone to the bathroom since before I had been shot down nine days earlier. I mentioned to a doctor that I was going to need something to help me have a bowel movement because I was so uncomfortable. The doctor soon returned with a small pill that looked like a chocolate jelly bean, which I swallowed immediately.

There was an orderly who walked to my bedside, took my chart with my name on it and spoke to me in his thick British accent, saying, "Hello, Frahnk." Not long after our brief introduction, he became real busy, real fast. Once that magic pill began to work – and it did – my insides went off like a bomb! This young orderly brought bedpan after bedpan after bedpan to me, with the same routine – me filling it up and him removing it and returning it to me. This went on for quite some time and I will never forget how kind and gracious this young man was to me throughout this ordeal. I will always be grateful to him for his compassionate care giving. After this most unusual 'getting to know each other' sequence of events, he became one of my regular caretakers, bathing me and feeding me.

He was a friendly "bloke," and took time to do little things to make me more comfortable in my current condition, that made such a difference. He climbed up to my upper bunk and taught me how to play cribbage. He brought books for me to read. Anything I needed, he was always right there to take care of me. In spite of his very thick British accent, we communicated very well, and he became a big blessing to me. I marveled that he and the other caregivers worked such incredibly hard, long hours – usually laboring 12 to 14 hours a day. We were all so very thankful for their dedication to our recovery and well-being. It turns out this young man was a medic as were so many others who daily cared for all of us patients. Many of the staff had enlisted into the RAMC (Royal Army Medical Corps), British troops who themselves had been captured and taken prisoners of war, with their assignment being the Obermassfeld hospital.

During the early part of my hospitalization, the only treatment plan was to keep the infection down. Drainage tubes were placed in my leg and early indications were that I didn't have any bone damage, but that I did have a slight crack in the bone. Thank God no main arteries were severed, but I did suffer a lot of nerve damage.

Eventually, the doctors began to devise a plan of action for my recovery, to help relieve my pain and discomfort, with the goal of getting me healed and back on my feet being their primary objective. Having had some time to review my case, the doctors reached a decision on how best to proceed with my treatment. The doctors discovered that gangrene had already set in to my wound, and they were afraid that it might spread to another part of my body. Infection had invaded my leg and needed to be treated immediately. There was not much medicine in the hospital during this time, and I wasn't sure how they were going to treat my wound.

In fact, the doctors never told me exactly what they were going to do in terms of treatment, they just did it. They prefaced their actions by saying something like, "This is going to help kill the infection." The doctors cleaned the wound as best they could under the conditions. Both of my legs, including my feet, were firmly encased in an aluminum or thin steel 'trough-like' apparatus that resembled a drain spout.

With my left thigh lying exposed and open, I watched as they took a jar filled with maggots and dumped them into the wound on my thigh. They laid towels on either side of the wound to keep the maggots in place once they were released onto the wound. The maggots went immediately for the wound, ravaging the blackened, rotting flesh. The doctors then covered the wound with the maggots inside in a bandage, wrapped tightly around my thigh. A tent-like covering was made with a sheet over the top of my legs and feet, and then they tucked the cloth underneath the aluminum trough.

The doctors were just as matter of fact as they could be – almost as if placing maggots inside my wound was just routine doctoring on their part, something they did on a daily basis, no big deal to them. I simply had to trust and have faith that they were doing the right thing and that this would help me. That's all I could do. If I gave it much thought I would recoil from the word "maggot" and the images that would conjure in my mind. As a boy, I remember lighting fires in our garbage cans at home to kill maggots. We would pour gasoline into the cans and light them with matches to burn the maggots away. Now, here I was with these tiny, disgusting creatures eating away at the rotted flesh inside my leg.

It was over a week that I remained with the bandage in place and the maggots busily doing their duty. I never felt the maggots while they were in there. A team of doctors returned after a week or so and removed the bandages. I watched with anticipation to see the look upon the doctor's faces. I was delighted to see their smiles of satisfaction, indicating that the procedure had worked. The wound had turned from a blackish color to a healthy pink color, indicating the flesh-eating maggots had stopped the invasion of the infection. They declared the procedure a success.

It was at this time that one of the doctors told me that the reason they tried this method was because there wasn't any penicillin available at this time in the hospital and they were limited in what they could do. The doctors at Obermassfeld were able to obtain the maggots from a local German doctor.

In the book, 'One and a Half Missions, the author Leland A. Dowland recalls this procedure being done for him while in Obermassfeld. He mentions one other fellow who had this done. While I know that I am not the person Leland refers to in his account, I am grateful for his recording and description of this unique medical procedure taking place in Obermassfeld. It helped me to be comfortable and confident in relaying my own personal experience of having gone through this, and helped solidify the validity of my account.

I wondered about where they may have gotten these maggots. I found out the following from Dr. Ronald A. Sherman MD, MSC, DTM&H, retired University of California at Irvine, "Most likely, the doctor (at Obermassfeld) could have done what several in the US did during the 1940s through the 1980s, find (or take the patients outside to attract) wild maggots in hopes that they would be good enough. They usually were. During the 1930s, many hospitals had their own insectaries where they reared medical grade maggots. I am aware of only one commercial laboratory in North America, Lederle Laboratories (New Jersey) which probably supplied maggots during 1935-1939. There may have been suppliers in Europe during the 1940s, but I do not know of any, and therefore

I doubt it. The maggots could have been raised at the facility for this purpose." Maggot Debridement Therapy (MDT) is the medical use of live maggots (fly larvae) for cleaning non-healing wounds. Medicinal maggots have three actions, (1) they debride (clean) wounds by dissolving the necrotic (dead), infected tissue; (2) they disinfect the wound, by killing bacteria; and (3) they stimulate wound healing. Historically, maggots have been known for centuries to help heal wounds. Many military surgeons noted that soldiers whose wounds became infested with maggots did better – and had a much lower mortality rate – than did soldiers with similar wounds not infested.[2]

My doctor was an English doctor, Major John Sherman (not related to Dr. Ronald Sherman above.) He was a prisoner of war also, captured in 1941 at the battle of Dunkirk and sent to work in the hospital at Obermassfeld. I credit him and his staff of medical doctors with saving my leg and my life. I am forever indebted to them.

Left to right: Capt. Vernon Barling, Capt. Bill Holden, Capt. Wooden, Major J. B. Sherman

With the maggot therapy behind me and my flesh beginning to heal, my leg would be ready to have necessary skin grafts to close up the wound. The doctors kept returning to my bedside every few days or so over the next month to take a look at my wound, checking on the healing process.

---

[2] Dr. Ronald A. Sherman, website: vcihs.uci.edu/path/sherman/home

One day the doctors said it was time to start skin grafts on my leg. They began the procedure right there as I lay in my bed. I wasn't required to go to surgery or have an operation. Knowing this part of my treatment was beginning made me very happy because I knew I'd be moving closer to my leg being healed completely.

To begin the skin grafts, the doctors turned me over onto my side the best they could. They painted a patch on my rear end with a purple-colored betadine-type solution, and then began scraping three-inch squares of skin off my butt. Once the pieces of skin were removed, they placed them into a saucer and added some kind of solution to the skin, mixing both together and then applying it directly onto my thigh wound. They did not cover the wound, but used the bed sheet to form a canopy over the area. I really didn't feel any pain; it was more like a brush-burn type of sensation. The mixture looked like grease that forms on top of a pot of soup that has sat for a day cooling off.

I wasn't given any type of anesthetic and was very much awake during the procedure. The doctors said, "Stay as still as you can, don't move your legs or anything else, remain still." They kept reminding me to remain still and I didn't move! Or at least I did the best I could, propped up on my side. I wasn't about to question anybody or anything. All I knew was that these doctors were taking care of me, providing professional medical care – and that was good enough for me. They repeated this procedure four times while I was in the hospital, each time pulling new patches of skin from my rear end, mixing skin and solution and repeatedly applying it to my wound. When the procedure was over all I could do was lie down on my back, find as comfortable a position as possible, and stay put.

After each application, they came back and checked both the wound and my behind. I never had any problems or complications. I don't remember being uncomfortable. In my mind, it was a simple procedure to help me. When I first arrived at the hospital my left leg wound was wide open, stretching across the entire top of my thigh, ten inches or more and quite deep. It turns out that a large piece of metal from an enemy shell had been buried deep into my muscle when I got shot. Amazingly, with the velocity of the shell hitting my thigh, it did not shatter my bone or hit a major artery, which would have caused me to bleed to death. At some point, I was given the piece of metal that had been removed in surgery, but I don't know what happened to it.

Thankfully, after each of these skin graft procedures, the wound was contracting as the skin was knitting together and healing. The doctors told me that I would still be bedridden for quite a while longer, so I had no expectations about being up and around any time soon. I remember asking them, "How long until I will be able to walk?" They explained that the wound was still draining, so as long as pus was still seeping out, there was no way I was going to be able to get up.

So I continued eating every single meal while lying flat on my back and that is not easy to do. The meager servings would be brought right to my bedside by one of the orderlies. I was so grateful for their assistance. I was painfully aware that I was not free to come and go as I pleased, that the Germans controlled the food supply, and ultimately decided what I would receive to sustain me during my recovery. The fact was that there just wasn't much food available for any of us, only a minimum amount of calories – enough to keep us alive.

For breakfast there was typically black bread with some type of a jellylike spread on top, served with a cup of hot tea (which was a wonderful treat.) The warmth of the tea was so good simply because it was hot – it was wintertime and I was cold a lot. For lunch there was usually some kind of black bread (again) and a flavored soup which was all mixed together. Dinner brought the ever-present black bread, potatoes, some meager serving of a bean or pea and usually some type of a vegetable. We received English and American Red Cross parcels that contained items like cheese and canned meats, biscuits, cans of dehydrated oatmeal and sometimes, powdered milk. Getting these different items was a big boost, and something we all really looked forward to.

A little more about the food that I was given: while I was a patient, I was given something called 'Welsh rarebit.' The cooks in this little hospital made this dish and as I understand, it's a British meal. They were able to make it because they got the ingredients out of Red Cross parcels. Included in the parcels were what we referred to as 'dog biscuits'. The cooks soaked the biscuits in water to soften them up, then used them in the recipe. It was pretty good, made with cheese and I'm not sure what else. After I first tasted it, it became a meal I really looked forward to. When they would bring my dinner plate to me, I would ask, "What are we having tonight?" When they answered, 'Welsh Rarebit," I would say, "Oh boy!" It's nothing really, just one of the routines I remember. The funny thing is that I always thought I was eating Welsh *Rabbit*, not rarebit. Occasionally I was lucky enough to receive two sardines on a plate and believe me, that was a big deal!

There were a few books that were available to us to share and read. The two books that I was able to read were, "How Green was my Valley" and "A Tree Grows In Brooklyn." I only had the books for two hours at a time and then they would be passed along to another patient to allow everyone a chance to get some reading time. It's not as though I could hide the books under my pillow and pull them out later – everyone was waiting for the books, so I had two precious hours of reading and then they were off making the rounds. To say the books were highly treasured by me and the others would be an understatement.

Since I had learned to play cribbage, this became a pastime that I also looked forward to when the orderlies had some rare free time to bring the board up to my bunk.

There were no calendars available so the only way I knew the date was when I got a copy of a German newspaper with a date on it. A newspaper like that would be passed around among all of the patients – of course we could only decipher a few words or phrases. The only other way we received information was when new patients would arrive from the battlefields. As they shared firsthand accounts about battles won or lost, we listened intently.

A record player had been delivered by the Red Cross with a small collection of records and the player rotated to different places throughout the hospital. We heard the sounds of Bing Crosby, Harry James and Deanna Durbin.

For many of us disabled patients, the days were just unbelievably dull and boring. We had no contact from home, no letters, no entertainment or distractions. Added to this was the constant hunger, the waiting for our wounds to heal and the battle against depression and lethargy. I gave up smoking cigarettes while a patient in Obermassfeld. There really weren't that many to go around and they were a highly valued and often traded item for those patients still wanting a smoke.

It was now November and December of 1944; I hadn't written any letters and hadn't received any letters from home.

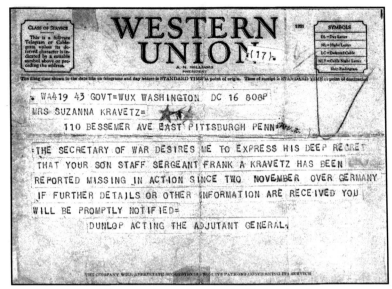

Telegram sent to my parents from the War Department

I didn't know at that time that the war department had sent them a telegram.

At this time, intense fighting was taking place at the Battle of the Bulge, and the hospital was being overrun by casualties coming in from the battlefields. Wounded servicemen were arriving every day at the hospital and the staff just laid them on the floor, anywhere they could find a spot. You can't imagine this scene. There were so many wounded that they were lying in the aisles with very little room in between. They were being brought in faster than the hospital staff could keep up with, the place was overwhelmed with new arrivals. I recall the incredible and horrifying sound of the moaning and groaning of the injured. Guys were literally dying left and right.

Prior to Hitler's massive winter offensive, which began on Dec 16, 1944, it was widely believed that Allied Forces would quickly bring Hitler's war machine to its knees. But information brought to the hospital by the new patients relayed devastating news that Nazi Germany was not ready to quit fighting. Our hopes were dashed to learn that the Germans were, instead, overrunning our troops.

I often think about everything I had experienced during this time. Terribly horrible things that happened to other people, but that I had never in my wildest dreams expected to have happen to me. Yet, here they were, my reality. Yes, I had some rough times. At times it was hard – maddening, and I would press my hands against my ears in an attempt to drown out the screams and the pain from those all around me. I couldn't avoid the others' misery and despair, it was everywhere, and it bothered me. There were quite a few blind patients who were in a nearby ward and they would yell and cry, "I'm not going home like this!" Some of the ambulatory patients would attempt to read to them, and as they read stories about home or something meant to comfort them, it would do the opposite, and they would scream, "Stop! *STOP* – I don't want to hear any more!" fraught with their own realization that they would never see their wives' or parents' or children's' faces again. And I couldn't move, couldn't get away from it all, couldn't help or change the circumstances of my fellow man. Yet it reminded me of how fortunate I was to have survived with the injuries I had.

I recall being in the hospital flat on my back when a guy in the bed directly across from me hung himself. Both of his legs were gone. I heard him screaming that he didn't want to go home this way, that he didn't want to go on. At some point during the night, his despondency took over and I awoke to see him dangling from his bed. As daylight poured into the ward, the staff put a curtain around his bed to shield us from seeing all the confusion and activity taking place. There was all kinds of commotion in the ward, with people coming in to assist. I heard horrible screams coming from so many of the other patients, my fellow human beings. There weren't enough doctors to ease the pain, discomfort and anguish all around us. It was hell on earth, that's all I can say, hell on earth.

Although I never saw a burial while at Obermassfeld, many patients did die while there. They were permitted a service and buried in a nearby cemetery. I was curious as to how a deceased patient would be buried and asked one of the orderlies who assisted to describe how it was done. He mentioned the dead were simply placed naked in a crude box filled with leaves and carried to their final resting place just away from the hospital grounds. They were escorted by German guards who fired their rifles as a final tribute.

Our morale went way down, because they were telling us, "We're losing the war." It was just terrible; an awful, very depressing time. It was sometime around December 16th. I didn't make friends during my time in the hospital. It just didn't happen that way since I was stuck in my bed and not ambulatory at all. Other POW's who were in different stalags were together in a prison camp, they had opportunities to get to know each other and form friendships.

Christmas Eve soon rolled around. Here we all were, British, Austrian, American wounded – all kinds of guys in my shoes, away from home and sad, stuck in this hospital on Christmas Eve, 1944. The Germans allowed us to have a Christmas Eve and Christmas Day celebration. We were given turkey and potatoes, pitchers of beer and wine. That went a long way to lift our sagging spirits and give us a taste of home.

After all of the enjoyable respite from the throes of war and the joyous celebration of Christmas, there was still one more surprise that we were thrilled about. The Germans arranged for a Midnight Mass to be celebrated. This was the only time during my captivity that I was able to attend Mass, and it was the only time I was out of my bed. I was carried to the front of the auditorium where there was a make shift altar and that's where my stretcher was placed on the floor. As the priest performed the Mass, with lumps in our throats, we prayed, sang, hoped, and sought Divine intervention.

They also had a few gifts that they passed around the hospital. I received a picture of Ebbets field which was the home of the Brooklyn Dodgers Baseball team. I thought, "What do I want with a picture of the Brooklyn baseball team's field?" The answer was, "Nothing" – so I traded that item, actually bartering with another guy for a pipe. And even though I didn't have any tobacco, I kept the pipe with me for when I would have tobacco again and would be able to smoke the pipe.

In spite of this temporary diversion, the news of Germany's massive offensive – the Battle of the Bulge – which surprised and caught Allied Commanders off guard – soon overshadowed the gifts and the celebration of Christmas. The morale at the hospital slipped to a low ebb. When I first arrived at the hospital, conditions were somewhat bearable. But by Christmas 1944, the hospital was jammed with new patients, most of them wounded and captured in the Battle of the Bulge, Hitler's last gasp effort to turn the tide of WWII in Western Europe.

While captive in physical terms, and wanting not to be held a prisoner in my mind, I battled to take my 'captivity captive' – a phrase used by an orderly who worked at Obermassfeld. I learned to embrace a reading from the letter of St. Paul to the Philippians, "Brothers and sisters, I know how to live in humble circumstances; I know also how to live with abundance. In every circumstance and in all things I have learned the secret of being well fed and of going hungry, of living in abundance and of being in need. I can do all things in Him who strengthens me. Still, it was kind of you to share in my distress. My God will fully supply whatever you need, in accord with his glorious riches in Christ Jesus.

To our God and Father, glory forever and ever. Amen."
(Philippians 4:12-14, 19-20.)

A brief time later, I experienced one of the biggest
disappointments of my life as a prisoner. I was still bedridden
and one of the orderlies had placed a tag on my bed indicating
that I was slated to be put on a Swedish Red Cross repatriation
boat to go home on January 1, 1945. But very soon after that
I was taken off the list. Because there were now so many more
seriously wounded men that were a higher priority needing
treatment, they needed to board the ship first. My tag was
removed from my bed and given to another soldier, and I went
way down on the list to go home by boat. I had almost tasted
my freedom, and then it was taken away again.

Around this time I made the acquaintance of a serviceman
named Harold Sturman who had part of his foot shot off and
had a cast on his leg. He was scheduled to be put on the
repatriation boat and would be going home. My parents had
no idea of my plight during this time since it had been months
since I could get any kind of word to them. I asked Harold if I
could leave a note in his leg cast that would get back to the
states and hopefully, to my parents. The guy agreed, and there
were others who placed similar notes in his cast for the trip
back to the United States. The note simply stated to my family
that I was in a hospital, was OK and that I would be home as
soon as the war was over.

Soon the New Year 1945 arrived, and with it my continued
desire to get better, survive, and go home! But my plan was
sidetracked by my coming down with a pneumonia-like illness
shortly after the start of the New Year. I started shaking and
shivering, chilled to the bone and unable to get warm or to
stop my body from trembling. I was soon transferred to a
barrack type of unit away from the main hospital and placed

in an isolation ward – a section where they took all of the patients with pneumonia.

The building was a tar paper shanty with ice on the windows. There were many, many patients in the ward. I can't say for sure if I was actually diagnosed with pneumonia, but I can say for sure that I was real sick with a high fever and was barely conscious throughout most of this ordeal. I was covered with large, round, heated stones, like you would find in a creek. These were lined the entire length of my body on both sides up and down, even placing them clear up under my arms to the armpit. I was packed in these heated stones from my toes up to my neck. After the stones were in place, I was covered with towels, wrapped up like a mummy in an attempt to get me and keep me warm. This routine of replacing the stones and towels was repeated several times throughout my stay in the isolation ward. I was given hot liquids of tea and broth which the orderlies helped me to swallow.

I'm not sure how long I was there, but at some point, my fever dropped, the chills disappeared and I was transferred back to the main hospital. My daily routine continued with no change as January turned to February 1945. February 14th, on Valentine's Day, one of the orderlies came in and this was the first time since I was shot down on November 2nd that I was able to sit up in bed. It had now been three months of lying flat on my back, never getting up, even eating while laying down. The day had finally arrived where I could get up! I couldn't believe it.

When the orderlies helped to lift my body up and slide me toward the side of the bed I became very dizzy, very quickly. One of the attendants literally had to hold me up for awhile until the dizziness began to fade and I could adjust to being upright. Next I got to dangle my legs over the side of the bed.

It turns out my leg muscles were so stiff from inactivity that they shot straight out forming an L shape, there was no elasticity at all. But oh, how wonderful it was to be sitting up! It only lasted a short time but I sure appreciated it. This also was the first time I got to eat while sitting up. I felt like a new person. The other guys were watching me, happy for the progress I was making and I was the center of attention for a while.

The orderlies then said to me, "We're going to start you with therapy as soon as we can." Therapy did begin and it consisted of putting my legs stretched out on the bed, and then they added weights. They used little bags about the size of a small sack of sugar or flour, filled with sand, each with different amount of weights. They would put the weights on the instep of my foot and I would slowly lift the weight bags. I don't know how long I continued this routine. The therapy was every day, twice a day for quite some time; working hard on getting my feet to bend again and my legs to strengthen. Eventually I regained sufficient strength in my legs to satisfy the orderlies that I had progressed enough to now get me out of bed. I was given a set of crutches and began my first baby steps away from my bed. The orderlies were with me every step of the way. I walked slowly and hesitantly but with a smile on my face; it felt so good to be up and walking again. There were no goals for walking a certain distance on my crutches; I just walked around the ward sometimes holding on to the other beds as I maneuvered around. I was putting weight on my wounded leg a little at a time, but there was still pus coming out of it, so it was still draining. I continued to learn how to walk again and get steadier on my crutches. I was gaining confidence daily and also gaining back some muscle strength.

About this time, I received word that I would be leaving Obermassfeld Hospital and would be transferred to a new location. It made sense, because I was out of the bed and ambulatory and the bed was now needed for another wounded soldier or airman. But instead of being on a ship headed for home, in the back of my mind I knew I would be sent to a prisoner of war camp. There weren't many other options for me at this point.

On March 1, 1945, after months of lying on my back recovering from my leg wounds, it was time to leave the hospital that had become my home. I reflected long and hard upon the months spent at Obermassfeld and now I was leaving.

Upon departing, the young British orderly who had so compassionately cared for me wished me a hearty and heartfelt, "Good Luck, Frank!" I simply can't say enough about him – he was such a blessing to me, along with the other selfless caregivers at Obermassfeld.

Many years after the war, I tried to locate this young man so that I could offer my sincere thanks for all of his work on my behalf. Sadly, I was not able to ever contact him. Instead I reached a fellow British orderly by the name of H. L. Martin, who penned his memoirs of his time at Obermassfeld, entitled "Lasting Impressions". His recording of the history of Obermassfeld is priceless.

Finally no longer captive to my bed, using my crutches and feeling a bit wobbly, I walked out of Obermassfeld Hospital. It was a great feeling to be upright and walking after all those months of being a bedridden patient.

There was no ground transportation to get us to the train station so several of us who were able to walk journeyed a short distance through town on our way to the Oberursel

Railroad station, accompanied by armed German guards. I enjoyed being outside again, smelling the crisp air and seeing how pretty the countryside was. But as I walked, I couldn't forget the many scenes etched in my mind forever of the sights, the sounds and the sacrifices made by one human being in the compassionate selfless care given to one scared, now skinny airman from Pennsylvania. A lump remained in my throat as I moved on.

Chapter Twelve

Barbed Wire and Bugs – Nuremberg Prison Camp; Stalag XIIID

I hobbled aboard the train, took my seat and reflected on where I had just spent the last three months of my life; wondering, apprehensively, where my next destination would be. It didn't take long for me to get an answer. When the train eventually stopped to pick up a few more prisoners of war, I found out that this train was taking us all to Stalag Luft XIIID (13-D) in Nuremberg, Germany (Stalag Luft means, "camp for Airmen".)

I really had no idea what to expect. Of course, I thought of cells and imprisonment and barbed wire, but I couldn't comprehend what being a 'prisoner of war' would mean to me. Up until now I was a patient, then a prisoner-patient in a hospital setting, but not in a prison camp. I wondered what kind of medical attention I would get, if any. As the train raced down the tracks, I tried to just appreciate not being in a hospital bed, and accept this next part of my journey.

Arriving at the train station in Nuremberg, I grabbed my crutches, walked off the train and immediately noticed how the station had been severely damaged by bombings and stood partially in ruins. Guards from the Nuremberg Prisoner of War Camp met us there and began walking us to the prison camp, as there was no transportation available. There were several of us who had just been released from hospitals, so we were all plodding along, me on my crutches, others just shuffling along dealing with their injuries and sickness.

Along the way, we passed the Nuremberg Stadium where Hitler held rallies and delivered several of his speeches. It was here that he recruited masses of people into Nazism, convincing them to follow him and his radical ideas. As I looked at the stadium, I briefly reflected on the significance of this one man's power gone out of control and how it had destroyed so many lives, and certainly how now his decisions were impacting my life.

The walk was a short distance from the train station, maybe three kilometers. Approaching the site, I could see the barbed wire encampment, and guard towers with the German soldiers' rifles rising as we got closer to the gate. This scene was the embodiment of what I had lost – my freedom. I was now held captive by the enemy under their terms. The front gates were opened and our German guards marched us into the compound, handing over our prisoner paper work, to the Commandant in charge of the camp.

The Commander went inside a building for a brief time, then came back outside and announced which barracks we were assigned to. We were all assigned to different barracks, and a guard escorted me to mine. Walking across the grounds,

I saw building after building of wooden boxlike structures spread across the compound as far as I could see. Eventually my guard stopped in front of one of these buildings and pointed to the door. I entered the barracks and was greeted immediately by a fellow prisoner, the barracks leader, who walked over and introduced himself to me. The rest of the men in the barracks also welcomed me into the fold. Everyone was an American and they were all very warm and receptive toward me. I was relieved to be among other Americans at this point and to be able to speak English and communicate easily.

The only items I brought with me were the crutches I was using and a satchel I received while at the Interrogation center, which contained a toothbrush, tooth powder, soap and a comb. I was shown to a bunk and put my stuff on the bed.

Conversation soon began with the other guys asking me where I was from. I told them that I was from Pittsburgh and asked if anybody else in the barracks was from that area. There weren't any others from Pennsylvania or even from nearby states like Ohio, West Virginia, or New York.

The get acquainted talk shifted to being asked where I was shot down. I shared the basics of my being shot down, parachuting, then being taken captive and eventually taken to a hospital for recovery. They asked me how I was coming along with my injuries, and I said I was doing OK. It turns out that I was the only one in the barracks recovering from wounds received in battle.

I was asked about what I might have heard from the front, but I didn't have any outside information to bring them about how the war was progressing or anything like that because I had been in hospitals and we didn't get very many updates.

The guys then shared with me about how things were handled in the camp – what the daily routine was and what was expected. I learned when and how chow was distributed, when we had to be in bed for lights out and how roll calls were conducted. It turns out that I was now a "kriegie" – a slang term used by prisoners of war. It was a shortened version of the German word kriegsgefangener, which meant war prisoner.

After taking care of this business, they asked me if I wanted some coffee or a bite to eat and I let them know that I had eaten a little on the train ride and I was OK. I wasn't really aware at that point of how bad the shortage of food was within the camp. I then just tried to adjust to my new surroundings, and continue to get acquainted with the guys.

I couldn't help but notice how dismal, dingy, dark and dirty the barracks were. But that was just the tip of the iceberg, for I would soon experience the filth and deteriorating conditions of the camp in a more personal way.

As nighttime approached, I tried to crawl up into the upper bunk I had been assigned upon my arrival into camp. I was having a tough time and struggled to hoist myself up with my bad leg. One of the other fellas saw my plight and offered to switch with me, giving me his lower bunk, and for that I was grateful.

As I settled in for my first night in prison camp, one thing I noticed right away was how cold it was there. Cold and dark. There were a couple of dim lights in the room and a potbelly stove in the middle of the barracks. The way it worked was when coal was available we would get a little heat. When the coal ran out, and more wasn't given to us, some of the guys would go out and get some wood. Guys would be assigned to a work detail, accompanied by German guards, to go out and chop firewood from the woods that surrounded the camp. Toward the end of our stay at Nuremberg firewood was getting more and more scarce. Guys started to tear lumber off of the wooden structures in the compound, mostly one board at a time, which allowed them to hide the stolen wood under their coats for safe delivery to their barracks without being seen. A lot of the wood was taken from the outhouse building.

Sleeping in prison camp proved to be an entirely different ball game. There were 12 men in a box-type arrangement of wooden beds, with some wire stretched underneath the boards, creating a hammock type of framework that was wavy and lumpy. At some point, alternate bed slats were removed to provide heat for the stove, which left an uneven sagging in the bedding. There was some sort of a sack-like material filled with straw for the so-called mattress.

It was so cold in the room that guys would buddy up with someone else to take advantage of the body heat. I went to sleep with all of my clothes on and soon found out about the routine of sharing a blanket with two other guys to help us keep each other warm. The blankets were thin and filthy. The body heat went a long way in keeping us from getting too cold to sleep. But – it also went a long way to give lice a place to reproduce!

It didn't take long before I first noticed the lice in bed when I started scratching, and itching, and scratching and itching and scratching some more. I could actually feel them biting, like little intruders on my skin, and I could see them crawling on me and my clothes. I realized everybody was scratching and everybody had lice, fleas and bedbugs; and these constant companions did their part to drive us crazy with the itching. This was part of my discovery of just how filthy dirty the camp was.

At night, a German guard came by and closed a small window in the barracks from the outside with a wooden bar.

That was it – you were locked in. Once the guard shut that window you were in the barracks until morning, and you were not leaving. Bathroom needs were taken care of courtesy of a bucket in the room. Believe it or not, I actually slept pretty well the first night in prison camp. I guess after the long day I had, exhaustion set in and mercifully, I was able to sleep.

Before I knew it I heard the sound of a guard yelling, "Appell, Appell," which is the German word that means roll call. Shortly after this shout from the guard we shuffled outside and assembled to stand in lines while we waited for the guards to take a head count. The guards didn't count right away. They would make it miserable for us, sometimes making us wait for over an hour before they completed their count. Or if it was raining, they took special delight in having us stand there getting soaking wet. I wasn't used to standing for any length of time and with my crutches, it was difficult for me.

We lined up in rows with so many in a row, maybe 50 or 60 guys. A German guard in front would count, "eins, zwei, drei, vier"… and so on, eventually shouting out a number to a German guard in the back who was also counting along the lines, a kind of multiplication game. If the numbers added up from front to back, side to side, row to row, and everybody was there – meaning the counts were right for all the men that were assigned to the barracks, we'd be dismissed, if not, the counting would begin all over again.

Once back in the barracks after roll call, I would walk with my crutches, back and forth, back and forth. It wound up being my own physical therapy and I did it every day. If there was nice weather I would go outside the barracks and walk the perimeter of the camp. Most days I would find somebody else to walk with, exchanging small talk as we walked. We talked about our families, sports, food, whatever would help pass the time. The daily walking routine helped me to clear my head mentally and speed my healing physically.

On warmer days you'd see guys out in the compound trying to get some physical activity in. One thing that guys would do on nicer days was to rinse their clothes out with what little cold water they could get then hang them out on a line to dry.

There weren't many rules within the camp. The place was so overcrowded that the rules were kept simple, and showing up for a daily roll call was one of the main rules. Estimates of the prison population at the time were 10,000.

The Allied Armies were advancing from the west and the Russian armies were advancing from the East. As a result, many POW camps were being evacuated and the prisoners were moved into other camps which were already overcrowded, which was the case at Nuremberg.

I was introduced to the joys of the outhouse area, which was quite far away from our barracks. Bathroom choices were limited, there was one outhouse building to be used by three or four barracks of guys. The Germans never really cleaned them, and there was no lye available. As a result, the toilets were always filled and filthy with a smell that was horrid. Sanitation was virtually nonexistent, and of course, privacy was not available. As a result, most of the time guys simply used slit trenches. Being on crutches I found this was not an option for me. Slit trenches were nothing more than a dug out hole in the ground with boards stretched across that you could straddle and do your business. Guys would just dig a new slit trench when needed, covering up the old one as necessary – a foul and primitive way to relieve one's self with no options.

The camp had one wash house that serviced two barracks, where I would go to get water. There were two running cold water spigots for *all* of us guys – it was not enough. When I went in to brush my teeth or wash up a little, I was only able to splash a few drops of water into my mouth or onto my face, that's all.

In prison camp, I quickly grew a scraggly beard and a moustache that resembled the handle bar variety. There was nothing in camp to properly shave or groom with, so the best I could do was when somebody scrounged up a pair of dull, old scissors, every so often I'd borrow them and hack away at the days-old growth.

I soon learned firsthand how the distribution of food was handled. The German guards would bring the food into the barracks, then one of our barracks guys would take the ration of bread, (which was a black bread mixed with sawdust, leaves, straw and sugar beets) margarine and sometimes jelly to the tables with benches for guys to sit and eat. Portions would then be evenly divided for a group of four guys. This way everybody wasn't running to get the food in one giant rush. This system made the distribution easier and a bit more civilized.

Sometimes, on better days, there were soups or stews and when these were available; it was prepared in a big kettle outside. We'd grab our tin cans and stand in line until it was our turn to receive the ladle-full of soup. If we were lucky we'd be given a potato in the soup line and most of us would stick them in our pockets to eat later. Occasionally when I would receive this meager bowl of watery soup, there were beans in it (similar to a garbanzo bean) and sometimes I would notice a tiny yellow worm moving on the bean which I suspect was some type of maggot. I forced myself to look past the worm, put the spoonful in my mouth, and swallow the soup, worm and all. The way I looked at it, the worm was an additional source of protein and I needed it.

The guys in my barracks that had been in camp before I arrived told me how bad the food rationing had become. The camp did receive some Red Cross food parcels, but not very often. I never got my own food parcel while in Nuremberg. Now and then I was able to share with other guys who had received a parcel before I got to prison camp.

In those parcels were sugar, cigarettes, coffee, crackers, and maybe a chocolate bar. Portions were almost always rationed and we were very aware that we might need to dip into the stash later. We all learned how to squirrel food away to stretch it out and use later. We rationed everything – we had to. Some days we got fed, some days we didn't. There was barely enough to live and survive, and not more than that. That's just the plain and simple truth. Because of this, we were always hungry and very often, as you can imagine, our conversations revolved around food. Especially when talking about those wonderful home-cooked meals we would get once we got home!

One very precious commodity in camp was coffee. Coffee was so appreciated by everyone, and we purposely made it weak to stretch it out. Instead of putting an entire teaspoon of coffee into some water, we'd use ½ teaspoonful of coffee. Usually we only had German ersatz coffee which was made out of roasted acorns – a sort of imitation coffee, not the real thing, and it tasted like shit. By comparison our good old American coffee tasted fantastic and was a huge treat welcomed by all of us. This was my first experience with something called 'instant coffee' and I treasured it. The brand was George Washington Instant Coffee, supplied in a two oz. package by the military through the Red Cross. It was weak, but very enjoyable. Sometimes British parcels had 'loose' tea, not tea bags, and we would drop a pinch of that into water.

At other times, the Germans would bring horse drawn wagons with buckets of potatoes into camp. The potatoes would get boiled and we'd get a thin slice or two of bread and that was it. I made my own homemade version of a three pronged fork/spoon combination that I crafted out of a piece of wood.

There was a very small stove to cook on and we all took turns using the stove. I was really intrigued with the simple ingenuity of the cook stove and very much impressed with how efficiently it worked.

The British were instrumental in making a lot of these types of items to use, being that they had been in the camps a lot longer due to the fact that Britain entered the air wars earlier than the United States. As early as 1942, the British Royal Air Force had over 1,000 aircraft in the sky in a massive bombing over Cologne, Germany. As a result, the British became prisoners of war early on in the war.

Another activity that took place in the barracks was playing cards, which I took part in a lot. I learned how to play bridge. That helped to pass the time and ease the boredom. All of us in the barracks got along real well and there were never any personality conflicts of any kind. Some of the British prisoners of war had a few cribbage boards with them and I joined in. I was grateful that I had learned how to play the game while at Obermassfeld hospital.

There was a little library in the camp, mostly started by the guys that had been in prison camp for a while. There were only a few precious books available. I learned that the library was located in another compound, pretty far away from my barracks and there were always long lines of guys waiting to try and get a book. As a result, I never had a book the whole time I was a prisoner. It's hard to describe, but just existing became what was important. Not even getting a book mattered.

Yet even as I struggled with the day-to-day sadness and despair, I never once had any regrets that I signed up to serve.

In the barracks there would be hand-drawn maps that were posted showing the latest battles and strategies of the war. We would gather around and discuss what might be happening and how close we were to being rescued. Our man of confidence would come into the barracks and read from the BBC (British Broadcasting Company) and also pass on German version updates that were heard on a clandestine radio hidden in camp somewhere. Wherever the radio was, after listening to a report, the news was written down on something, and copies were then made by rewriting so that they could be taken barrack to barrack to be read to others. Guys coming in from the front would provide the latest news, too.

Once we received these very latest communiqués, a considerable amount of time was spent by all of us trying to decipher the news we heard and strategizing – guessing, really – how long until we would be liberated.

I never heard of anyone planning an escape from prison camp. The guards up there in the towers were always watching the perimeter of the camp all day and night, armed with machine guns at the ready. They were always there, a constant presence and reminder. The towers had search lights that the German guards would shine on the barracks during the night. As we'd lie in bed at night trying to sleep, freezing cold, battling lice and bed bugs, sharing blankets, we'd all have to watch as the search lights circled and shone in the barracks like a light show throughout the night, reminding us that we were prisoners at the mercy of our captors. So, no – there weren't any escape attempts. As daring as that may sound, it was just asking for death.

I did witness the deaths of fellow prisoners while in camp and watched as they were taken outside of the gates and buried, getting their final resting place. Information would be passed along and you'd hear, "Someone from Barracks 56 died." Then some guys would be pall bearers, another prisoner would serve as the chaplain and a small, informal service was permitted. The Germans were required to document the deaths. Those times were very sad, thinking about a young airman who died in a prison camp in the enemy's country, alone, no family or friends to bid him farewell.

Most of the days were spent just laying around in the barracks trying to pass the time away bullshitting with someone. In the daytime, we'd often try to sleep because the routine was so darn boring and monotonous. However, during daytime attempts to sleep (same as at night) we had to deal with the fleas, lice and bedbugs, as the mattresses and blankets were loaded with them.

I tried to shake my clothes outside to rid myself of them, but that didn't work. Some guys would take their underwear off and rinse them out in cold water, hang them outside to dry, put them back on, hoping against hope that the cleaning ritual worked. If it snowed, I'd go outside and rub snow all over me and that seemed to help…temporarily. But, unfortunately, the way it worked was the warmer you were, the more you'd be bitten, so it was a "damned if you do, damned if you don't" situation. We all had to get warm at night because it was winter and freezing cold in the camp and to have any chance of getting sleep instead of shivering all night getting warm was key. But in the warmth was where the bed bugs and lice manifested themselves – in the heat among the blankets and bodies. With no change of clothes, and no real way to rid ourselves of the lice, you just lived with it.

It was horrible. It is recorded that the winter of 1944 in Germany, when I was in prison camp, was the coldest winter Germany experienced during the war years.

To take my mind off of the entire experience, and attempt to think about other things, I wrote letters. We were allowed three postcards and one letter per month. I used them all up. I wrote to my parents and to Anne. I found out after the war that they never received any of the mail that I sent from prison camp. I guess the Germans took our letters that we had written to send home, said, "To hell with them," and just didn't send them.

The letters were found after the fact, after I had come home. My brother John wrote a letter to me while I was in prison camp that I didn't receive until I got home. I always looked forward to the letters he sent home from the service before I entered the Air Corps.

Letter from Frank's brother John

The article shown at the top of the next page appeared in the local newspaper, *The Braddock Free Press* and describes the information that my family knew at the time that they learned from the War department telegram.

The daily thought that my family didn't know what I was going through bothered me. I wished they could have known that I was doing OK and doing all I could to come home.

S/SGT. FRANK A. KRAVETZ

S/Sgt. Frank A. Kravetz, son of Mr. and Mrs. George Kravetz, of 110 Bessemer avenue, East Pittsburgh, recently reported as missing in action since November 2, just a year to the day he embarked for overseas duty, has turned up as a prisoner of war, according to word received by his family in a wire from the War Department.

PRISONERS
Germany

Sgt. George C. Boschoff—Mrs. Lois Boschoff, wife, 309 Kennedy St.
Pvt. Theodore M. James, Leechburg.
Lt. Edward A. Jones—Mrs. Edith E. Bishing, mother, 335 Hastings St.
Sgt. Frank A. Kravetz — Mrs. Suzanna Kravetz, mother, 110 Bessemer Ave., East Pittsburgh.
Sgt. Roy F. Marshall, Point Marion.
Corp. John F. Pates, Washington.
Pvt. John B. Rock Jr., Beaverdale.
Sgt. Robert S. Scott — Mrs. Mary Scott, mother, 5637 Elgin St.
Corp. Michael J. Serrian, Farrell.
Pvt. Fred A. Shaffer, Falls Creek.
Pvt. Andrew J. Stascak—Mrs. Mary Stascak, mother, E. Deer Twp., Creighton.
Pvt. Gustaff B. Swanson Jr., Punxsutawney.
Pvt. Albert C. Zientek—Mrs. Catherine Zientek, mother, 126 Forty-first St.

Braddock Free Press newspaper announcement
that Frank was Missing In Action

Barracks and prison camp life continued, and I never changed barracks, yet I never really got close with any of the guys in the barracks. I never wrote down any of the names of the guys who were in with me. It's hard to explain. I guess we were just friends for the time being, helping each other to survive, and stuck in a situation with all of us having the same goal – hoping to be liberated some day, that's all. We were just living day-to-day in a very boring, lousy existence wondering when it would ever end. I can say for sure that thought was always on my mind…the question of when is this going to end, when will it all be over?

I hated the Germans because they were the enemy, the ones responsible for all of our anguish on a daily basis. All of us prisoners had animosity toward them because they were the enemy at all times. When our planes were flying over and bombing the German industries and rail yards nearby we were all hoping our boys would beat the hell out of them! As we watched the planes going over our heads on their way to their targets all of us guys were yelling wildly and cheering them on.

To combat the hatred and hopelessness we would get together within the prison camp for religious services. It gave us a chance to pray together, say the rosary, and be encouraged by each other's faith. There is no doubt about it, prayer and faith played a big part in my surviving it all.

Along with that, my mind and my heart were filled with thoughts of Anne. My heart was all out for her and I really prayed that I could come home and we could have a life together. When I left the United States, Anne was the last person I saw before heading off to war – that really made me think about her a lot. Our good-bye left a deep impression on me. I had so much love for her in my heart and I wanted to be with her, not away from her. In the barracks, I would talk about Anne and tell the guys that she was my girl back home. I still didn't know if we would be together when I got home, but I looked forward to it coming true. That thought was a big part of my hope.

In spite of all of the difficulties with day-to-day living, I managed to not get sick while I was in prison camp. My biggest concern was keeping my wound clean, which under the circumstances, wasn't easy to do as there wasn't much water and sanitation was nonexistent. I was doing my best to take care of myself, nurse my wounds, and get better. I wrapped a towel around the wound on my thigh, as pus was still oozing out. The prison camp had a small sick call area and at some point, I went there to get some sulfur powder, new compresses and bandages.

I never saw a doctor or had any additional medical attention after I left Obermassfeld hospital or while in prison camp. Never. That's why I don't know how I'm alive, really. All I can say is that the good Lord was watching out for me.

At Obermassfeld, they took what clothing I had left of my flight suit, put it in a bag and kept it until I left the hospital. Everything I was wearing before I was shot down, from the waist up was in that bag. The clothes that I was wearing from the waist down were destroyed when I was wounded. That clothing is what I wore the entire time I was a prisoner of war. Every day, day in and day out, and each night, too. I never had a change of clothes. That's hard to believe, but it's true. Some guys I know only had the clothes they got shot down in for their entire time as prisoners of war.

The only clothing I had with me was my olive drab underwear top and shirt which was long-sleeved along with the top of my heated flying suit and a jacket. The Germans gave me a knit wool cap that you could pull down over your ears, bottom underwear, long johns, a pair of pants, a pair of socks and a pair of shoes, because I didn't have a pair of shoes after being shot down. These clothes were provided by the Red Cross.

Shortly after I arrived in prison camp, in late February and early March of 1945, bombings were experienced in prison camp a lot, both day and night. The city of Nuremberg was being bombed and we could see the planes flying directly overhead as they headed for their targets. On February 21st and 22nd, 1945 Mustangs swooped over camp, really, really low. Our morale went way up because we knew our guys were in the area, in the fight to come and free us soon!

The bombing of Nuremburg took place on three consecutive days, the 22nd, 23rd and 24th of February. I hadn't been in the camp very long. Those three days and nights were just terrible. Morning, noon, and night the bombing went on. The camp was three kilometers from city, approximately six miles – so the intense bombings were right upon us. Of course, our Army Air Corps knew that we prisoners were in the camps nearby and so they used precision targeting of their bomb run destinations. Needless to say, we were happy and proud with our fellow airmen and their ability, skill, bravery and daring.

To this day, those bombings were some of the worst experiences I encountered. To be subjected to something like that is unbelievable and very hard to describe. First there was the wailing warning of the air raid sirens, followed by the whistling of the bombs dropping out of the planes. As the bombs detonated on the ground on impact, they created a powerful explosive sound that was horrible, just horrible. Imagine Fourth of July fireworks that you might have observed – only a million times louder.

The British were dropping their bomb loads at night, and they brought the blockbusters – the 5,000 pound bombs. The Americans conducted daytime bombings. This combination came relentlessly, day and night, and just knocked the shit out of everything, very close to camp. If 800 to a 1,000 bombers were over a target with a full payload of bombs being dropped – well, that's a hell of a lot of bombs being dropped and exploding, an awful lot of destruction and damage. In addition there were many antiaircraft batteries operating around the camp.

History records a lot about the extensive bombing raids on Nuremberg. It is said that Nuremberg was Hitler's favorite city. Concentrated efforts to bomb that city took place quite often with the British RAF leading the charge.

The concussion bombs, "88s" were the bad ones. When they were dropped they literally shook the ground. You could actually feel the earth moving and shaking. Some of the bombs that fell were so close to the perimeter of the camp they may as well have been dropped inside camp. At the same time the Germans were firing antiaircraft weaponry back up at the planes that were doing the bombing. It was continuous ear-blasting percussion all around with no escaping it.

Our prison camp, thank God, was never hit while I was in camp. As soon as the bombing started, the German guards retreated into shelters and we were left to scramble and find places to try and find cover. The German guards in the towers had bunkers right at the base of the towers. There were many trenches dug throughout the camp that we used during the bombing raids and these were the only shelter we had. The guys who were in prison camp before my arrival had worked hard to dig and form those trenches, and as a result, they clung to them as their own. Now the ground was too hard to dig into and there were just so many men in the camp that when the bombing runs began I just crawled under the prison camp barracks building. I didn't feel any safer there, the fact is, there was no place to go and feel truly safe, but you did what you could do. I lay on the ground and I could feel the ground shaking beneath my body and I could see the sky lit up with the bursts of never-ending light and explosives. It's the most terrifying thing you could ever imagine.

Flak would fall; pieces of bombs would fall, raining down all over the place. Only those who have witnessed an air raid of planes dropping bombs, along with antiaircraft guns lighting up the sky, flares shooting into the sky and spiraling planes on fire plummeting to the ground can relate to what I'm trying to convey. The sound of those bombs being dropped out of those planes and then exploding on the ground with such ferocious impact was horrifying.

As I found myself caught in the middle of the bombing runs, I'd press my hands over my ears to protect my eardrums and try to muffle the deafening sounds. We were told to not close our mouths during the bombings. Instead we were warned to open our mouths wide – just like when a doctor tells you to open wide and say, "Ahh." And that's what we did, we held our mouths open. They said that it was better to open your mouth rather than stay 'tight-lipped', gritting your teeth. I guess it helped protect our tongues and teeth from the rattling effects of the bombing, as well as helped our ear drums withstand the pressure.

It seemed as though the bombings lasted forever. I recall one particular night bombing raid in March where there were so many bombers in the air flying over our camp to their targets that the drone seemed to last forever. I couldn't see them, but I could hear them on their missions. There was no way to prepare for the sound that would follow as they dropped the bombs on the city of Nuremberg. With the city so close, I could see flames erupting in the city, creating a firestorm with smoke rising as the city burned.

Once the bombings were over and we were back in the barracks, all of us would be thanking God that it was over, trying to relax and calm our shattered nerves. We all knew that the intense air effort was helping us to win the war, but it was tough to endure, helplessly sitting through the bombings. I can say this with certainty: I don't ever want to hear anything like the sounds of bombs bursting in air ever again!

It was Lent during this time in late March, and I was able to attend Catholic services of the Stations of the Cross. As I did, I thought about my family back home preparing to celebrate Easter Sunday. Lots of us in camp were having high hopes of being liberated soon by our troops advancing from the south west.

Easter Sunday fell on April 1, 1945. The war would be over in a month, but I had no way of knowing that at the time. We had received clandestine reports that came into the barracks leader that the troops were in Hanover. The British were on the move as well as the French and Russians, and they were all closing in on Germany.

As the Allied Forces closed in from East and West Nuremberg camp received many POWs coming from other camps that were being evacuated.

At this point, more German guards were posted all around the camp.

We knew we'd soon be moving out of Nuremberg because the prisoners that just arrived into camp after marching from Sagan (Stalag Luft 3) would tell us what was taking place, explaining all of the movement and activity. When they arrived, the population of the camp doubled immediately. The food situation became really bad at this point, as there was almost nothing to eat. When the guys from Sagan got to Nuremberg, we heard firsthand of what was going on with the war.

The general consensus of the time was, "Well, it's getting so crowded in our camp, they're going to have to move us, too." We took the continued crowding and moving of prisoner of war camps as good news that things were going well for the Allied movement, and that the Allied forces were getting close to Berlin.

The Germans figured it wasn't going to take long for us to be liberated from camp, so the idea was to move all prisoners of war further south toward Munich which was five or six km from Nuremberg. Fellow airmen like my friend Walt Pawlesh in Stalag 17B were moving out of their camp before us and were moving south.

We prisoners of war became pawns in Hitler's schemes. Prisoners kept getting moved to keep us from being liberated and rejoining our troops to fight for victory. The only thing Hitler had left to do was march us south.

By April, Allied troops were moving toward Berlin from all sides. Germany was getting smaller and smaller as the war fronts to the east and west created a crushing vice, closing in. There was nowhere for the Germans to go, they were trapped on all sides. They had two choices: they could keep fighting, in which case we'd overrun them and kill them all; or they could surrender.

On April 3rd orders were received that we were to prepare to leave camp the next morning. German guards came to the barracks and told us to gather up any of our personal belongings, anything that we wanted to take with us, only things we could carry – because the camp was being vacated. I watched the guys in the barracks construct quickly assembled knapsacks, rolling thin blankets and gathering some bits and pieces of food to put in sacks. I prepared only a blanket and some food to stuff in my pockets – German bread, potatoes, biscuits and my can to drink with. I wanted to travel as light as I could because I was in no condition to be carrying anything large or heavy. I only had the clothes I was wearing on my back, so getting my wardrobe together was no big deal – I had no wardrobe. Plus, I would have the extra burden of using my crutches.

Our barracks leader read the orders to us and told us that we had a choice to travel by train or go on foot. Anybody that wanted to use the train had to sign up. I was still using my crutches to get around at this point. Some of the other fellows who had experienced travelling by train advised me not to go by train because trains were being strafed by our fighter planes and it would be safer to walk. The Germans weren't putting any markings on any of the train cars to signify that they were carrying American prisoners of war. I heard this from quite a few guys who had come in from other camps that emptied out and so I knew this was taking place.

As soon as it was mentioned, I thought to myself, "I ain't going on no train that's going to be strafed," so I made the decision to walk, and the guys offered to help me along the way. Everyone said, "I'm walking, I'll take my chances." Some said, "There might even be a chance to escape."

I know that I was not alone in being glad to get away from camp and the horrific bombings that we all endured. Everyone was weary and our nerves were shot from the experience. We glad to be getting the hell out of there.

On April 4, 1945 as we prepared to leave our barracks, we could see outside as other barracks were systematically given orders that it was their time to move out.

Soon it was our turn. Our barracks leader called out our Barracks number and said, "You're leaving – it's your turn to go out the gate now!" We walked out the door, into the compound and out the front gate of the prison camp. That first step outside of the camp felt almost like freedom itself. I was now out – out of the confines of the dingy, cold, lice-infested barracks. Outside the confining barbed wire fencing and out in the fresh air!

The one month that I was at Stalag 13D was short by some standards, but the experience I had left a lasting impression on me. The hardships of being in a German prison camp were life-defining. The lack of food and water, inadequate clothing, filthy living conditions, boredom, sickness, bugs, the unknown and the fear-all these things that I lived with on a daily basis plus the inability to do what I wanted to do left me numb and emptied of my humanity in a way. All I could do was pray, and I did.

I had never been that low in my life. I knew I would never forget what I had been through. I was grateful I wasn't a prisoner of war for a longer length of time. I can't even fathom what that must have been like for those who where there for a much longer period of time. I know that my trials of being a prisoner fashioned my outlook on how I would live the rest of my life. Now, if I was just able to survive the rest of this ordeal and get home…

Chapter Thirteen

STEPS TO SURVIVE –
THE MARCH TO MOOSBURG

The date was April 4th, 1945 – just 35 days after leaving a hospital bed in Obermassfeld on crutches – and I was starting on a forced march from Nuremberg prison camp to Moosburg. A lot of fellow marchers would be joining me; as the Germans emptied other prison camps, those guys wound up at Nuremberg. In April, 1945 there were 30,000 men in camp.

The truth is I really could have cared less where I was going. I was still a 'rookie' as far as being a prisoner of war was concerned. My enemy had been telling me what to do for quite some time – it was part of my life now. To me, this was just another trial I was going to have to go through and something else I was being forced to do. The other guys were seasoned, having been imprisoned a lot longer than me.

I had learned in prison camp that there were so many other things to be concerned with on a daily basis that you just do whatever is best for your own welfare. I was glad to get out of prison camp, out into the open where the sun was shining on me. Most of the guys felt this way; that it was a relief to be out of the hell-hole that was Nuremberg Prison Camp.

The Allied Front was moving forward, capturing ground, and the Germans were losing ground and retreating. We POW's weren't fighting, of course, but if we could get to the point where we could be liberated and turned back over to our forces, then they'd give us guns, we could fly planes again and we'd be a larger force fighting them again – we were all potential manpower. They had to keep moving us – it was military strategy on the part of the Germans.

There was an agreement for the march – that in return for us being responsible for keeping order during the march, the Germans were to have full control of the column and to march us no more than ten kilometers per day (or around 12 miles.) I started the march on crutches. I was the only guy in my column using crutches. I had them with me in prison camp for my walking exercise while there and knew I would need them for the march. I got a lot of help along the way. Guys helped carry some of my stuff, such as my jacket or blanket – doing whatever they could to make it go easier for me. I knew I needed to travel light because my wound was still healing and the crutches made it hard to carry stuff. When I needed to lean on someone, or take a break, a fellow POW was always there to assist me. I don't know their names, but I'm thankful for their good deeds.

There was no snow at this time of year; the weather was fairly mild for early spring. Our column marched in groups of three men across with about 100 prisoners proceeding down country roads through lots of little German villages. It was just a marching walk, not a forced march, no cadence or anything formal in step. We just picked 'em up and laid 'em down for mile after mile after mile. Nothing organized. If someone fell back, then they just stayed there in that part of the column. There really wasn't anybody in charge of the march of the Americans. When the German soldiers told us to stop, we stopped.

Occasionally you might hear casual, "OK, let's keep it together..." or comments like that. We were allowed to talk while marching and carry on conversations with each other. But marching buddies changed every day, as columns dropped in and out. Most of the talk was about how we thought we'd be liberated even while on the march. As we walked, I looked in front of me and behind me. There were hundreds and hundreds of guys that I could see in my range of vision. Ultimately there were thousands upon thousands of us prisoners walking these German roads at any given time.

I began to feel pain from travelling with crutches. They made every step so hard, and everything was starting to hurt. My hands, my arms, and underneath my armpits were getting raw from the rubbing of the crutches. I was just so hindered and frustrated. I had not been putting much weight on my injured leg up to this point, but I decided to try and do without them, so I threw them away and was going to attempt to finish the march without them. I said, "The heck with them!" and tossed them aside. Although it was difficult at the time, I realize now that it was a good decision because it was the best physical therapy program to rehabilitate my leg – slowly, the leg got stronger. Man, did it feel good to be walking without those two wooden supports! With each step I savored the feeling of being out of prison camp, feeling stronger and happy about my decision to ditch the crutches.

Being part of this grand fellowship of Americans on the move – hopefully the move to freedom – somehow encouraged me. I can honestly say that the march from this point forward was what gave me the incentive to go on. As we continued walking, I slowly was regaining strength in my leg. We had no idea how long we would be marching each day, and we were permitted ten minutes rest every hour. Sometimes the breaks would be longer, but ten minutes was the average. The German guards were tired as well, and we all eagerly looked forward to the breaks.

Our first stop on the first day was in the afternoon and we were given some bread and time to rest a bit. The very first day out of Nuremberg Prison Camp, we were seemingly attacked by P-47s – our own Thunderbirds that headed straight to the column. As the planes swooped down, we all just instinctively dove into ditches off the road – none of us really knew what was going on. The planes disappeared as quickly as the appeared. The planes didn't fire at us. We all determined that it was our guys who recognized us as American prisoners on the road and they were acknowledging us with a little 'friendly fly-over'. Upon that realization we all jumped up and cheered and hollered at our fly-boys in the air. Back on the road, I was glad that our walk was getting us further and further from Nuremburg and all the bombing of that city that we had just experienced in camp.

As evening approached and it started to get dark, the German guards began to search out areas where we could get off the road and stop for the night. With no flashlights available, getting the logistics worked out as to where we would stay had to take place prior to nightfall. Some nights we just slept out under the stars in open fields with German guards posted all around. When this happened, everyone kind of 'huddled up together' with each other in the woods off the side of the road and tried to sleep. In these situations, I really become aware of how I was just living for the moment, and not thinking too much about what was coming next. It becomes an acceptance thing. The truth is for me, I was just so tired that all I wanted to do was sleep and I didn't care where I got to do that. My estimate is that we marched for ten miles or so that first day.

While I don't recall the sequence of each day and night on the march, I vividly recall the night that the Germans found the first barn for us to stay in. A barn was a real convenient way to get a lot of guys under cover in one place. A small group of us were told we'd be sleeping in a hayloft. I was about to experience a great moment in my life. At this point, I was

Operation Halyard, photo by J.B. Allin. Reprinted with permission.[3]

utterly exhausted and didn't want to move another muscle or take one more step. The barn was very inviting. I climbed the ladder up to the hayloft, and plopped into a three ft. pile of soft, warm hay that smelled so good and felt like I was on a cloud. Oh my God...that was the most wonderful, peaceful thing I had ever done in my life, to sleep in that hay. I thought I had died and gone to heaven after such a long hard day on the road. Soon I was fast asleep. I will never forget that moment and what a welcome relief that hayloft was. It is still so vivid and etched in my mind forever as I recall it now.

There was also a time on the march when we experienced a tremendous downpour where we all got soaked to our skin. Everything and everyone was drenched, mud was everywhere.

---

[3] Reprinted with permission by Mim Bizic, from her father Milan M. Karlo's *American Serb Life Magazine* in 1948 Original photograph taken by J.B. Allin.

That was some very difficult marching for us all. We were thrilled when, once again, the Germans ushered us into a big dry barn where we were able to stay for a few days waiting out the rainfall. It was really a blessing to be able to rest our aching muscles and be off the road for an extended period of time. The first thing we did was busy ourselves getting our soaking wet clothes dry. We wrung them out and hung them up in the barns rafters to let them drip dry. We were now down to our skivvies, and that's how we once again plopped to sleep on that soft, mattress-like hay of the barn. During this time of heavy rainfall, we didn't march for a day or two which allowed us to get some much needed rest.

Back on the road after the rain, we marched again in some nice weather, cooler temperatures and sunny skies. We were all doing better due to the couple of days of inactivity.

By now we were in a different part of the column of marchers. POW's were being dropped off at different points along the way because they couldn't keep up or because of an illness. Other marching prisoners could meet up with our column at any given point. The Germans were always emptying out other camps and getting them on the march. Again, we were all potential manpower if Allied forces caught up, so the strategy was to keep moving us.

While marching, I'd be walking next to a guy and he and I would strike up a conversation as we walked to pass the time away. I didn't make any lasting friendships while on the march, I just had walking partners that were sharing the same time passage in life as me. As I walked, I was just so satisfied that I could do this. I knew that I could survive this walk. My mind was made up and I just kept going, determined and persistent.

Guards would alert us to the fact that we could get some food at the next town, and prepare us for that. That gave us something to look forward to. We were passing through peaceful, farm type settings, it was actually pleasant to be walking and seeing the beauty of the countryside and not the ravages of war. Also along the march at times, German horse drawn food trucks would stop to give us something to eat. We had our cans with us, and we'd walk up to the truck and get some soup and potatoes.

Guys did have trouble keeping up and German guards struggled, too. For the Germans it was not easy marching all that way with rifles on their shoulders, and they weren't eating very well, either. They were only in slightly better shape than we were. We usually managed to find some potatoes or rutabagas by rummaging through the fields and farmlands we stopped at for breaks. When we could, we cooked them over a little cook-stove for dinner.

At some point on the march, I was allowed to go to a small Catholic church that was packed with POWs and say my prayers. Outside of the church there were people who passed food items on to us. It was close to Easter Sunday and people were very friendly to us. A beautiful, peaceful time in a quaint setting – away from it all for a short while and very appreciated. All along the march I noticed very beautiful, wayside shrines dotting the roadsides; most of them had crucifixes on display.

We were told we could wander about the town near the church and we soon found ourselves trading soap, cigarettes and coffee for bread, eggs and potatoes. Germans were always interested in trading for our American cigarettes. They would say in their thick, broken German accents, "American cigarettes, American cigarettes"…they wanted our cigarettes because American smokes were the best. There were always extra cigarettes to trade and barter with. We had received the items we were trading from Red Cross trailer trucks that had greeted us on the road as we marched. At times along the march, we received Red Cross parcels of spam, powdered milk, raisins or prunes, biscuits and chocolate bars. The usual distribution was one parcel for four men.

Whenever we arrived in a town, we had an opportunity to scrounge for food from the local Germans. The German townsfolk didn't speak much English and we didn't speak much German. All we could really do was to show them what we had to trade. By this time, we all knew a few German words like, broat (bread), fleish (meat) lire, (eggs), and schwebel (onions). I learned these words and I'll never forget them. When we marched through, the German townsfolk usually observed us – I don't really think they were afraid of us, it was more of a curiosity. When we got to a German farmhouse (they were a little more compassionate) we were often given an egg or a couple of turnips or rutabagas. Some guys left notes with the German families they came in contact with, signing their names stating, "These people treated us well and shared their food with us." Our guys wanted people who came behind them into these villages and hamlets to know that these townsfolk treated them well and helped to take care of them.

While I can't remember exact days, I passed through the small villages and hamlets of, Berching, Belingries, Neustadt, Pfeffinhausen. I never saw any animals or wildlife on the march; I guess the sound of all the marching kept them away. Hop fields were everywhere you looked – field after field of them, distinguishable by their many tall shoots that looked similar to bamboo poles. At the time, I didn't even know what they were.

Some days of marching were longer, some shorter. One clear weather day with crystal clear blue skies, I noticed something sparkling and shining in the trees and lying in the fields. It was chaff, shredded metallic foil thrown from Allied bombers. It looked like Christmas tree tinsel. Our guys deliberately threw it in great quantities, using it to try to render enemy-detecting devices ineffective.

At one particular stop, I was caught up with the beautiful, lush, green landscape covered with flowers and a crystal clear stream. Lots of guys were heading for the stream to bathe their swollen, aching feet. I never saw anybody offering first aid during the whole march. I really don't remember having any blisters, but a lot of guys suffered with them. I bathed in this stream and boy, was that water ever cold! But I didn't care because it provided such relief from the bed bugs and lice. I stayed under the water as long as I could, which I suspect wasn't that long.

I am not sure of our location on the march when we heard that President Franklin Delano Roosevelt had died. He died on April 13, 1945. The Germans let us have a ceremony in the field, where a small service was conducted and Taps was blown. It was a sad and somber time. We all felt bad that our President had died and we wondered if it would have any impact with the war.

Up to this point, we had hope that if we could just stay alive, we would be liberated. As I moved along, able to keep going, I realized how much the daily walking I did while in Nuremberg helped to strengthen me physically and I was glad I had put in the effort.

When we first started marching we didn't know where we were marching to. Somewhere along the way, somebody figured it out, or somebody overheard something. Eventually we put two and two together, and knew that Moosburg was where we were headed. While marching near Gammelsdorf we saw a sign that had 'Moosburg' on it and this is how we knew we had another 62 miles of marching to get to our final destination.

I, for one, was glad to see the sign that said Moosburg, because it meant we'd be in a camp again. At least in a prison camp setting we could rest our aching legs and feet and give our bodies the rest they so desperately needed. We really had the mindset that it wouldn't be too much longer before liberation and being in prison camp seemed like a safe option until that happened.

Near the end of the march we wound up crossing a small bridge that spanned the Danube River – it was muddy, and even though I knew it was famous for the *Blue Danube Waltz*, it seemed like nothing special. Where we crossed, the river was more of a tributary; the other end of the river was the beautiful wide section for which the waltz was written. As we walked over the bridge, I saw bombs lined up along the sides. To me, they looked similar to the bombs we dropped out of our B-17s on German targets. The Germans wanted to blow the bridge up if they were being overtaken, so our troops and tanks couldn't get across the bridge to come and rescue us. Everyone I talked to about this experience said they also saw the bombs on the bridge. They were allowing us prisoners to pass on through in order to get to Moosburg. But after we crossed, the Germans intended to blow it up so our troops couldn't follow after us. The advancing American troops got there before the Germans had the opportunity to blow up the bridge and defused the bombs.

We arrived around the 18th or 19th into Moosburg, having completed a 90 mile trip with an estimated 10,000 men on the march. The march was difficult and I was glad to be somewhere in a camp again. As I entered Stalag VIIA, more questions surfaced in my mind. "Would Moosburg be the final chapter in my being a prisoner of war? Would the war end soon? Just what were Hitler's plans for us? Would there be enough food to feed so many of us?" It appeared as though Moosburg brought more questions than answers.

Below is a map[4] of the march route and the ground we covered sketched by Bob Neary. My thanks to Bob for his record of the march, which helped jog my memory.

Map showing the forced march of POWs from Sagan to Moosburg

---

[4] Permission to use this sketch granted by 392nd Bomb Group, www.b24.net

Chapter Fourteen

HELL'S JOURNEY CONTINUES – MOOSBURG – POW CAMP – STALAG VIIA

Tired, but happy to have completed the march, I walked into the second prison camp I would be a POW in – Stalag VIIA located in Moosburg, Germany. My best guess is that I arrived somewhere between April 15-19, 1945. Again, I was greeted by the now familiar guard towers, barbed wire fencing and German soldiers armed with rifles.

By the time I got to the camp, the place was a wreck. Buildings were old and falling apart – bursting at the seams. The whole camp was jam-packed with prisoners everywhere you looked, creating a lot of disorder.

We were all carbon copies of each other: dirty, gaunt, ragged clothing, tired and hungry. Someone pointed to our group of arriving marchers and said, "OK, you go over there, you go down there, you stay here" – giving us directions as to where we'd be staying within the camp. I was assigned to a barracks at this point. No matter where a prisoner wound up sleeping – inside or outside – they were body to body because of how crowded it was. Guys who slept on the floors of the barracks and guys who slept outside used wood shavings as mattresses. Some guys managed to put up makeshift tents, sleeping there and some slept in foxholes.

To my great disappointment, the same as in Nuremberg, the lice, fleas and bedbugs were very much a part of Moosburg, too. Stalag VIIA was a disaster.

By this time, Germany was losing the war and Moosburg had become a massive center to hold POW's who had emptied out from every other camp around. There was no end in sight as every day new prisoners by the hundreds kept pouring into the camp. Eventually, the barracks were filled with 500 guys as a camp that was built to hold 10,000 was now packed with more than 100,000. The camp was originally built to hold meetings and provide housing for Nazi party gatherings and now sadly, it was filled to overflowing with anxious prisoners of war from all over the world. One account said the camp resembled a 'giant hobo village' and that is an accurate description.

The mass of humanity that wound up in camp was hard to believe. There were many different nationalities represented in Moosburg: Americans, British and military personnel of every Allied European nationality including Russians. Because there were so many in the camp, there was very little food. We were scraping the bottom of the barrel and begging for something to eat. Fortunately, guys who were in camp before we arrived shared scraps of food with us and that helped a lot. The Red Cross parcels that were delivered were what we relied on for survival, as there were no food supplies left in camp whatsoever.

There were gangs of people everywhere – just out in the open milling around, sitting on the ground. Any little bit of space that was available quickly became occupied. With this many people in one small space, every problem in camp intensified.

Nowhere was this more evident than at the bathroom area. What we had to use for bathrooms was sickening. They stunk to high heaven and I could barely stand to walk in the place. There were no lights inside, no heat and certainly no privacy! A long row of holes spaced closed together was your choice and usually there weren't any available or you waited your turn in long lines. Any "deposits" dropped right into an open trench beneath. They were always filled to overflowing, hardly ever getting emptied and there was nothing to keep the place clean or sanitized in any way. It's a wonder we all didn't die from some dread disease just from using those holes to do our business.

On a positive note, my leg was stronger after all of the walking and I didn't need any medical help, so I was in pretty good shape in that regard.

The word within the camp was pretty exciting. They said that our troops were somewhere very close, within 50 miles of the camp – to me that meant one thing, they are on their way to get us! The anticipation and excitement could be felt – there was a buzz in the air. There were over 100,000 prisoners whose one thought was in one accord – the single thought that we were going to be liberated. In the meantime, we just waited – some more patient than others.

There were some POW's who entertained the thought of 'just getting to the other side', since now our freedom seemed inevitable. But German soldiers were still in the guard towers, waiting to mow down anyone trying to make an escape attempt. Anybody that bolted or tried to make a run for it would not have made it. Two very large fences were covered with barbed wire. Between the main fence and the guard rail in the immediate foreground was an open stretch of about fifteen feet that was off limits to prisoners. There was a warning wire two feet off the ground and there was an outer fence. But in the middle was what was referred to as 'no man's land.' As soon as a prisoner got into this area, they would be shot immediately. This kept guys from making that move to go out.

Twenty four hours a day we were under the guard's watch. They roamed around the compound with German shepherd police dogs, and at night they shone bright spotlights at varying times all throughout the camp, searching for any prisoner that had escape on his mind.

Days were filled with lots of time on our hands and nothing to do. I decided to try and get a little exercise for my leg, but by now there wasn't much room within the prison compound to even walk. We were, however, permitted to walk around the inside perimeter near the fence that surrounded the camp.

As I walked, I could see the road that went right past the camp, and as I peered through the fence, I would see wooden carts go by stacked with dead bodies. There were so many bodies on these carts that they would be falling off the carts as they moved down the road. I assumed they were the 'war dead', those killed in action. I was wrong. I was to find out many years later, that this was not the case.

These carts that I observed rolling past the prison compound were actually the bodies of those who were killed in one of the many concentration camps run by Hitler set up for the annihilation of the Jewish people.

The entire time that I was overseas in combat, captured and recovering, I was unaware that this atrocity was taking place. It wasn't until the war was over and the much publicized Nuremburg Trials began that I realized the extent of the evil that Hitler's war machine had inflicted upon the Jews. Dachau concentration camp was close to Moosburg, I assume they came from there. These were hard images to shake from my mind.

New guys continued to arrive in camp, bringing their versions of how the war was progressing and we all eagerly listened. It was pretty basic stuff; the Russians were advancing on the eastern front and the Allies on the Western front. Word was they should arrive soon. Although none of us could pin down an exact date or time, these reports brought a measure of hope to us. We needed it because there were still so many uncertainties surrounding us. In the back of our minds we wondered, "Will the Allies liberate us in time, or would time run out just as we could see the possibility of freedom on the horizon?"

For the thousands of American and British prisoners of war in Germany, the last few months of the war were the most tense. It became clear early in 1945 that the Allies were winning the war, but the uncertainties that went along with the victory became troublesome. Would they be liberated or would their captors execute the ultimate power over them by killing them all. With all the uncertainties of war and the gruesome nature of World War II up until then, the concerns of the prisoners of war were very real, and merited. History would later reveal that in early 1945, Hitler ordered all British and U.S. Air Officers gathered up and held hostage in chief downtown areas in Berlin and several other major cities. The plan was apparently an attempt to curtail the Allied bombing attacks, which were having a crippling effect on Germany's war effort by 1945. Hitler's directive, however, was never carried out. Another order was more direct, this time coming from Joseph Goebbels, Minister of Propaganda, who suggested to Hitler during the closing months of the war that all interned Allied airman be killed. Although such mass executions never occurred, news of Goebbels plan left Allied commanders scrambling for a solution to protect the POWs.

This caused some guys to plan to escape – but we were continually reminded to 'hang in there' – that our troops were not far away and our rescue would be soon. Most of us chose to cling to the belief that our rescue was imminent. We didn't speak about it but many also feared that we could starve to death if something didn't happen soon. Supplies were so low that even water was being rationed. That's part of why it was so difficult at the end – there were so many prisoners and no food. There just wasn't anything to eat, it was terrible. We were waiting to be liberated. That's all.

By the last week of April, we could hear artillery and small arms fire outside the camp. I was very confident that hostilities would end and in my prayers to the Lord I asked for freedom and to protect those who were preparing to face the enemy to release us. I was upbeat.

Chapter Fifteen

LIBERATION –
FREEDOM GAINED

It was April 29, 1945 – a little cold; but a beautiful, sunny, spring day. I slept pretty well the night before and felt ready to face just another day in prison camp. But there seemed to be something different about this day. All around me my fellow 'kriegies' seemed a little more anxious, a little more on edge.

Behind the scenes of the prison camp, a meeting is taking place to set Moosburg Prisoners free. The following account describes this:[5]

"At one minute before six a.m. a strange group strode into the headquarters of Combat Command A to meet Brigadier General Karlstad, combat commander. It consisted of a German major, representing the commander of the Moosburg allied prisoner of war camp; Colonel Paul Goode of the United States Army; and a group from the British Royal Air Force, the senior and British officers respectively,

---

[5] Reprinted with permission from the 100th Bomb Group Foundation with additional acknowledgment to Captain Frank Murphy, Dave Kanzler and Cindy Goodman, Editor of Splasher Six.

imprisoned in the Moosburg camp. As well, they were joined by a Swiss Red Cross representative; and Colonel Lann, my battalion commander. The German Major brought a written proposal from his commander for the creation of a neutral zone surrounding Moosburg, all movement of Allied troops in the general vicinity of Moosburg to stop while representatives of the Allied and German governments conferred on disposition of the Allied prisoners of war in that vicinity."

"The German proposals were rejected and the party was given until 9 a.m. to return to Moosburg and to submit an unconditional surrender offer – or receive the American attack at that hour. The German command would not submit an unconditional surrender, instead German SS (Schutzstaffel, protection guard) troops moved outside the city and set up a defense perimeter. They opened the fight and we were ready for them. Every tanker, infantryman, truck driver, clerks and cooks took up arms."

In camp there was a lot of activity going on; P-47s and P-51s were spotted over head and guys were discussing rumors that Patton's 3rd Army was rapidly moving towards camp and that the regular German army was seen taking up positions around camp. We can hear tanks moving and grinding their way toward camp. We begin to hear rifle shots in the woods outside of camp.

Germans were making their last stand for control of us and soon the rifle shots turn into a full blown battle as now small arms fire and machine guns can be heard everywhere. I dove for cover on the ground as did others, scrambling for protection by going under the barracks and anywhere we could go to get to a safe spot. The Allied Forces were fighting for the city of Moosburg and as the fighting continued, smoke was seen rising from the city. Troops were moving from Moosburg city to Moosburg prison camp. Our artillery was close and as nerve-wracking as it was to be exposed to the fighting, we knew that this was necessary for our guys to come and get us.

This intense fight for our freedom, for our lives, went on for an hour or more. We were so grateful for our soldiers battling on our behalf. It didn't seem real that our liberation might really be close, but we waited expectantly.

We continued to stay under cover as best we could, observing all that was taking place around the camp. Then, at some point, it got quiet – no more shots could be heard. Slowly and hesitantly we began to emerge from our bunkers, barracks, makeshift fox holes and hiding places. It was assumed that the quiet signified that Moosburg had fallen, the fighting had stopped and our fighting men had won the battle.

Amidst the quiet and wondering what was going on, we waited – something we had become very good at. We all began to hang around in the compound near the gate, watching expectantly, not really knowing what to anticipate. The next sound I heard was music to my ears and every other guy in the compound. It was the sound of a great big, bruising American tank rumbling up the street toward the camp!

Within minutes, the first tank came crashing through the front fence of the prison camp, smashing the gates and crushing the barbed wire fencing. I almost couldn't believe it – how wonderful this whole scene was playing out before my very eyes!

I watched as my fellow POW's jumped onto the tanks wanting to get as close as they could to their liberators, the 14th Armored Division, those responsible for us no longer being prisoners, but free men. The clapping and cheering was deafening, everyone went crazy with joy and excitement!

Our emotions ran the gamut as we hooted and hollered, laughed with joy and cried with no shame. I yelled, jumped, and shouted along with thousands of others, "The war is over, the war is over, we're free, we're free!"

German guards were scrambling down from their towers and surrendering. Now they would be prisoners of war.

"Frantically trying to defend himself against being crushed by the mob of ragtag rabble climbing all over his tank, the besieged sergeant driver of one of the 14th Armored Division Shermans declared that he had never seen such "a crazy bunch of ragged-ass people."

"Scenes of the wildest rejoicing accompanied the tanks as they crashed through the double ten foot wire fences of the prison camp. There were Norwegians, Brazilians, French, Poles, Dutch, Greeks, Rumanians, Bulgarians, Americans, Russians, Serbs, Italians, New Zealanders, South Africans, Australians, British, Canadians – men from almost every nation fighting the Nazis. All combined to give the 14th Armored Division the most incredible welcome it ever received. The tanks were finally slowed to five miles an hour as they went through the camps – the press of men in front of them was so great. Men cried and shouted and patted the tanks."

"You damned bloody Yanks, I love you!" shouted a six foot four Australian and threw his arms around the driver."

"A weary bearded American paratrooper climbed on a tank and kissed the tank commander. Tears streamed from his cheeks. An American Air Corps Lieutenant kissed a tank. "God damn, do I love the ground forces," he said. "You were a long time coming, but now you are here!"[6]

There were no words to express the feeling of these men. As the German guards were formed in columns of four and marched away, each man carrying two or three loaves of black bread, some of the tankers took the bread from them and tossed it over the fences to the Allied prisoners and they also tossed their own K and C rations.

German prisoners taken included boys of nine, fully uniformed and armed, and girls of 17 or 18 – also uniformed, armed and capable of shooting you just as easy as a regular.

What happened next is a once-in-a-lifetime experience, for sure. Every POW in the camp turned their attention toward the city of Moosburg and as we did, I witnessed the most beautiful sight I have ever seen. It was just after noon and we watched as our American Flag, Old Glory, was raised on the top of a church steeple in Moosburg. After seeing the flag of our country raised in triumph we shouted, raised our hands in victory, danced, hugged each other, cried and saluted the flag, singing a spontaneous heartfelt rendition of our National Anthem and God Bless America. So many of our thoughts, feelings, emotions had been in lockdown for so long, but not now, not here – we thrust every fiber of our being into this moment and rejoiced!

Flag raising at Moosburg
photo reprinted courtesy of USAF Library

To this day, I can still see our flag being raised, with our Stars and Stripes flying against the blue sky and the Swastika coming down. I will never forget the moment I witnessed that flag go up over the city.

I include the following poem from R. H. Owen, POW Stalags III and VIIA, which so accurately captures this most glorious event:

OUR FLAG WAVED SO BEAUTIFUL

On The Raising Of Old Glory At Moosburg – (Stalag VIIA) Germany

April 29, 1945

Tanks rumble in the night
And we sensed freedom was coming.
How soon it would happen
We did not know,
But our faith told us all would be right.
Then with the rising of the sun
Our freedom thundered in on that
beautiful April day
Of cold sunshine and breeze
We listened to token gunfire beyond the trees
And knew liberation was not far away.
Our forces had given an ultimatum
For the Germans to free us all,
But they held onto our freedom
And did not reply
It was then came up the war cry
That sent our army forward
Into Moosburg, barbed wire prison town,
Where anxious village square, church steeple,
And flag pole flying the sinister swastika.
Was disrupted by one lone rifleman
Firing as though to say
"I shall hold for one last moment their freedom."
With the exchange of angry fire,
Shooting ceased and we at the gate rejoiced
In loud hurrahs.
And then, quiet came in our hearts,
As men cried and fell down on their knees
Thanking God for their liberation,
Burned in my mind forever
Will always be the picture of our flags
Going slowly up that flag pole –
Waving so gently in the breeze.

– R.H. Owen, Clinton, MS;
POW, Stalags III and VIIA

[6] Reprinted with permission from the 100th Bomb Group Foundation

Fellow former prisoner of war, Claude Watkins states it this way, "Liberation, the good guys came and took you away from the bad guys! Your country had the will and its military had the initiative, the guts and the ability to kick butt and win to get you all the marbles."

At a national convention of former prisoners of war I attended years later, someone who had been to the 50th anniversary of the liberation of Moosburg brought back a special edition newspaper of the event and gave me a copy. The headline reads: The 'Moosberger', which was the German spelling. A photograph was included in the account of the liberation showing a scene in the prison camp where I was standing that day. There was also a picture of the same liberation scene in the American Ex-Prisoner of War history book with a caption beneath the photo asking: "Can you find yourself?", but I couldn't. I had the photo enlarged and looked at it closely with a magnifying glass–but I must be just on the outer edge of the photo. One thing is for certain–I know I am there, for sure!

Official estimates of the total Allied prisoners freed at Moosburg were 110,000 including an estimated 30,000 Americans. Picture a football stadium with 100,000 people in it. This is what the scene was like in terms of how many prisoners were being set free in one glorious day.

After the flag was raised, and within a few hours of our troops arriving in camp, General Patton rolled in sitting high in a command car. His very presence was awe-inspiring. I stood there staring at General Patton, our liberator, appearing larger than life. I couldn't believe it – but it was true. We were chanting his name, "Patton, Patton, Patton." Thousands of us were cheering as though we were at some major sporting event. Some guys fell to their knees, overcome with emotion, weeping unabashedly at General Patton's very significant appearance and what he represented.

He got up and stood tall in that car, and with a bullhorn in hand he spoke. "Gentlemen – you're now liberated and under Allied Control. We're going to take care of you; we're going to get you out of here." I listened and embraced his every word. Patton said he was going to get a field kitchen in here as soon as possible and get us some 'good chow'.

General Patton told us to, "Stay put, and do not go roaming around the countryside because there are still lots of mines around, sniper fire and still some gunfire action. You fellas aren't in any kind of condition to be traipsing around." We were all thrilled to have him in the camp sharing such wonderful truths with us.

After his appearance, it began to hit me, "I'm going home, I'm really going home!"

Soon some of the Infantry guys, our liberators, were giving us candy bars and cigarettes. Some soldiers actually liberated their brothers; it was like watching a scene from a movie. You couldn't take your eyes off the scene for fear you'd miss something so I just stood there watching every wonderful moment. It is an event that I will never forget. It was just so overwhelming, and the feelings that were stirred up deep within us all – they just got the best of us. Everyone's minds were flooded with thoughts, and at the top of my list was, "I wonder how soon I will get home?" Not far beyond that thought, was my next question, "How soon will I get to see Anne?"

Later that day a field kitchen was set up in the prison camp. We were given hot chocolate and white bread. As we came through the chow line, the guys serving us gave us their chocolate bars, whatever extra food they might have had with them and they gave us their 'dog biscuits'. These dog biscuits, as they were affectionately called, were nothing more than a snack type of cracker that was an easy food to carry into combat.

At this time of liberation, I weighed just 125 pounds. It seemed unbelievable to me since I had to lose weight to come under the 175 pound weight limit to enlist.

We hung around, happily enjoyed the treats we were given by 'our guys', watched the camp be restructured under the command of our forces and not the enemy, and waited anxiously to hear what was next.

For the next day or two, we remained in the camp until all of the planning and logistics of moving us out of our barbed wire prison could be worked out. To pass the time, we talked and prepared to leave the camp. Our conversations were totally about our liberation, how they would get us home, how quickly it all would take place and what the end of the war would mean to each former prisoner of war. Our thoughts were consumed with happiness and loved ones at home.

It was true, the war was over, but it was hard to comprehend. I joined my fellow prisoners – all of us rag-tagged, bug-bitten, bearded, and filthy; but finally in the very real process of getting back home. Our forces (99th Infantry and others) had basically claimed the town in a military government takeover and our military just chased the townsfolk of Moosburg out. They, in turn, took their belongings and went someplace else – who knows where they went?

The US military had taken over hotels, inns, and houses within the town and found us places to sleep that were finally outside of the prison barracks! But before this could happen, groups of us were taken somewhere just outside of the camp into a field and given a much needed delousing.

So, within a day or two of the liberation of our camp, our delousing completed, our commanders told us, "OK, everything is clear and you can go in to the town of Moosburg." In town the Army had set up different supply stations for us to go to for food, water, and first aid.

Our liberators would announce, "There's room for four in this house." We went in, found whatever food we could and helped ourselves to it. The owners had been chased out by our liberating forces and weren't there so it really didn't matter. To the victor go the spoils of war, so it was said. We were just happy for food and a place to sleep that was not overrun with bugs and filth. The opportunity to be sleeping somewhere other than a prison camp was indescribable. We stayed a few nights in that house. It was so satisfying to sleep in a real home, a real bed and not in a prison compound. I don't remember anything about the guys who may have been with me, no recollection of who they were. I do remember that in this house we were staying in a few of us sat down at a dining room table to eat some of the meager portions of food we found and that was a real treat.

Eventually many of us went into the town looking through the stores, mostly for souvenirs. Everything was vacant and wide open for our use. The town of Moosburg was all shot up from rousting the Germans out of the buildings so there really wasn't much of anything of value left. Some of the houses had been ransacked, presumably by others who left the prison camp on their own and began going through the town of Moosburg.

Allied prisoners could be seen all through the town just enjoying their freedom and being able to go wherever they wanted. Some perhaps a bit more mischievous than others, who just got into cars and drove to France, not wanting to wait for the army to complete our liberation process.

There wasn't much adventure for us, we were playing the waiting game and the real adventure for me would be getting out of Moosburg and heading toward home. The army guys were always reminding us that it wouldn't be long and they'd get us out of here.

On May 5th orders came and we were loaded onto trucks and transported to a Luftwaffe Air Base in Landshut, Germany where we stayed for a few days. We were all dirty from the filthy living conditions we had been in and our personal hygiene was virtually nonexistent. So one of the first things they did was take us to a huge staging area with outdoor showers.

This entire process was like running the gauntlet. Before getting into the showers, we stripped naked dropping our clothes into a pile on the ground where they were immediately thrown into a fire and burned. Next someone sprayed us down with a powdery delouser of some kind designed to kill any remaining lice or bugs that still clung to our bodies. After this we were guided to the showers and, once done, someone handed us towels to dry off with. Once we were dried off, someone was right there to hand us new clothes. After this whole process was done I started to feel like a human being again.

It was springtime and we slept on the ground – it wasn't too bad, but it did get cold at night.

We anxiously awaited the arrival of planes that were coming to the Air base to load us up and take us to France. We all joked that we didn't care if the planes arrived at night we were getting on them! American pilots were flying in whatever planes were available to come and fly us out of here.

On May 8th, a group of us got on board a C-47 heading for Rheims, France. This was the first time I was back on a plane after being shot out of my B-17, and I couldn't have been more excited. My thought was, "I'm headin' home!" We were all thrilled to be on this plane that was getting us closer to home. We were all so happy that once on board we all began cheering, "We're getting out of Germany and into France!" As we flew low level over Germany we could see below us all of the damage that was done as a result of the war. It was a sobering sight; buildings were just shattered – blown to bits.

The plane landed in Rheims, France at a camp called 'Lucky Strike' on the edge of the Atlantic Ocean. This is when we found out that the surrender to end the war was signed that very day.

This memory of regaining my freedom will never diminish in my mind. It's hard to believe that all of the hardships and struggles of the last several months were over. Even today, I still think, "I'm thankful to the good Lord all the time for being liberated and being able to come back home."

Chapter Sixteen

LADY LIBERTY –
HOME SWEET HOME

Camp Lucky Strike in Rheims, France was a former WWII German airstrip and was one of several camps built around LeHavre at the end of 1944. It served as the principal camp for liberated prisoners of war as well as repatriated soldiers. It was also the Headquarters for Allied Supreme Commander General Dwight D. Eisenhower.

The camps were in use at the beginning of the war, too. The camps were named after different brands of American cigarettes. This was done for security purposes – if the camp was being talked about on the radio as "Lucky Strike," "Pall Mall," or "Camel", we weren't giving the enemy strategic locations of the camps.

We were delivered to the camp via large trucks, all of them filled with joyful former prisoners of war. I just kept delighting in the fact that I would soon be going home and that this was all part of the process.

It was a large area filled with a lot of army tents everywhere you looked. There were thousands of POW's arriving daily to the camp. Having so many POW's released at the same time presented some delay in being able to get everyone transported out. Logistically, it was a challenge, as at times there were 100,000 men in the camp all requiring lodging and food.

I was given a barracks bag, mess kit, underwear, fatigues, casual clothing, shoes, and a blanket. We were assigned four men to a tent in an area used only for former prisoners of war. There were also big mess halls close to our tent where we were given hot meals. I remember how nice and warm it was in those tents.

I soon learned that I was now a RAMP, or Recovered Allied Military Personnel – a term given to all of us Allied POWs.

I had several interviews that involved a debriefing type of questioning. There were hundreds of us lined up for this process. Most of the information was basic and included questions concerning our date of capture and the camp we were held in. Here in Camp Lucky Strike we were waiting for the ships that would take us back to America.

We were given permission to go into town and do whatever we wanted. We didn't have to pay for anything, everything was free. If I wanted chocolate milk, I'd just go get some. It took some getting used to, as only days before I, and other prisoners, were scrounging for food to stay alive.

There was a carnival at Reims at this time set up like an amusement park with a Ferris wheel and merry-go-round that the kids were riding and enjoying. I will never forget as I watched this wonderful scene, so far removed from all I had just left behind. I had a soft ice cream cone like you'd get at a Dairy Queen at this carnival – I never had one before in my life – what a treat! Basically, we all were just sight-seeing. Camp Lucky Strike wasn't set up that far from town and when we went in to the town we were treated by the townsfolk like the liberators that we were.

I don't recall anyone walking up and kissing me, though!

We were wearing clean, new Army uniforms that had been issued to us, but of course, many of them didn't fit right. It was almost like getting something out of a Goodwill box. We really were a bunch of sad sacks, but the uniforms were clean and we were glad to have them.

Eventually I was able to get a good haircut and shave, and I chose to leave a moustache on my upper lip. A lot of guys were copying the mustachioed and popular look of famous World War II airmen like Colonel Gabreski and Hollywood movie star Clark Gable.

We really didn't know how long this freedom we were experiencing in France was going to last, so we just enjoyed it as much as we could. Back at camp, we passed the time waiting to hear about our next leg of the journey by playing cards.

In the beginning of June, I received the orders I had long been waiting for and I boarded a truck for LeHavre, France. This truck ride delivered me to the dock where a boat was now ready for our arrival to begin our voyage home.

Upon arrival at the dock, I could see the 'Liberty Ship', which was a supply ship that was going to be my ticket home. Liberty ships were originally built to carry weapons, ammunition, food, tools, vehicles – all of the things that might be needed for the war effort all around the world. But now, at the end of the war, these ships were used to carry large numbers of troops home. I can tell you that it was not an ocean liner or cruise ship in any sense. It was just a transport vessel, set up to take passengers and supplies. There weren't even any bunks to sleep on.

The boat was so crowded that there was very little to eat on board. Every once in a while someone would make an announcement that there were some "goodies" available and we'd scramble to whatever location aboard ship they were being given out.

We were on the water for ten long days. I will, however, hand it to the Navy guys stationed on the ship. At one point during the trip, they provided us with some good, old-fashioned military fun while out on the open seas. I heard and felt the "BOOM" of cannon fire from the hold of the ship. I thought to myself, "What's going on, why is someone shootin' right here in the middle of the Atlantic? Could there still be German submarines going by? Didn't anybody tell the Navy the war was over?" It turns out that the good ole' sailors on board were just having some fun shooting their guns at the icebergs off in the distance! The ship was jammed with POW's – and once we found out why all the firing was being done, we all had a good laugh at their antics.

Mostly though, to pass the time on board ship I sat up on the deck getting some sun. I admit that part of the trip was nice. Other parts, however, not so much. We travelled in a three-ship convoy, and I did not like the constant up and down, up and down motion of the ship caused by the wake from the other ships. I wasn't used to Navy life, in addition to the sea sickness, everything was cramped and small. Guys would just relieve themselves over the side of the boat. I had no shower for ten days. I just kept thinking that all of this was a very small price to pay for the trip home!

It was day ten of this journey, and we were coming into New York harbor at daylight. It was June 16, 1945. After this trip this flyboy said to himself, "I'm never going on a boat again!" I wanted nothing to do with water travel after that, I said, "No more!"

I couldn't believe I was finally back in the United States, but yes, it was true! There was such an anxiousness to get off of the ship, but we had to hurry up and wait some more. The ship was just sitting out in the harbor waiting for our turn to come in and for a dock to become available. The set up was similar to planes waiting at an airport for a runway to become available for landing or takeoff.

There was a lot of activity in the harbor, so many boats coming and going, bringing so many of us home. It was actually a wonderful scene to watch, to realize so many fighting men were finally getting back from the war.

Finally, our floating home moved forward to an empty pier and docked. As the ship docked I saw the Statue of Liberty. I will never forget seeing this wonderful symbol of freedom and liberty. I and everyone else on the ship erupted into shouts of joy, with hundreds of us of cheering and shouting – it was quite a scene!

Next, the gang plank was lowered and the systematic and orderly unloading of all us from the ship began. I watched as man after man came down that plank, walked off the boat, stepped onto the ground and immediately bent down and kissed the earth. Everybody did it. It was a natural response. Then it was my turn. I walked down the plank onto American soil and did what every other returning soldier did – I knelt down and kissed the ground. What a great feeling that was!

The dock was so crowded and nobody cared one bit. It was one great, big, wonderful homecoming and our joy was evident everywhere! I didn't expect anyone from my family to be there in New York to meet me, and that was OK because I was home and it felt great. Soon enough I would be reunited with family. I savored the historic event I was part of for this moment and loved every minute of it.

Not long after docking, I was on an Army truck headed to Camp Shanks in upstate New York, which, after the war, was set up exclusively for returning prisoners of war. The army processed 290,000 returning American prisoners of war through Camp Shanks. Ironically, the camp was staffed by captured German prisoners of war. They were the ones who did all of the 'dirty work' for us – the cooking, feeding , laundry, cleanup – those types of things. A lot of the former prisoners were resentful of this set up. Not me. My whole mindset was doing the things that were getting me closer and closer and closer to home.

I received a barracks assignment, was issued clothes that were a better fit and given some good chow.

The next day after arriving, I got called in for an interview which was more or less an exit interview, where I was asked questions about my time as a prisoner and about my injuries.

On June 16, 1945 I was given furlough paper and $300.00 to go home with, which seemed like a lot of money to me at the time. Plus, I had six months of back pay coming to me from prison camp. (This was sent home to me while on my 60-day furlough.) I was told that I was 'on my own' to get transportation, as there were no Army busses available to transport anyone to New York City simply because of so many serviceman utilizing bus service.

At the time, I was buddying with a fellow who had also been a prisoner of war. He offered to take me to where his family lived, which was an apartment in Brooklyn, New York. I only stayed with his family in Brooklyn overnight so I didn't get to really see Brooklyn. Watching his homecoming scene really made me anticipate my own homecoming, which would be happening very shortly, I hoped. His family was glad to see him, and his brothers and sisters and aunts and uncles were all there to welcome him home.

I called home from his house and said, "I'm in the United States." My brother George and my Dad said they wanted to come and get me by car. I said, "No, there's so much confusion here, you'll never find me. I'll just come home by myself. I'm going to Philadelphia where I'll get a bus and be home in a few days. I'll see you then."

His family then took me to the bus station and helped me get pointed in the right direction by showing me how I could get a bus to Philadelphia.

When I went to the ticket counter and asked for a ticket to Philadelphia, I was told, "There are no tickets available and we don't know when any will be available." I soon found out that busses and trains were all booked solid.

At this point there were a lot of fellows in the same predicament as me. We began talking about what we could do next… how could we get home, what options did we have? We were so close we wouldn't give up now, just because we couldn't get train or bus tickets. Some of us decided we were going to hitchhike, and that's what I did. It seemed reasonable enough, so I got out of the station and to a main road and began my hitchhike home. I first hitchhiked a ride out of New York. This guy drove me five hours, where he then dropped me off. I said so long to him and then headed into whatever town I was near. Knowing I had to head west, I'd get to a highway and hitch another ride west. I would explain to whoever was providing the ride that I was heading to Pittsburgh, and asked, "Can you get me to the Lincoln Highway?' That was my strategy, to pretty much follow the Lincoln Highway as best I could, and that's what I did.

I was in my uniform and I had my B4 bag with me as I hitchhiked. I always thought that the B4 bag was fancy. It was leather and canvas and it opened up so that you could hang it up with your clothes and all of your belongings in it. I had my socks and underwear and all of my toiletries in that bag.

Of course, this hitchhiking adventure wasn't all one ride, either. There were several fairly long rides, but never the entire way. As a result, after some of my rides, I slept on front porches along the way. Some of the folks who gave me rides let me sleep in their houses – total strangers. People were so kind in welcoming home a returning airman from the war. They were thankful for our military victory and in some small way they wanted to repay us. This is what I experienced.

The closer and closer to home I got the smaller my moustache got. My father was always telling us boys to be clean-shaven and well groomed. This was in the back of my mind and by the time I got home, I only had a very slight moustache.

At some point down the highway, I ran into somebody who said, "I'm going to Harrisburg, PA." And I said, "Oh boy, I'm going to Harrisburg – now I'm really getting close to Pittsburgh."

There was a stop somewhere before we got to Harrisburg, and I recall the next ride after that was pretty long too, and I think my final ride was from Harrisburg all the way to Irwin, PA. From Irwin, PA there was one more ride needed – and I got it. I hitchhiked into East Pittsburgh, Pennsylvania.

I had the driver drop me at the end of thee East Pittsburgh side of the Westinghouse Bridge at Center Street. From this drop-off point I walked to my house at 110 Bessemer Avenue.

I met a couple of people along the way who shouted out to me, "How ya' doin, Frank?" "Welcome home, Frank!" and similar greetings. That was my first taste of what it felt like to be welcomed home and it felt terrific. I didn't call anybody even though I was so close to home. It was daylight as I walked up to the porch and knocked on the front door and that was it.

I don't remember who answered the door, but it didn't take long for everyone to come flying out onto the porch to mob me and welcome me home. Everybody was there and I was just so happy and thankful to be home again!

One thing I'll always remember is that young Henny, the oldest son of my brother George and his wife, Myra was there sitting on the front porch. He was probably only two years old. It was such a change, coming from the horrors of war to that innocent child, just sitting on the front porch grinning at me. Life seemed surreal, and I wasn't sure which reality was the true one for a while.

I knew two things for certain, I was home and I was tired. I don't remember when I decided to call Anne. We weren't going steady or anything, but we had dated prior to me going off to war and she was a very important person in my life. My memory of our times together helped to sustain me and give me strength while in prison camp. She was the last person to see me off to war as she had been the one who took me to the station when I left for the service. Now that I was home, I wanted to reconnect with her as soon as possible.

I had found out that another fellow Anne had dated, Dave Cinna, was killed on Iwo Jima. I didn't know what was going to happen in our relationship. I called her and had a chance to talk to her, arranging a time when we could meet. Soon after, I went up to see her at her parent's house. Anne and her mom and dad were so glad to see me and that was nice, how warmly they welcomed me home.

I received my six months back pay check for $1,200 at this time. This was especially good timing as Anne and I started going out together again for the next sixty days of my furlough. And I fell hook, line and sinker for her.

NOVEMBER 2ND, 1945

FRANK A. KRAVETZ
HONORABLY DISCHARGED
FROM THE MILITARY

Chapter Seventeen

MENDING A BROKEN BODY

After I was welcomed home, I spent time getting reacquainted with family, neighbors and the people of East Pittsburgh. So many kindnesses were extended to me and among them was getting invited to their homes for dinner – something I really enjoyed. During the day I had friends and classmates from East Pittsburgh that were coming home from the war too. We'd get together and do things like go to a ball game and hang out. I started to work around my house a little bit, helping at home with different things that needed to be done. At this point in my life it was just so wonderful to be home. That's all I wanted and it meant so much to me.

After Anne's work day was over, I'd pick her up at National Biscuit Company in East Liberty and we'd be off to do something together. Anne had lots of friends so there were always two or three couples going out to have a good time. Dorothy Marino was a real good friend of Anne's (who was a cousin of NFL quarterback Dan Marino.) Dorothy was dating Russ Foster, who also had also been serving in the Air Corps in

Europe and who had recently come back from the war. They were one of the couples we enjoyed going out with a lot.

I wore my uniform on these dates, as I wanted people to know I was home from the war, and this was one way to do it. I must admit, there were a lot of advantages to being seen in public in uniform. For instance, I could get on a streetcar and the conductor would say, "Just come on board, no charge." It was a small way they could say, "Thanks," to a returning serviceman.

We went out to dinner, dances and nightclubs, traveling all over the place. There were lots of nice, little nightclubs all around the area. There was one right across the Westinghouse Bridge, the 413 – that had a talented piano player who we liked going to see. We took rides out to South Park, rode horses, went on picnics and took trips to Kennywood Park. Just in my hometown of East Pittsburgh there were three movie theaters where we would go to see the first run movies.

We kept busy – it seemed like every night was a different adventure going somewhere, doing something. Whatever it was, we were out on the town, living life to the fullest and it was *great* therapy for me.

Being with Anne was my life at this stage of the game – that's just the way it was in my heart and soul.

Frank and Anne together again

Being with her meant everything to me; I didn't want to be with anyone else.

Nobody knew I was a prisoner of war. I didn't talk about it – not at home, not to anyone. At this stage of my life, I was enjoying being out with friends, having fun, and moving on with my life – trying to forget about all that took place as a prisoner of war. This was therapy for me; I didn't want anybody talking about it. I was happy to be talking about other things. I didn't want to dwell on my war experiences because it was too sad, too hard. Even later on, I didn't talk about the war. I didn't want to tell anybody anything about my experiences. Part of my thinking was, "Who is going to believe me?" People weren't going to believe that something like that could happen to somebody. I'm serious about this.

I went to a bar with some guys and they'd ask me, "Where were you in the war?" And I'd say, "I was in the Army Air Corps and I got shot down over Germany." Right away, some of these macho guys would say, "Oh, prisoner of war, eh? Well, *we* fought to the bitter end, *we* never gave up, *we* fought to the death." At that point, I didn't say any more about being shot in the tail section of a bomber, wounded in a crippled plane that was going down, or being thrown out of the plane with a parachute wrapped in my arms, or my wound freezing being what probably saved me from bleeding to death. I was getting mad. And I'd just say, "Shut up – you don't know what the hell you're talking about," blowing off a little steam.

From that point forward, I placed that in the back of my mind and said to myself, "I'm not telling anybody – because they're not going to believe me anyway." I thought, "They're not going to believe I had the same clothes on my back for three months, or that the meager rations of food were just enough to keep me alive." I firmly believed people would say I was full of bull if I talked about any part of my experience, so I just didn't say anymore. I became introverted and protective of my experience.

Other guys would be saying stuff like, "Oh, we were in this battle and that battle and we fought and did this and that." Then I'd say, "Oh, I was in a prison camp." Their response would be, "Oh, you had it nice!" Right then and there, I realized their perception was that I had it easy in prison camp. I was getting mixed feelings that I might be exaggerating, or that I had it nice and easy while they were still fighting. So I learned not to talk about it. It's that old form of self-protection where you just kept things to yourself. I kept it away from my brothers and sisters too. I didn't want anybody to know how difficult it was. It wasn't until years later, when I started going to the VA and hearing the stories from other prisoners of war, that I could start sharing my experiences of the horrors we faced and survived.

I didn't even talk to Anne about it. She knew I was wounded, but I never dwelled on it. Really, that was the best part of my therapy – not talking about it. For me, it was still there in my mind, but I didn't "let it out" like I can talk about it now. I just wasn't talking to anyone about it at the time. There was an unspoken belief held by those who had not been a prisoner of war that if you were captured, why, then, you gave up and were somehow less than a true soldier.

At that time it wasn't popular to be a prisoner of war – or at least that's how I thought about it. When I came home, there was no band playing, no fanfare in the streets. No one saying, "Here's a bus for you to come home." Of course, the War Department did send a telegram home to my family stating that I was a prisoner of war, so they knew. But it was an unspoken thing between everybody. I was home. We didn't talk about it, it was too tragic. It was swept under the rug like it never happened. Everyone's perspective was, "He's here, he's with us and that's all we care about." It was that kind of atmosphere. So I just moved on. I just moved on.

My life was enjoying my time with Anne and with our friends – just having fun. I did not ask Anne to marry me at this time. My 60 days of leave was coming to an end. I realized that I had to go back and I became very depressed. I withdrew a lot. My relationship with Anne was the only thing that gave me peace. I just wanted to be with her more than I wanted to be with others. At times, I really had to push myself to double date or go out with groups of people. In a way I was selfish, I guess.

I had the, "I don't want to do this (whatever the 'this' was) – I want to do what I want to do" mentality. In prison camp, I was always told what to do, where to go, losing my freedom to make personal decisions. Now I very much wanted to connect with my personal freedom of choice.

At this point, I was caring for my leg wounds by myself because my wounds were still open. I wasn't sure how I'd get along in another hospital setting. My dad, 'Pap' Kravetz, took me down to see our family doctor, Dr. Travaskis, whose office was located in East Pittsburgh. Pap wanted the family doctor to look at me and see that I was doing all right and coming along with my wounds. At this point, I hadn't showed my father my wounds and I was reluctant to do so, but he wanted to see my injuries. During my appointment, the doctor examined me, and my father spoke up and said, "I want to see it" (the wound). He repeated determinedly, "I want to see it." I said, "Pap, it's OK, you don't have to see it." But he insisted so strongly that I relented, and pulled my pants down with the bandages still on my leg.

The doctor carefully unwrapped the wound and then it could be seen. My father gasped and said, "Oh my God!" There was pity in his eyes and I could tell his response was one of total sadness and anguish over seeing the wound I had gotten accustomed to seeing every day. After this, nothing more was said.

I told the doctor that I would be going back to the service for rehabilitation, and to a military hospital in Florida for therapy and more operations. I mentioned that once I was discharged, I'd return to him so he could keep an eye on the wound. The Army Air Corps wasn't going to discharge me until I completed all of my recuperation at the hospital. After I finished all of the rehabilitation my enlistment obligation would be complete.

My whirlwind time of being together with Anne went on for two months, June 16th to August 15th. And now, the closer it came to my time to go back – just thinking about it made me very sad. After having all of the freedom and good times that I was now experiencing from being back home, that was all that mattered – I didn't want to interrupt any of it. Soon enough, my 60-day furlough came to an end and orders were sent to my home that I was to report to Miami Beach, Florida.

The military sent train tickets to my home. I asked Anne once again to take me to the train station to leave. She took off some time from National Biscuit to take me and she was more than willing to do so. Pap was working second shift then at Westinghouse and honestly, I didn't want anyone else with me. That was it, that's how I wanted it. Anne and I had just spent a lot of time together for the past 60 days, having a real good time, and that's what cemented our relationship.

Now it was time to go – something I had to do, but didn't want to do.

I wore my uniform to the station – it was late afternoon as I kissed Anne good-bye and boarded the Baltimore & Ohio Railroad from the Southside of Pittsburgh. I was so sad, it was breaking my heart to leave her, but I reasoned, the sooner I completed my military obligations, the quicker I could return to Anne. I had overnight accommodations, a Pullman sleeper car, like when this whole adventure began in what seemed lifetimes ago.

As I recall, I was the only serviceman on the train with a lot of business men types – big wigs enjoying a first-class trip. While chatting with them over dinner, I told them about where I was going, and about my service, and being a war veteran.

Everybody was very friendly to me and welcomed me home, acknowledging my service. A lot of guys were coming home, but I was going back – and I was kind of depressed. But once I got on the train and got treated so well – the porters were good to me and I got a good night's sleep – I felt better and the sadness eased up a little.

At this time I was walking fairly normally, but still did not have the full extension of my leg. I couldn't run if I had to and I still had a little tightness to my leg.

First stop was Washington, DC, where I had to switch trains to the 'Silver Meteor' going to Miami Beach, Florida. The 'Silver Meteor' was a streamlined train, fantastic transportation. And this was another sleeper, so I had wonderful overnight accommodations again, which I appreciated very much.

There was always somebody to talk to and that helped the trip go by a little faster. I felt very important, like there was significance to my life – a sense that I had accomplished something of value and purpose.

I had been to Miami Beach before, just three or four days early on during my training. When I arrived in Miami Beach, we were quartered in the hotels that were designated for military personnel. I had travelling papers with me. There was a replacement center that I reported to somewhere in Miami Beach – a headquarters type of place. Once I checked in there, they gave me orders as to where I was to report next. I had accommodations in Miami for a few days where I enjoyed the beach until I did receive my assignment to go to the Don Cesar Convalescent Hospital in St. Petersburg, Florida. I was transported by bus – the 'Tam-Miami' bus line, a straight shot from Miami to St. Petersburg. I didn't know what to expect at all. When the bus pulled up in front of this huge, bright pink building right on the beach, I thought to myself, "Boy this is like being in heaven!" The sight of this place was really overwhelming. The Don Cesar, well-known as a 'pink palace' luxury hotel, now converted to a military hospital, would be where I would get the attention I needed to recover from my war wounds. I got assigned to a hotel room that was set up with double military bunk beds. I got a lower bunk because of my leg injuries.

I began the process of getting acquainted with yet another place which was to be my home away from home. One of the things that I really enjoyed was that you could simply walk right out on to the beach from the hotel. I wasn't allowed to go into the water to swim because of my wound still being open, so I just sunbathed and enjoyed being near the water. There was a concern about getting an infection in my wound and I sure didn't want that to happen. Kind of ironic, really, when you think of the filth I survived in the prisoner of war camp, but I listened to their counsel and stayed out of the water.

During this time I had the pleasure of meeting Joe DiMaggio of the New York Yankees. Joe was in the service during the war and was sent to Don Cesar hospital for a medical discharge. He was looking forward to getting back to playing with the Yankees. All the guys were aware that he was in our midst, as he was a very popular figure at the time. He was on the beach catching a baseball, playing ping-pong, joining in the activities just like he was one of the guys. He was a real nice guy who was sympathetic toward us because we were all wounded and recuperating. He participated in everything right along with us. I remember catching fly balls on the beach with him. He went to the mess hall with us, going through the chow line. I'd hear guys in line saying, "There's Joe DiMaggio."

Ping-pong tables and basketball hoops were set up right on the beach – that was so nice and relaxing playing right near the surf – all kinds of activities to help in our recovery. There was a lot to keep us all busy, including crafts of all kinds. They gave us silk from parachutes and we made scarves. They would cut a piece of silk to the right size for a scarf and then we would have to 'fray' the edges. Then we finished off the project by painting the Mighty 8th logo on it. I remember that really well. Guys were sending them home to their girlfriends – I may have brought one of those scarves home for Anne, I'm not sure.

They started on my therapy and I was assigned to a psychiatrist. August 22, 1945 – I was 21 years old. The psychiatrist was the first doctor I saw. These are his written notes found in my medical record: "Wounds, flak, left thigh and right ankle – severe, sustained in combat mission over Germany on 2nd November 1944. Partially healed. Approximately 65 small metallic foreign bodies right ankle and approximately 40 such bodies in the left thigh. No bony destruction by x-ray." My thigh bone was slightly cracked, but it healed, so there was no more break in it at this time. The bullet glanced off my femur. I was also being treated for shell-shock. During this psychiatric exam, I lay down on a couch and the Psychiatrist administered Pentothal (truth serum). I didn't know what the hell I was saying. Here's one excerpt that I read later from my records, "His only worry is about getting out of the Army, he only has 48 points. He's still single but says that he will get married next summer. He has known this girl (Anne) for many years." I guess I blurted out a lot about wanting to get home, mentioned what was bothering me, those types of things. This psychiatrist was a Captain in the Air Force, a good doctor, kind and compassionate to me during treatment.

I went through all of the psychiatric evaluations and the result was they classified me as 'P/N', which was Psycho/Neurosis/Neurotic. That was the military's term for what is now referred to as PTSD or Post Traumatic Stress Disorder, but at that time they didn't call it that. I was awarded a 10% service connected disability for that, and 20% service connected disability for my wounds.

I still had a little limp when I walked. For the physical therapy part of my recovery I'd go out on the beach and do all kinds of exercises, calisthenics, and take walks on the beach. I cooperated and did everything I could to get myself in shape except swim. Some guys could go in the water for swim therapy, but I still couldn't due to the condition of my leg wounds. There were amputees and lots of other visible types of wounds. My leg wound was covered with bandages and still had some open, seeping areas, so I could not get it wet.

Eventually I was told I needed some more skin grafts for my leg. It was a more pleasant experience having this procedure done back home in the good old US of A, as opposed to the last grafts I had done while a prisoner-patient in Germany.

It was discovered that the reason my wound was still open was because there were still foreign particles in my leg. By injecting dyes into my leg, they could take contrasting x-rays which revealed pieces of my flight suit actually imbedded inside my leg. When I was shot down, I had on all of my flying gear. When the shell came through my suit, it pushed the springs from the nichrome wire which was part of my heated flying suit inside my leg. I saw my x-ray and could see about an inch and a half spring inside my leg, like a coil. To reach the pieces, the docs had probes that they put into my open wound to pull those pieces of uniform and the wire they could get to out. In a way, I was lucky, my imbedded particles showed up on an x-ray – wounds that were caused by wood bursts from a splintered tree wouldn't show up on an x-ray. The doctors also did a procedure to dissolve some pieces of my embedded uniform. These procedures finally helped close most of the open wounds on my leg. But even after all of the skin grafts I received, there was still about a half inch hole remaining where pus was still draining. I would not be discharged to go home until the entire wound was clean and closed.

I was really surprised to find out about my shredded uniform pieces being in the wound. I saw the x-rays. They removed most of the pieces that were close to the surface, but some of the pieces are still in there. Some of the other pieces worked their way out on their own. I'd be walking around and I'd say to myself, "Oh, I got a nail in my shoe," but that wasn't the case. What was actually happening is that some of those foreign bodies that were lodged in my ankle would work their way down and out, and I could feel them, like a nail in my shoe.

Once they made the diagnosis and I knew they were going to continue to take x-rays and clean my wounds until it closed, I knew I still had some rehabilitation in front of me. Just at this stage of the game, I found out they were going to close the Don Cesar Hospital, because they were building permanent military-based veterans hospitals all over the country. The Veterans Administration took over the Don Cesar, Plattsburgh, San Antonio – many different facilities. They wanted to send me to a recovery quarters – a Military Hospital for the Air Force in San Antonio, Texas. I asked, "Is there anything in the East, so I could be closer to home?" They said I could go up to Plattsburgh, New York. I received travel orders to go to there directly from St. Petersburg, Florida by train and given a per diem for expenses.

I arrived at the train station in Plattsburg, and someone from the air base picked me up there. Plattsburg had an air base with a hospital. This was a real small place, especially when compared to where I was just stationed at the Don Cesar. It was one floor and maybe had 50 beds at the most. Most of the servicemen who were there were like me, transitioning out of the service to get back home, but needing more medical attention before they could be discharged. For me, the main medical need was to receive more skin grafts on my leg. I would not be discharged until my wound was closed, and there was no more festering or draining. I wasn't bedridden and that was good, because I could get around OK. There was no type of military duty – I was strictly there for treatment. If I wasn't receiving medical care, I would go to the day room and shoot pool, or would read books, stuff like that. I would write a note to send off to my family. It was a relaxing time. After all I had been through it was like a vacation, really.

I went to a high school football game. Plattsburgh High School was playing somebody and they provided a bus for us guys to attend the game. We talked to the football players and the cheerleaders and told them that we were soldiers and they gathered around us to hear our stories. The students were very interested in us and what we shared with them about our war experiences. The Parent's Club took us into the high school and provided us with hot dogs, chips, and pop, catering to our every need – making us feel so welcomed. It was like being a carefree teenager once again and it was great. The fact is we weren't too far removed from being teenagers ourselves. This was just a nice time for us to experience a piece of the good old hometown America.

Another activity they provided for us was a boat ride to Lake Placid. The hospital was right on Lake Champlain. The whole Lake Placid area was beautiful. It was around September, and we were taken to the area where the Olympic Ski jumps were. There was no snow on them at the time, so we climbed up a ladder to get to the top of the ski jump. The reason I was able to make this climb was because I was getting stronger, which meant I was also was fairly close to being able to get my medical discharge. At the top there were pieces of board going across the slope horizontally so you could have a place to get your footing. This is the part of the jump where there would normally be snow and ice before you take the jump. So there we were, at the very top taking it all in, and it was high! I really didn't know anything about the sport of snow skiing, it was just another experience for me to get to enjoy. Never would I ever believe or little did I think at that time, that someday my kids would be involved in snow skiing. But there I was at the top of this very high ski jump looking out and down. It was quite an experience, really interesting.

There were people in the town that volunteered to take us guys in for Sunday dinner, to invite us into their homes for a little taste of home away from home. Those times were really nice and appreciated by all of us. I'd wear my dress uniform, and wearing that uniform went a long way in those days! There was respect for the uniform, plus I had a lot of pride in wearing it. I sat down to a good meal and nice conversation. My hosts would ask me all kinds of questions, and we just enjoyed a good time around a dinner table. I don't remember any specific family names or anything, but I remember how nice it was, and how good it felt to be in someone's welcoming home. These were total strangers taking us in and I was very appreciative, very appreciative.

There was also a USO club in the area, and we went to dances and gatherings in that club.

I can say that the evenings for us were always busy. There was always something for us to do, to get out, and enjoy time away from our rehabilitation. We were on our own to do what we wanted. There was a noncommissioned officer's club and we would go there to hang out, plus there were dances we attended.

I don't think I called Anne during the time I was in Plattsburg, but I did write to her. There were letters from my family, and I sent return cards, telling them what was going on and how I was doing and when I expected to be home.

One day the doctor came in and said, "OK, we're going to get your papers ready and discharge you." They did give me a list of things I had to do prior to my discharge, like getting my back pay and discharge papers, things like that. It was a busy few days preparing for separation from the military. I had been there about a month and was discharged officially on November 2, 1945.

I got my ticket for the train, made my arrangements for transportation, and that was that: Plattsburg, to New York City, to Philadelphia, then the Pennsylvania railroad back to Pittsburgh. I had already told my parents when I expected to be home and I treasured the fact that this time I was finally going home for good.

When I arrived in Pittsburgh, my mom, dad, and my brother George met me at the train station in downtown Pittsburgh and brought me home. My other brothers, Johnny and Mickey, were still living at home at the time, and they, too, were back from the war. We didn't talk about the war much at all. We were all trying to forget the war. We were back into our civilian interests and glad for them.

Mickey went his own way with the guys that were back from the war and my brother Johnny was engaged to Agnes – they were to be married in January, 1946. At the top of my list after coming home was getting an engagement ring to give to Anne. I got it at Kappels jewelry store in East Liberty.

I had received some mustering out pay (this is any money that you have coming to you from your time in the service.) I was getting paid the entire time I was in the hospital, and with that pay I went down right away and bought both of our rings. That was a priority with the money I received, plus some additional money I had saved, too.

Lots of couples were getting engaged and I would soon be joining the ranks. Anne and I went to a Pittsburgh Pirates baseball game at Forbes Field. I said, "I have something for you," and I gave Anne the ring during the middle of the game. She put it on, and that was it. This was just between Anne and me at this point, our little secret. And we kept it our little secret until Christmas, 1945.

I officially gave Anne the engagement ring at Christmastime. She had the ring on when she came up to my house and, of course, everybody was looking at the ring on her hand. It was now publicly announced that we were engaged. We made plans to be married the following September, 1946.

Chapter Eighteen

A Civilian Again

Now that I was discharged and engaged to be married, it was time to move forward with my work and career plans. I was debating whether I was going to return to the University of Pittsburgh to finish my degree in Engineering or go back to Westinghouse and continue my work there. I had already completed a two-year apprenticeship as a machinist prior to entering the service. I thought that going back to Westinghouse might be my best option.

This next part of my story is one that I don't talk about very much, because it wasn't a very pleasant experience. In order to return to Westinghouse after my time in the military they required me to undergo a physical examination before they would hire me. I really didn't think too much about it, and set up an appointment for the exam.

During the exam, my military discharge papers were reviewed. Included in the papers was a diagnosis of 'P/N', which stood for Psycho-Neurosis, the common term now known as 'PTSD' or 'Post Traumatic Stress Disorder.' In those early years after the war it was the way the military acknowledged combat stress in a veteran.

The interviewer said that Westinghouse wouldn't accept me back into the workplace with this condition. I couldn't believe what I was hearing. They were refusing to hire me and I immediately began my own defense by telling him, "I'm only receiving a 10% service-connected disability compensation for the diagnosis, that's nothing. There's nothing wrong with me."

The interviewer didn't budge and repeated his point, "But your discharge papers say you are psychoneurotic and therefore we can't hire you." I was so angry that I got up from the exam and walked out.

I immediately drove to the Veterans Administration Regional Office in downtown Pittsburgh. I met with a VA representative and began to ask him questions about what was recorded on my discharge papers. I said, "Why is this 'P/N' on my record that I'm receiving 10% disability for – what does it mean? Are you guys saying I'm neurotic or what?"

The representative answered back, "Oh, no, you're OK, we're just giving you a 30% disability compensation recognizing your combat wounds and another 10% for combat stress."

I asked him, "What would it take for me to get that 10% rating taken off of my record?"

He replied, "Your signature."

I said, "Where's the pen?" I signed the paper and the VA removed, with my consent, the 10% Psycho-Neurotic rating.

I then went back to Westinghouse with the P/N diagnosis no longer a part of my record and was accepted for employment. I was told to report to the apprentice program and see the supervisor of Trades Training, Mr. Dearbeck. He said that he would give me one year of credit towards completion of a four-year tool and die apprenticeship.

I figured that was a good deal. He then explained to me that I would be going back to classes and would still be an apprentice until I completed the program. The supervisor also said that with this type of experience, I'd be better off down the road in terms of job and promotion opportunities. I was subsidized at $90.00 per month from the government for attending school – the same reimbursement as if I were attending a four-year college. If I needed anything for my classes like books or tools for use in the shop, I turned my expenses in to the instructor and received reimbursement for my purchases for the program. This did turn out to be the best move that I made for my career and my future.

With the 30% service connected disability I was receiving from the VA, the $90.00 per month subsidy for my government education, and my apprenticeship pay I was doing pretty good financially at the time. I settled in to what thousands and thousands of other guys were doing at the time, enjoying being a civilian again and getting on with my life after the war.

One day I received a call from the military base at the Pittsburgh International Airport asking me if I wanted to come up and be formally presented with my Purple Heart medal. That seemed like a lot of bother for another piece of metal, so I told them just to drop it in the mail to me, which they did.

Almost immediately after returning home I was asked to join the Veterans of Foreign Wars. There were so many of us who had returned from fighting overseas that it was a kind of word of mouth thing with other guys talking about it. Some local veterans began a drive to organize a local Post in Bessemer Terrace – a part of East Pittsburgh Borough. In order to move forward with this, the local group had to apply for a charter from the National VFW headquarters. My brother Mickey and I were signatories on that original charter to bring a local VFW to our hometown.

Frank and his brother Mike
in their VFW Uniforms

We had no building of our own at the time so we held meetings in Barman's, a local bar on the corner of Bessemer and Main streets. It quickly became a popular place for veterans home from the service to hang out and enjoy a few drinks. It didn't take long before someone would place a piece of paper in front of some newcomer and say, "Sign up for the local VFW we're starting." The bar was also used to hold our early organizational meetings.

In no time at all, from our little borough, we had over 260 guys signed up who agreed to join the VFW. The bar became too small too fast and we began meeting in a big older ten room house with a large lot that was made available to us after the older couple who lived there relocated. I was committed to the VFW and became active pretty quickly, attending meetings, planning fund raisers and working events like street fairs and picnics.

Since we didn't have our own club in those early years, Christmas and anniversary celebrations were held in different nightclubs in the area – the most popular ones being the Vogue Terrace and the Holiday House.

We eventually built our own Post home building. It was rewarding to have worked so hard on the planning committee and finally see the fruits of our labor. I served as both junior vice commander and then senior commander before becoming the commander of Post 5008. I served four more terms. A lot of guys didn't step forward to help, but I always did and enjoyed it. I was humbled by the fact that my fellow veterans thought enough of me to ask me to be a leader in an organization with the reputation of the VFW. That, more than anything else, prompted me to become involved and stay involved.

I was proud to be part of a group who had the same membership requirements – we had all served our country overseas in Europe, Japan and all over the world. Along with the other members, I was proud of my service and contributions to the war effort. The VFW was a natural place to fit in with people who shared those experiences. Even though the VFW was well known for its military membership, and there were lots of opportunities to discuss my time in the service with other men who served, I chose to not talk about my days in the service. Not at the VFW, not anywhere. Instead, while at the club I stayed busy with responsibilities which helped me keep my mind occupied and put the thoughts of war behind. Part of my reason for the silence was that my story, I felt, was just so hard to believe.

A lot of guys did talk about their days in the service, and weren't shy about it at all. As an example they'd say stuff like, "Oh, I killed at least ten Germans," or "I was on Iwo Jima and wiped out a machine gun nest." Their stories were of the real, 'macho type' stuff. I wasn't about to tell them I was a prisoner of war – it just wasn't popular to be a POW. At that time the mentality was like the old Phoenicians, 'You come home with your shield or on your shield'. In other words, you fight to the death, period. This attitude was prevalent, and lots of returning veterans prided themselves on being blood-and-guts fighters.

The truth is, many simply did not know what a prisoner of war was or what we might have gone through. As I mentioned before, I wanted to spare my family the heartache of retelling my story of being a POW because it was too sad for them, so I learned, very early on, how *not* to tell my story.

One of my strategies was to just make a big joke of the whole subject. For instance, someone would ask me if I ever wanted to go back overseas where I served. I would answer, "Why would I want to go back? The last time I was there, they put me in jail!" (ha, ha) It was an attempt to deflect the attention anyway from anything that could draw me into the discussion of the subject and perhaps have to face cutting or snide remarks. When I got back to the states, I put my happy face on, but for the most part it was a façade. Sure, outside I appeared 'happy-go-lucky'; but inside, my feelings were being locked up with a key turning the lock tighter and tighter.

Maybe my family of origin had set me up for this. All of my material needs were met, but very little love was dished out, and never an external sign of affection – no hugs, no kisses. That was the norm for that generation – feelings were very rarely talked about and emotions were not easily expressed.

Now with Anne, that was changing. I finally felt real love and affection and began opening up a little. My life changed altogether when I was making plans with Anne for our future. My goals were different, new and promising. I was moving on.

Wedding plans were at the top of our to-do list. Anne and I travelled to Monessen and Rices Landing, PA to attend a few weddings of relatives from her side of the family. We observed what these couples had as part of their wedding, took note of some of the different orchestras and bands that played and began making a list of what we wanted for our big day. One thing was certain – when Croatians and Slovaks (really any of the Eastern European families) got together there was always a big wedding. Ours would be no different.

We also travelled to Washington, DC to visit my brother, John, who took us to the Yugoslavian Embassy where Anne's cousin, Charlotte Muzar, worked. It was at the Embassy that we were able to buy whiskey for the reception for one dollar a bottle.

The hall we booked for the reception was a Hungarian hall in East Pittsburgh. A short time prior to our wedding day, we stopped in to check on our reservation. We discovered that the hall was double-booked. I confronted the owner of the hall and said, "You made the mistake and now we already have our invitations printed, naming this hall as the place for our reception. The very least you can do to make this right is pay for the printing of our new invitations that will need to be sent out." Fortunately we located the Slovak Social Hall in North Braddock near St. Helen's church. We received our money back for the mistake that was made and continued with our plans.

Anne and I were getting along so well together, enjoying each other and were anxious for our big day to arrive. There was yet another important item to plan for – the honeymoon. Since I had been stationed in Miami Beach prior to being assigned to the crew I would be flying with during the war, I had the experience living in a first class hotel on the beach. During my training time there, we marched up and down

Collins Avenue, the main street of Miami Beach; and our physical training took place right on the beach. The hotel restaurants were converted into mess halls where we had delicious meals prepared. It was the most wonderful vacation I ever had. I told Anne about this time in the service and suggested we go to Miami Beach for our honeymoon – but there was an obstacle in our way. I went to the supervisor of the apprentice program at Westinghouse and asked if it would be possible to delay the start of my program until the first of the year. I knew a new class would be starting then, and I wanted more time for our honeymoon. The supervisor didn't approve of my proposal, saying Westinghouse wouldn't allow it. I continued to give my reasons for the request. The supervisor's secretary, who knew Anne and me, overheard our conversation and came to my rescue. She spoke up saying, "Don't be an old grouch. Don't you realize what Frank went through during the war? Let the kids go on their honeymoon! We can enroll him after the New Year." This is how we were able to have six wonderful weeks to start our married life.

When our day finally arrived, I was truly overwhelmed by everything – it wasn't a dream or a distant hope, but rather that it was really coming to be. On a gorgeous blue sky day, September 7, 1946 Anne and I exchanged our wedding vows at St. Mary's Croatian Catholic church in Rankin, PA becoming husband and wife.

Mr. & Mrs. Frank Kravetz – September 7, 1946

The thoughts of coming home and getting married to my girl had kept me going through my dark days of hospital stays and prison camp, and now my long awaited dream was coming true.

Our reception was a really joyous occasion, and many friends and relatives celebrated with us. Everyone was so happy, and so were we.

After a fun-filled reception, we headed to Miami Beach for our honeymoon. I had purchased a 1938 Dodge from Anne's uncle for $300.00, so we were all set for our drive to Florida.

There were no motels, so we stopped at guest houses along the way, as well as one place that had little cabins that we really liked. We both loved to travel and were enjoying sharing our accommodations as newlyweds.

Once in Miami, we went to the beach, night spots, restaurants, and tourist attractions; cramming as much fun and excitement as we could into our new start as a married couple. When our whirlwind honeymoon ended, we moved in with Anne's parents until we could find a suitable place of our own. Anne's dad worked second shift and I was working the daylight shift at Westinghouse. We were still going out in the evening with friends, so we weren't really sitting at home all that much.

It was only a short time into this living arrangement with my in-laws when a neighbor, Bob Eisler and his wife Caroline, made it known that they wanted to sell their house and move to California. Bob had worked as an engineer for Westinghouse during the war and his wife worked full time. They would often work seven days a week, saving their money so that they could make the move to the west coast. Thinking that we might be interested in buying their house, Bob spoke with my in-laws.

It turns out that this neighbor wanted to do something special for a deserving veteran and, knowing I was back from the war, he put me first on his list of people to which he wanted make the house available.

We were very interested, went to look at the house, and immediately knew we wanted to buy it. We agreed on a price and signed the contract. Between my paycheck and the small compensation I was getting from the VA, we become homeowners. This is going to be hard to believe, I know, but for less than $50.00 a month, we were able to obtain a mortgage.

'Home Sweet Home' – it was a small dwelling, only three rooms and a bath with a small back yard, but it was all ours. To this day it remains our home. Our new house was located in the little borough of Chalfant.

Two of our neighbors, Bill Puskar and John "Bones" Zenuh, came to me and asked, "Why don't you join the Chalfant Servicemen?"

I replied, "Oh, I belong to the VFW."

They insisted, "Yeah, but you live in Chalfant Borough and really should join."

Because of Bill's influence on me, I did join. The organization was very involved in doing things for the betterment of the community and improving our hometown, it was a chance for us to give back to our home town in the way of service.

To become a member the requirement was that you served, but not necessarily overseas. Surprisingly enough, there were enough guys in a small town like Chalfant who were in the military to generate a good group of active members. The organization eventually bought a little house in the neighborhood that became our meeting place. We sponsored Little League teams, held street fairs, raised funds for the local ball park – things like that. It was a very rewarding experience for me.

One day I heard from one of my former crew mates, Bill Rhodes. Bill remembered that I worked for Westinghouse and he contacted me about getting some Westinghouse appliances for him and his wife. I had mentioned to Bill that as an employee I could get a 25% discount on items and so I ordered an electric roaster, a toaster and other small household items for Bill and his wife Ruth.

They drove down from Madison, Wisconsin to Pittsburgh to pick up their stuff and stayed with Anne and me for a few days. We took them around to see some of the sights like Forbes Field and the Mt. Washington Incline, enjoying a nice time visiting together. It was so great to reconnect with Bill; the last time I saw him was on a dusty road in Germany as he was being taken to a prison camp after enduring a pretty severe beating at the hands of the enemy.

Anne thought it would be a good idea to get established with a family doctor and suggested I go to the same doctor her parents had been seeing, since they really liked him. His name was Dr. Tipping and I did schedule an appointment to see him. On my first visit, Dr. Tipping warmly greeted me, asked me to get undressed down to my skivvies and get up on the examination table. As he left the room so I could get ready, he said that he would return shortly. When he reentered the room – he looked over at me with my legs dangling off the table and said, "What the hell hit you?!" I proceeded to tell him my story of being shot out of a B-17, that I had lots of surgery and maggot therapy. It turns out that Dr. Tipping was an infantry combat doctor who served in World War II. He was very sympathetic and understanding, having a personal knowledge of what I must have gone through. Starting with that very first exam and every visit to his office afterward, he established a routine. After I entered the examination room, he would swing open the door and announce to his staff, "No phone calls or interruptions, please." He showed me so much respect and compassion. We would exchange stories and I felt so comfortable with him. I knew I was in good hands.

After one exam, he was a bit concerned about the wound and referred me to an orthopedic specialist. The specialist admitted me to the hospital so that my leg wound could be reviewed, to see if I needed reconstructive surgery. The team of doctors decided that it would not be necessary at the time, but if, my leg gave me any problems any time in the future to just let them know. I so appreciated Dr. Tipping and I enjoyed the office visits to see him. He became not only my doctor but a trusted confidant.

Soon, Anne suspected she might be pregnant and made an appointment with an Obstetrician/Gynecologist where her suspicions were confirmed. We were thrilled with the news and awaited the grand arrival of our first child.

On Good Friday, March 23, 1951 our first child, a boy, Robert Francis Kravetz was born. This event of becoming a father overwhelmed me. After the reality of it all settled in, it was now time to celebrate. On my way home from the hospital I stopped at a liquor store and bought a bottle of whiskey as well as a box of cigars, then the celebration began. My first stop was the home of my in-laws, John and Catherine Cerjanic to tell them they were now grandparents. I then went through the neighborhood spreading the good news.

In April of 1953 the play, 'Stalag 17' came to Pittsburgh. It opened on Broadway in 1951 and toured in many cities. The show played at the Nixon theatre and all former prisoners of war were invited to attend one night as special guests. At that time, about 300 former prisoners of war from Western Pennsylvania and surrounding areas attended the show. I enjoyed seeing the play and knowing that the public was getting a chance to see a little of what we all went through in prison camp. This play depicted, accurately, what it was like in a prison camp. Tragedy, comedy, intrigue – all of it playing right before my eyes, and I was captivated watching it.

I can still remember the scene where the guys in the barracks scrounged up a tree that they were decorating with whatever they could find to hang on the branches. In walks the actor George Tobias wearing a pair of ragtag, droopy, long underwear – he pointed to the tree and said, "Who the hell brought that in here?" The prisoners happily replied, "It's a Christmas Tree!" George Tobias says indignantly, "A Christmas Tree? Even a dog wouldn't piss on that tree!" (The inference being the tree was so scrawny and ugly.) It was a very funny scene.

I was totally pleased with the presentation. At that time, nobody was talking about what had happened to prisoners of war and I still wasn't speaking about my experience very much. This play was one way of letting people know what it was like in a prison camp. It was a very good performance and I was glad for the recognition of former prisoners of war.

Also in April of 1953, Anne discovered she was pregnant again. Anyone reading this book can recall how overwhelmed I was with the birth of our son. Well, read on.

After visiting with her obstetrician, the doctor told her that she was going to have a multiple birth – two for sure, maybe three. I was at work when Anne found out this good news. She drove to the Westinghouse plant in East Pittsburgh and waited in the car until I finished my workday. When I got in the car, I gave her a big kiss and asked her how it went at the doctor's office. She told me the good news and we were both so excited, hugging each other and crying with happiness. On January 4, 1954, Anne gave birth to twin girls; Cheryl Anne and Lynne Catherine – wonderful additions to our family.

Having a family ushered in a whole new era in my life. I never really experienced love until I met Anne. With her and I now having a family of our own together – loving, cherishing and raising our children – I felt I was really living. I wasn't just existing and going through the motions. This was the best time of my life and I threw myself into my role wholeheartedly.

I loved being a civilian again and was putting the war behind me.

Chapter Nineteen

FINDING MY WAY

Those were good, productive years; full of optimism and living out the American dream that we combat veterans lived for while fighting the war; that we fought to preserve for all Americans. I immersed myself in my family, work, church and various social activities; putting the war behind me and moving forward.

In the 1970s a local newspaper ran a notice about a convention coming to Pittsburgh held by the *American Ex-Prisoners of War* – a group I had never heard of. My curiosity was piqued and I decided I would attend.

I walked in to the meeting, glanced around and realized I didn't know anyone in this room full of people. I listened to the presentations and the various topics being discussed and began to learn more about the organization. I came away from that gathering with a lot of useful information about resources and programs that were available to support former POW's.

One of the men I met at this gathering was Walt Pawlesh, who was the National Convention Chairman. Walt was very involved with the organization and responsible for bringing the convention to Pittsburgh. He showed me the ropes of how the organization was run, explaining the mission and goals. I continued to learn about the group as well as the benefits and services they provided. By 1979, a second convention was held in Pittsburgh and I assisted Walt in the planning process. The convention was well attended by veterans and former prisoners of war from all across the United States. It was eye-opening to realize just how many of us former prisoners of war there were.

In the spring of 1981, the nation held its breath and prayed for the release of the hostages held at the American Embassy in Iran. The release became reality, and the former hostages were brought back to the United States, and then sent to Walter Reed Army Hospital, where they received the red carpet treatment for everything they had been through in captivity.

It was at this time that the American Ex-Prisoners of War organization's national officers, who had been lobbying for the cause of World War II former prisoners of war for years, took the matter to the United States Congress. They simply said to Congress, "How about us now?" Our un-met needs and health issues had been put on a back burner.

At the Congressional hearing the organization presented the facts of all that had been done on behalf of the returning Iran hostages, and then asked; "Now what are you going to do for war veterans and former prisoners of war – we still need help, too?" Combine this with the fact that prisoners of war from Vietnam were receiving compensation and benefits for their time as prisoners of war, but still not World War II or Korean POW's.

So many issues had never been addressed such as PTSD, and the many medical conditions that were presumptive disorders that resulted from poor diets, lack of treatment, inadequate living conditions and the length of time POW's endured these many hardships. To complicate matters at the time, if a former prisoner of war filed for additional assistance or compensation and the Veterans Administration discovered the former POW was holding down a job, they took your compensation away. So just exactly what did former prisoners of war like me do? We stayed as far away from the VA as possible. Many of us simply did not want to jeopardize losing the little bit of service-connected compensation we were receiving.

In 1981, Congress passed Public Law 97-37 entitled "Former Prisoners of War Benefits Act" (38 U.S.C.541). This law accomplished several things. It established an Advisory Committee on former prisoners of war and mandated medical and dental care. It also identified certain diagnoses as presumptive service-connected conditions for former POWs.

In December of 1982 President Ronald Reagan signed into law Public Law 97-37 which mandated the Veterans Administration to call all former prisoners of war from World War II and the Korean War into the VA hospitals for a 'protocol examination.' The examination provided former prisoners of war to undergo complete physical examinations, and then to be able to file claims for compensation for service connected disabilities.

The narrative that goes along with the prisoner of war protocol examination gives a good overview of the concerns:

"This is the protocol for conducting initial examinations on former POWs, Approach these veterans with the greatest sensitivity

because the POW experience likely resulted in a great deal of psychological and physical trauma. **Details about beatings, torture, forced marches, forced labor, diet, disease, brainwashing, extremes of hot and cold, and anxiety may be significant parts of the veteran's history; eliciting these details requires that one establish a trusting relationship with the veteran."[7]

When I think about it now, we didn't know what PTSD (Post Traumatic Stress Disorder) was. All of us had it and all of us had it recorded on our service records as Combat fatigue or P/N (Psychoneurosis). Typical symptoms include episodes of repeated reliving of the trauma in intrusive memories ("flashbacks") or dreams, occurring against the persisting background of a sense of "numbness" and emotional blunting, detachment from other people, unresponsiveness to surroundings, anhedonia, and avoidance of activities and situations reminiscent of the trauma. Commonly there is fear and avoidance of cues that remind the sufferer of the original trauma. Rarely, there may be dramatic, acute bursts of fear, panic or aggression, triggered by stimuli arousing a sudden recollection and/or reenactment of the trauma or of the original reaction to it.

The onset follows the trauma with a latency period which may range from a few weeks to months (but rarely exceeds six months). The course is fluctuating but recovery can be expected in the majority of cases. In a small proportion of patients the condition may show a chronic course over many years and a transition to an enduring personality change.

For me personally, the timing of the passage of this law was good. It allowed for the local VA hospitals to reach out to former prisoners of war. In my own life, I still struggled in some areas. Something wasn't quite right and I couldn't put

---

[7] Reprinted from Department of Veterans Affairs http://www.publichealth.va.gov/docs/vhi/pow.pdf

my finger on it. It was even harder to try and explain. A nagging uneasiness seemed to surround me and I often struggled with painful thoughts and memories. One thing I wrestled with was nightmares, which replayed bothersome and repetitive scenes that would often wake me from my sleep.

I dreamed a lot about falling, obviously because of my experience of falling out of the B-17. I would wake up and realize that the terrifying free fall I was experiencing yet again was only a dream. Another recurring dream I had was that I was lost in a maze and couldn't find my way out. This was from all of the uncertainty that accompanied my day-to-day existence as a prisoner of war, never knowing what would happen next. These dreams really shook me up and left me rattled. My wife would shake me awake asking, "What's the matter?" Because I had shared so little of what I had been through with her, she had no idea where all of this was coming from.

Other things lit the fuse for me and it didn't take much to set me off. Watching people wasting food bothered me a lot, still does. Or when someone would make a comment to me like, "Why don't you just forget about the war, put it behind you, and move on, – after all, the war is over." Statements like those made me really angry. But I kept it all to myself, burying it inside. I wanted to get an idea of where all the bad dreams and anger were coming from. I wanted to be rid of the nightmares, thoughts, and nagging questions that invaded my mind. It just seemed that it was easier to push it to the back of my mind and not deal with it. I would discover though, that you don't just "get over it" as others would suggest, nor can you just forget it ever happened.

So I responded to the VA request, made an appointment at our local Veterans Hospital in Pittsburgh and took the protocol exam. I also connected with the program for former prisoners of war.

I began to learn about this thing called PTSD.[8] I attended the PTSD support group and soon was able to understand how my experiences in the war and being a prisoner of war affected me and my entire life. Armed with this new knowledge, I began the process of healing that continues to this day. Attending the sessions allowed me to be with other guys who experienced the same things that I did. It was then that I realized they would be the only ones who could possibly understand what I was feeling and struggling with. I began to forge some strong and deep friendships with these fellows that helped me so much.

In our group therapy sessions, guys would share their stories of heartache, sadness, regret, pain, etc. – letting it out and getting it off of their chest. I watched and listened as they dumped their hurts, fears and anger, and their pent-up feelings. As they began to talk about their experiences, they loosened the death grip their past had on their lives. They could finally experience freedom, gaining courage as others acknowledged their trials and provided supportive empathy. Their honesty and level of sharing was a tremendous encouragement to me and propelled me deeper into my journey of healing.

Some of the other former prisoner's stories were filled with terror and horror. For example, one wounded infantryman was captured and taken to a German bunker. While in the bunker, German soldiers held a pistol to his forehead asking him questions, trying to extract information from him about his unit. It was a cruel game of Russian roulette, where he never knew if the gun was loaded or not as the questions were asked, gun barrel pressed against his temple.

---

[8] For more information on PTSD, see the Reference Section at the end of the book.

Another was a ball turret gunner whose plane caught fire and he was terribly burned – his face was covered with gauze bandages so that only his two eyes could be seen. In this terrible and painful condition he wound up in a prisoner of war camp; coping with imprisonment and a long, painful ordeal.

There were many stories similar to those two examples with which I could fill page after page. Before I heard these men share their experiences I really believed that nobody would believe my story, mainly because of how others had talked about their actions in the war. I'd hear bragging about various war time experiences such as, "I was in this big battle and that big battle." I wasn't in any big battles, or so I thought. After hearing these guys talk, I reasoned, "I was just in an airplane flying by and got shot down," downplaying the entire episode. And as I mentioned, there was a certain stigma attached to being a prisoner of war – that somehow we gave up, surrendered. But people who said this stuff didn't realize that I was shot down by the enemy while fighting. And yes, it was unnerving being so many thousands of feet up in the air fighting for my life with the enemy shooting at us. It seemed like so many people who had not experienced what we did just couldn't realize what the hell we were doing up there fighting the war from the air.

I believed in my heart of hearts that my cause was noble and just as important as the big battles of the war that received so much attention, but I couldn't conceive of others believing what happened to me. I actually thought if I told anyone my story that they would accuse me of making it up. But after talking to so many other former prisoners of war in this valuable program, I gained the courage to share a little portion of my story. What I would invariably find is that another former POW would respond by saying, "Frank, I absolutely believe that because I experienced almost the same thing, let me tell you about it." And that's when I started saying to myself, "Oh my God, they *will* believe me, because similar things have happened to them!"

I can't describe the feeling of having that acknowledgment from others of what happened to me. Their validation was a turning point for me in how I thought about myself, my service and my story. That I, too, had a story to tell. In my group therapy sessions I learned about survivor guilt, numbing, and how other guys coped with their problems. I heard guys talk about how they would never buy a German made Volkswagen car or eat a bowl of rice. I listened to the Army veterans talking about what it was like to fight the war while crawling around on their belly and seeing their buddies being shot right in front of their eyes. I hadn't experienced that. But I was able to listen to their stories and realize they did the same thing I did only in a different way. It became a brotherhood that was beyond belief, establishing a bond that can't be broken. It was then that I started to lighten up and realize there's a road to be walked to receive the healing necessary, and I was determined to continue on the journey.

I began to gain some clarity about becoming a POW. The truth is, I became a prisoner of war while doing an honorable thing, not necessarily heroic, but honorable nonetheless. But I wasn't doing it alone, I was part of the military, following orders, engaging in combat and being captured was just an unfortunate circumstance of war.

I started to understand why I controlled my anger. Dr. Kelnhofer, a fellow former prisoner of war and Ph.D., in his book, *Life after Liberation* states, "We learned to accept indignities, even pain, without displaying any emotion. Eventually, after suppressing our natural feelings every day in captivity, it became an automatic response, enabling us to endure discomfort and physical punishment without thinking. We became accustomed to behaving in ways that were not normal until the abnormal became our norm for survival."[9]

That was the truth and it was quite a revelation. When I connected my behaviors and responses to my new understanding of PTSD, things started to make sense. I learned that it was normal to become emotional when speaking about things that took place so long ago, yet were still so traumatic. I realized that, as a human being, I needed to be able to *feel* and not suppress deep hidden memories of my prisoner of war experience. I had to gradually come out from my safe hiding places and stop concealing my fears from others and myself, as well as the suffering that took place in my life. Essentially, I had to learn to become an ex-POW.

As I gained trust in the VA's Program for ex-prisoners of war and saw how much it was helping me, I also began to take advantage of the health care that was available to me at the VA. To this day I receive excellent and compassionate treatment from healthcare providers of all different specialties. I can't thank them enough for their professional help which has allowed me to live a healthy and productive life. These dedicated caregivers deserve recognition for all they do for veterans. I continued with my treatment and programs at the VA and participated in our local Pittsburgh chapter of the American Ex-Prisoners of War.

In 1985 Anne went with me to Milwaukee, Wisconsin where I attended the AXPOW Convention. I was still on the fringe of my involvement with the organization and used the opportunity while in Wisconsin to visit my former crew mate, Bill Rhodes, who lived in Madison. I hadn't seen Bill since back in 1947, soon after the war when Bill and his wife, Ruth,

---

[9] *Life after Liberation* by Dr. Guy Kelnhofer; Publisher and Editor Amy Lindgren, Banfil Street Press

visited Anne and me in Pittsburgh. This reunion so many years later was wonderful and we all had a great time catching up with all that was going on in our lives.

Each year when the National AXPOW convention was held, I would travel to various cities to attend. In 1994 in New Mexico, I was elected as a National Director for the Eastern Region and was appointed as a National Service Officer.

This is when my involvement really went full speed ahead. I worked hard at making improvements, assisting my fellow POW's and became well-respected in the organization.

The American Ex-Prisoners of War Veterans Organization was and is very unique in that spouses and next of kin are regular members and very active. I was now totally immersed in working with the group and totally dedicated to my roles and responsibilities.

I had been going by myself to the conventions and learned that many spouses of the POWs attended with them. I asked Anne to come along with me to the National American Ex-Prisoner of War Convention being held in Des Moines, Iowa in 1995. I mentioned to her that I thought it would be an opportunity for her to meet some nice people and to do a little traveling.

I was delighted that Anne agreed to accompany me to Iowa. She took to the organization like a duck to water. The best part is that it was her first opportunity to be around other former prisoners of war and their wives. She was able to hear others' stories, share experiences, and spend time talking and making new friends with whom she had so much in common.

I am so thankful that Anne immersed herself along with me and my involvement with the American Ex-Prisoners of

War. She embraced it wholeheartedly and was able to meet so many of the wonderful people that I had met at previous meetings and conventions. Anne was learning right alongside of me all of the complexities of the whole 'ex-prisoner' of war experience and it brought clarity and added another dimension of depth and understanding to our relationship.

This camaraderie that we experienced opened up a whole new wonderful lifestyle for both of us, and her personality was in full swing with all of our new-found friends.

As a prisoner of war in the hospitals and camps, there wasn't much of a chance to make friends and I was so involved in physical survival that I had made none. My friendships with other prisoners came now, at this stage of my life, with these guys with whom I had so much in common. It was wonderful to have deep, committed friendships.

I met a National Service Officer who reviewed my claim and re-filed on my behalf for additional compensation. He told me when I got back home to make sure I went to the VA and ask to see *all* of my records because by law we had a right to access to our military medical history.

This was the first time that Anne had been able to discuss the details surrounding my claim. She, in turn, provided her account of what she watched me go through on a daily basis; sleepless nights, flashbacks, physical ailments – those types of things she was able to verify. This process went a long way toward moving my claim forward.

When I did go to the medical records department at the VA hospital, an employee brought out my file folder and said, "Put a paper clip on all the pages you want copied." I did that and eventually wound up with medical records from my rehabilitation stays in both the Florida and New York hospitals.

Having these documents in my possession turned out to be invaluable to me.

I eventually received the ruling on the claim I had submitted in Iowa and I wasn't satisfied with it at all, as I was turned down for certain conditions I included in my submission. I requested a hearing before the Board of Examiners at the local VA Regional office and soon received a date scheduled for the hearing.

I drove down to the meeting and entered a room with many VA personnel who were all seated around a large conference table. I began to tell them about my story and the details of my experiences in the war. In the middle of my statement, one of them interrupted me and blurted out, "You don't have to do this, Kravetz, we know what you went through – we have your files right here." I was so mad that this guy had the nerve to presume to have the slightest clue as to what I had endured. And then, for him not to even have the common courtesy to hear me out just infuriated me! Their whole attitude was that they didn't want to be bothered with details at all.

My anger reached the boiling point and I reacted, yelling out, *"BULLSHIT!!"*

I then insisted on giving them a detailed description of my leg wound. To which they replied, "There's no need for that – we have your x-rays right here we don't need anything else from you." These guys simply weren't budging on recognizing the severity of my service-connected injuries and health-related problems.

I had really prepared for this meeting, having poured over my records – and I knew what needed correcting. The Federal Government had declared over twenty presumptive service-related conditions and I figured I had at least six of them. I wasn't going to lose this opportunity. I then became adamant and insisted that my version of what happened be included on my permanent record and I made them listen. I was in a real dogfight and figured I had nothing to lose. I had just become so frustrated with their nonchalant, disinterested attitude that I had to do something.

Once they said they had my x-rays and wouldn't need any more evidence, I thought I'd provide them with some anyway. I stood up, unbuckled my belt, and dropped my trousers down to my knees exposing my leg wound. Twenty men in the room fell silent. Essentially the hearing had come to an end.

I recognize that there were so many guys that were worse off than me from their war related injuries... guys that were blind, double amputees or lived with some chronic, life-threatening disease. But I reasoned that I, too, had earned the right to receive compensation and I was willing to fight for it. Having laid it all on the line, I left the hearing, drove home – and I waited for the ruling.

I received the results of that hearing and still hadn't reached the desired percentage I wanted. It continued to be a long drawn out process, where I kept filing and re-filing, getting nickel and dimed to death, with a 10% increase granted each step of the way, but never all the way.

Because of my work as a National Director and Service Officer with the AM-POW's, I wound up being at the Regional Office in Pittsburgh quite often for meetings and presentations. I got to know a lot of the employees and service representatives quite well. One day I approached the Director and asked if I could meet with her briefly. She agreed and we went to her office for an unscheduled, impromptu meeting. I mentioned to her that I wanted the opportunity to explain to her what I was going through trying to get my full disability compensation and the level of frustration I was feeling. I explained how I felt I was playing the game for many, many years and that enough was enough, then I asked if there was there anything she could do to assist me. She listened intently and said, "Well, let's just see what we can do."

One week later, my full disability was granted. The long, drawn out ordeal was over. I didn't have to keep fighting. The mounds of paperwork, record keeping, inquiries, mailings, fact finding, record reviews, doctors' examinations, as well as the months and years of disappointment finally came to an end. The entire process equipped me with a valuable hands-on, personal understanding of the steps involved and how much preparation and work was necessary to be successful. And now, since I had learned so much, I was ready to work hard for other POW's to get their claims reviewed and updated.

I had found my way, another opportunity was to open for me, and the ongoing story of Frank Kravetz, former prisoner of war was moving ahead.

Chapter Twenty

MOMENTS TO REMEMBER

Since the end of the war I had made contact with Bill Rhodes, our waist gunner, and Herb Brayman, our ball turret gunner. I spent many years trying to find the other crew members and, in the process, I found out that our Pilot, Ken Guptill, and Copilot, George Keller, had died. After quite a few letters and phone calls I was able to connect with the rest of the crew.

A reunion of the 457th Bomb Group was being held in Reno, Nevada in 1979 and all five remaining crew members agreed to attend. Unfortunately, just prior to the reunion, Herb Brayman passed away. I was thankful that I had the opportunity to meet Herb and his wife when Anne and I attended a previous reunion in Burlington, Vermont.

After so many years, I enjoyed a wonderful reunion with Lt. Ed McNamara, Navigator; Staff Sgt. Virgil Smallen, Radio Operator; and Staff Sgt. Harry Connors, Flight Engineer. It was very important and very emotional for me to meet the crew members who saved my life, and to personally thank them for their selfless behavior and bravery on my behalf.

A friend of our radio operator brought his camcorder to the reunion and taped all of the interviews. During this reunion I was able to not only reconnect with my crew members, but also find out what happened on that fateful day that our B-17 was shot down.

I learned about how we were attacked by the enemy fighters, the hits our engines took, and the subsequent damage to the plane; as well as the desperate, lifesaving actions the crew took to help me after I had been hit. The facts that I had no way of knowing were finally shared at this gathering. I found out that Ed McNamara was on the same forced march as me and was liberated the same day, too. I heard the details of why and how my parachute opened in the plane; how I was rescued; that the plane crashed in Dedensen, Germany; and to which prison camps the rest of the crew were taken.

We laughed at some of the more lighthearted moments of our imprisonment and thoroughly enjoyed this wonderful opportunity to see each other alive and well after all we had been through so many years ago.

At the conclusion of the video tape session, with the camera still rolling, I spoke the following words, "Anne knows what this has meant to me, and she has been with me all my life, watching as this has been with me my whole life – the desire to get some answers. I came full circle to really hear firsthand talk from my buddies here… to know who saved my life, and I'm very appreciative; more than I can express. I thank you guys for being here, for sharing your stories and for what you did for me."

I include this so their families will know what they did and what heroes they were.

This reunion went a long way toward my healing, and I made giant strides in my life after this gathering. I gained so much peace from seeing these guys again and from having my story verified and validated. It meant so much to me, and my desire to continue moving ahead never waned from this day on.

After the reunion I continued working on assembling my account. I had been collecting photographs and articles – adding more and more to my collection. I began to think about writing my story.

Anne and I had many wonderful opportunities to travel. One of the first events we went to was a reunion ceremony of American and Canadian prisoners of war held at the Peace Bridge in Canada on September 21st, 1989. There were a lot of Canadians in prison camp right alongside of us Americans, many of them were Canadian flyers who had been shot down and captured.

Many years after the war, the Canadians formed their own organization of Ex-Prisoners of War, the same way we had. The Commanders from each group came up with the idea to bring the two groups of former prisoners of war together on the Peace Bridge. I thought it was a great idea and so we went to Canada.

There were large welcome signs for us upon our arrival at the hotel at which we were booked. All traffic was stopped on the bridge on the day of the event. Our Commander led our American group, marching across the bridge starting on the American side, and the Canadian Commander led his group from the Canadian side. Everyone was spit and polished – we were wearing our distinctive burgundy blazers and the Canadian's sported royal blue for their color. The two groups met in the center of the bridge and crossed flags, accompanied by a fly-over with American fighter planes and British Spitfires. A program was held right there on the bridge with thousands in attendance. A plaque was unveiled and dedicated. It remains on the bridge to this day.

We were all treated to a big banquet at the hotel complete with a full orchestra and lots of opportunities to reminisce with our fellow Canadian ex-prisoners of war. It was definitely a highlight for me, as it was one of the first occasions I had been proudly, publicly recognized as a former POW.

The AXPOW organization held reunions each year in the autumn, and we traveled to many great states and cities to attend. We always looked so forward to attending each year and getting to see our friends from all over the country.

In the mid 1990s plans were underway to construct a National Ex-Prisoner of War section to be added to the museum already in existence at Andersonville National Historic Site[10] in Georgia. I was on the Board of Directors at this time, and we made a decision to sell commemorative silver dollars to help raise funds for the project. We spearheaded the idea and wholeheartedly believed that there should be a permanent place for people to come and learn about our experiences as prisoners of war, to include Vietnam and Korean veterans also. At some of the initial meetings, some folks wanted to have the museum located in Washington, DC. But after considering the financial aspect of it and the tremendous amount of fundraising we would have to take on for it to be in the nation's capital, – there was a consensus to build it in Andersonville, Georgia – the site of the first prisoner of war

---

[10] For more information on the National Prisoner of War Museum see the Reference Section at the end of the book.

camp. Even though we thought not as many people would visit the site in Andersonville as perhaps might have in DC, Andersonville was and is a very popular site for tourists down south; and we knew that with the quality of the museum it would soon draw visitors from all over the country. All of the state commanders were on board with the fundraising and it became a very successful endeavor that we completed in about three years. With our input and suggestions, the National Park Service agreed to have the grand opening of the museum on April 9, 1998 – which is National Former Prisoner of War Recognition Day. John McCain, former prisoner of war in Vietnam and U.S. Senator, would be the guest speaker.

I had an opportunity on my way to one of my bomb group reunions in Georgia, to visit the construction site and see the skeleton of the building. It made me even more excited to see the completed project.

Our family travelled down for the big event, and prior to the dedication, we took a tour of the Andersonville Cemetery grounds – a very hallowed place. It was one of the largest military prisons during the Civil War. It was run by the Confederacy and held over 45,000 Union Soldiers, many of whom died from malnutrition, exposure and disease.

As I walked through the cemetery, I remember having seen the movie *Andersonville,* and I couldn't imagine the human suffering from all of the horrible wounds they suffered in battle, let alone trying to survive in such primitive conditions. I could relate in a deep way, because I had experienced being locked up and losing my freedom, but I also realized that what they must have endured was beyond comprehension.

The grand opening was replete with pomp and circumstance. Overflowing crowds, huge circus-type tents, a beautiful, clear blue sky day, a very impressive military fly-over, the familiar colors of burgundy worn by thousands of former ex-prisoners of war. As John McCain approached the podium, I was able to exchange greetings with him and soon the dedication program was started. It was perfect from beginning to end, replaying the history of how the museum came to be and recognizing all those who played an important role in seeing it come to fruition.

After the ribbon cutting, we ex-prisoners of war were allowed to go in to see the museum for the first time. Approaching the walkway to the museum, the first thing I saw were the distinctive guard towers that were part of every German prison camp, which had been recreated as part of the museum building. They were very realistic and I was instantly transported back in my memory to what I had come to intimately know as a prisoner of war – that as long as the guards were up there in those towers with their machine guns we were not going anywhere because the alternative was getting shot to death.

The opening exhibit really got to me. There were all kinds of rifles, bayonets and guns pointing at me as I walked in, complete with sound effects depicting some of the different ways a person became a prisoner of war. More often than not, the soldier was injured and this is when they were captured. This display was a real eye-opener designed to get your attention – and it sure did.

I contributed to two of the audiovisual displays in the museum. One was the thought I had of how prayer influenced me during my stay in prison camp and how I made my own rosary beads from a piece of string. The second one included my telling of how I coped with prisoner of war life and how I got captured. (Photo of one of the displays on next page.)

Seeing the Korean and Vietnam displays also impacted me in a powerful way. I didn't experience any of what they had to go through and I learned a lot walking through that section. I saw how others were treated during their time of captivity. The Camp O'Donnell & Cabanatuan Japanese Prison Camp display with the white cement cross was very moving.

Most of us were very emotional as we walked away from that experience. First of all, it's depressing seeing all of the hardships and cruelty that prisoners had to endure. Then, when I got to the liberation and freedom section of the museum and saw how the prisoners reacted being freed...it brought back a lot of memories. The entire visit through the museum was an emotional roller coaster ride.

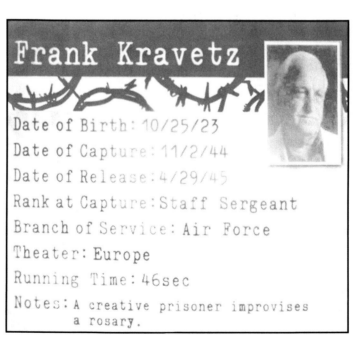

Audio Visual Display at the Andersonville
National POW Museum, "Courtesy
Andersonville National Historic Site"

The museum was set up to recreate, as much as was as possible, the experience of what we went through in the process of being prisoners of war. Once you left the museum exhibits, you stepped outside into a courtyard, where there was a very dramatic sculpture. It shows a gaunt prisoner stretching out, reaching for water, with a trickle of water dripping through his hands. Water was so scarce for so many of the prisoners' settings – and it was required for survival, for life – so this artistic image powerfully captured that reality.

Seeing this wonderful tribute to so many of us prisoners was very satisfying. Everyone involved should be commended for doing such a terrific job. It is a fitting memorial to honor former prisoners of war that will educate people for generations to come, and it was very rewarding for me to play a part in seeing this museum come to be. The fact that it was built for the purpose of educating people about how we lived under those conditions, how lucky we were to have survived at all, and especially to remember those who died while in prison so they will not be forgotten, makes the museum invaluable.

To be a part of the major war of our century that resulted in there being so many prisoners of war and for me to be in that group is part of my legacy, plain and simple.

Once our initial tour of the museum was complete, we were greeted by newspaper reporters, students, and a lot of attendees who wanted to interview us and get our thoughts. There was a lot of interaction with many of the visitors, many of whom were not knowledgeable about the prisoner of war experience and were very interested in finding out more. We answered questions and shared our individual experiences of being prisoners of war.

One of the ladies recognized me from one of the visual displays in the museum, and was quite excited to have the opportunity to get to ask me more about my time as a prisoner. She was awestruck to be speaking with the actual person whom she had just recently read about on the walls of the museum. It was all quite gratifying, that I was part of history – and a part that very few people have had the experience of – being a prisoner of war.

I'm at peace knowing our legacy will go on in such wonderful way. I am proud to have been part of founding a museum where people can go and get a very good history lesson on the subject of prisoners of war – that sets well with me. This visit was another piece in the healing process for me.

Hollywood called, and I had the opportunity to be involved with the making of a major motion picture, *Memphis Belle*. I completed a questionnaire that was in our American Ex-Prisoner of War magazine where the producers of the film were asking for input from B-17 crew members about their experiences. I was contacted by someone associated with the film and gave my personal accounts of what it was like on our air base in England, the missions I flew, my role as a waist gunner, and what it was like being a part of an aircrew aboard the plane.

Memphis Belle is the story of a young crew on dangerous bombing raids into Europe. This was a movie I could really relate to, as it followed the ten men on a B-17 bomber. It was difficult for me to watch. The memories of being aboard the B-17 high in the sky in combat came flooding back, and instantly I was back in the war. I got through the movie without closing my eyes, because that's the healing part – facing my fears and what I went through.

One scene in the movie shows the crew throwing a football around because their mission was delayed, so they wouldn't be flying for one reason or another. In my experience, none of our missions were delayed; however, because of weather, we had missions scrubbed, but we always knew the night before.

The movie also made a big deal out of the plane's nose art which featured a pin up girl. In the early part of the war all the crews gave names to their planes. Our crew thought about art work for our plane, but the war was at such a fever pitch for us that crews were just getting on whatever plane was available to fly. It's not like we had ownership of one plane. They tried to get us on the same plane, but if the plane we had just been on was damaged and in for repairs, then they had no option but to get us into another plane.

In *Memphis Belle* they were on the same plane for 24 missions, waiting to complete their 25th and final mission, after which they would be sent home. But as the war progressed and we were putting up over a thousand planes a day, the number of missions a crew had to complete to be able to go home progressed from 25, to 35, then to 50. By the time our crew began flying missions, the war had progressed to a much larger scale for the Army Air Corps, with commensurate consequences. In spite of the slight creative licenses taken, the movie was well done, and a good portrayal of what it was like for so many of us who flew as part of a crew on a Flying Fortress.

I first became aware of the plans that were in place to build a national monument for WWII Veterans through the AXPOW bulletin, our national publication. The organization provided updates and information on the progress of the museum, and I'd occasionally catch a newspaper article or see something on television that this project was progressing. I remember saying to myself, "Better late than never." There were other monuments in Washington, DC devoted to other aspects of WWII and I felt it was time to get this done, as well.

Congresswoman Marcie Kaptur from Ohio got the ball rolling after a veteran questioned her as to why there was no memorial for all WWII vets. The AXPOWs thought so much of her efforts that we presented her with the "Barbed Wire Award", an award given to an individual who has worked long and hard to introduce legislation and get it passed that benefits former prisoners of war. Senator Bob Dole was appointed as the National Chairman and my thought was, "If he's in charge of it then we should all get behind him and this worthy project." In my opinion, there couldn't have been a better man for the job. I immediately became a contributor and part of the effort to get this overdue monument built.

As the project neared completion, our AXPOW Organization made plans to attend the dedication ceremony as a group. I signed up immediately, as I did not want to miss out. There was a whole week's worth of activities in DC leading up to the actual dedication. On the day before the dedication our POW group was invited to the coliseum to watch a Salute to WWII Veterans Program put on by military performers that was outstanding. It gave me goose bumps and I was truly overwhelmed by the presentation they created to honor us.

The dedication of the World War II Monument took place on Saturday, May 29, 2004. The AXPOW's had four busloads of former POWs, their wives and families – around 200 people. We were all staying in one location for this historic event and we could feel the excitement.

When it was time to go to the ceremony, we boarded our tour busses and were given a police escort from the Pentagon location where we were staying to the WWII Memorial site which was located between the Lincoln Memorial and Washington monument. When we arrived, I was pleasantly surprised to see that our reserved seats were right up front. Media coverage was everywhere, the crowds were huge, and everything was done with excellence. Medical support personnel were there, as well as free water, food vendors, information booths, wheelchairs, escorts, shade tents – everything was made available to us. It was such a huge undertaking and the planners of this event left no stone unturned as so many assembled in our nation's capital to be a part of it all.

I was interviewed by both a New York Times reporter and a local newspaper reporter, and had lots of conversations with many people as we waited for the start of the ceremony.

In the meantime, back at my local VFW in East Pittsburgh, Pat Lanigan, a local funeral director and all around great guy arranged and placed a phone call to me in DC so that I could speak to those members and guests assembled at the club, who were watching the dedication, live on a large screen television. I shared that I was thrilled to be a part of it all and provided some firsthand, on the scene descriptions of what

was taking place all around me. It was very special to connect with my hometown VFW this way and it was such a wonderful gesture on Pat's part, of which I'm very appreciative.

Speakers at the dedication included

Frank being interviewed by reporters at the World War II Memorial Dedication

Presidents George H. and George W. Bush, Bill Clinton, Tom Hanks and Tom Brokaw.

I particularly liked what Bob Dole said as he spoke, "Of those veterans who died before seeing the monument dedicated," Dole said, "They won every battle, except the battle against time." Indeed, Dole captured the mood of the dedication when he said, "We have kept faith with our comrades from a distant youth."

It was a captivating program, perfect in every way. To be there with my family, having them share that day and all it meant to me, was very emotional and rewarding. It will go down as one of the best days of my life.

After the dedication it was time to walk over and see the memorial. As I walked past and saw the names of the great campaigns of the war etched in marble, my mind replayed so many scenes. The Freedom Wall, with the gold stars commemorating the over 400,000 who lost their lives in the war, made me realize that only by the grace of God was I fortunate enough to come home. In my own hometown with the entry of America into World War II late in 1941, the sons of Bessemer Terrace began to march off to war in all branches of our military forces. As the casualties began to mount this corner of America supplied far more than its share of heroes for the war effort – a total of 14 sons from my small corner of East Pittsburgh did not come home.

The scene was numbing in its scope and significance, and the tears flowed freely. There were large arches that represented the Pacific and Atlantic war theatres, as well as pillars that represent all the states. There were scenes carved into the marble of what took place on the home front, in the air, at sea, and on land.

Most significant are the words engraved on front of the monument that read, "Here we mark the price of freedom." The memorial was 16 years in the making and does not disappoint.

I knew that my name and biography were now forever on file at the World War II monument, and that I was again a part of history. I played a part and paid a price, but so many others paid a much, much higher price. I thought about them and honored them as I visited the memorial. My emotions were very mixed. There was, again, and continues to be today, a tremendous sense of pride at having served my country alongside thousands and thousands of others who also served and are reflected forever on that memorial.

Frank and Anne in front of the WWII Memorial Fountain

Chapter Twenty One

A STORY TO SHARE –
COMING FULL CIRCLE

My good friend, Jerry Alexis, invited me to go along with him to attend a program at Thiel College in Greenville, PA, where Jerry was scheduled to speak to the students.

I said, "I don't do that kind of stuff."

Jerry replied, "Well, just come along with me and during my talk, I'll introduce you to the crowd."

• 239 •

My thought had always been, "Who is going to believe some of the stuff that's part of my story, it's too unbelievable, they'll think I'm making it up."

At his urging, I did agree to go with him to his speaking engagement. Once at the college, I noticed the auditorium was full of students, and I took a seat in the front row while Jerry walked to the podium and began to speak to the students.

I was listening intently when at one point during his presentation; Jerry said to the audience, "I'd like to introduce you to Frank Kravetz." I was stunned. Jerry motioned for me to come up and join him on the stage. As I did so, he whispered to me, "Just tell them what you've told me about your story."

And that's what I did; I began to tell the students my story. It was the first time I had ever done so in front of a crowd of people. While I was talking, Jerry and his wife, Marge, who were sitting in the front row, were prodding me with verbal cues from where they were sitting: "Now tell them about how they threw you out of the plane," and I did. "Now tell them how they put maggots on your leg to get your wound to heal," And I told that story, as well. Jerry and Marge were essentially forcing me to dig up my story and speak it out loud. Jerry was a preacher, so he was good at public speaking and used to it. Not me. But they kept urging me to continue.

Before this experience, I couldn't... I *wouldn't* tell anybody the things I said at that college. But they kept asking me questions, and I gave an answer each time – hearing my own voice telling my story. I was so surprised at my own reaction to hearing the students' response to my story. They were so very receptive and I felt good about the whole experience. There was a question and answer session after the presentation. I wasn't sidetracked by any of the questions they asked and they were attentive and interested. I don't think they had ever heard any of the things that I shared with them, and their positive recognition gave credence to my war story, which in turn increased my boldness.

Around this time it was becoming popular to be asked to speak on the topic of being a prisoner of war due to the large amount of publicity the Desert Storm POW's had received. Jerry next invited me to Geneva College and then he continued to invite me along with him to other speaking opportunities to tell our stories.

Jerry was an army infantry rifleman and one of a handful of the 110th Regiment of Company B (28th Division of the Pennsylvania Army National Guard) sent to the front lines one month prior to the Battle of the Bulge. Entrenched in a foxhole, engaged in heavy combat, he survived German counter offensives along the Rohr River, Hurtgen Forrest area – only to be taken captive by Nazi ground troops 12 days into their attack. Upon capture, he saw an unarmed POW shot, then he waded waist deep through ice cold water to begin a 12 hour march to his first prison camp, Oflag 64, a camp for officers.

He was put to work on dangerous, dirty tasks such as digging antiaircraft placements. In five-and-one-half months of captivity, he was moved to seven different POW camps, marched an estimated 500 miles. In addition he rode another 1000 miles crowded in locked, freezing rail road box cars that were attacked twice by British fighter bomber squadrons. He was liberated at the end of 1945. He went on to serve 34 years in the army, retiring as a Colonel in the Chaplain Corps.

Jerry's war experiences are what prompted him to become a minister and I admire him for that. He has been a devoted man of the cloth for many, many years.

Public speaking became easier after each time I did it, and as I spoke, I remembered more and more about my story. So much had been suppressed, that when I was finally speaking about my experiences, my memory bank was jogged by the retelling of the events that took place. This allowed me to put more and more pieces of my life's puzzle together. I knew there were many things that I still personally wanted answers to.

I don't know why I was so compelled to go after everything I could find about my experience, but the fact is that I was. I thought at some point that it would have been nice to have gone back to Germany to the airfield at which I was stationed, or to visit the POW hospital I was in; but I didn't, and it's not a deep regret. I continued to collect lots of information that pertains to my story.

I read so many articles and stories about the day I was shot down; I just couldn't get enough. To finally learn how big the mission was that day was a real eye-opener. I came across the November 3, 1944 New York Times front page headline that reported the events of the November 2, 1944 bombings. Over 2500 planes took part in this massive air assault. For our mission to make the headlines of a major newspaper the day after the battle spoke volumes about the size and significance of the battle. Meeting with my crew mates at various times and places after the war and hearing their firsthand accounts was priceless, it filled in many gaps. I particularly could relate to my Navigator, Ed McNamara who said, after we were moved out of prison camp on the march to Moosburg, "I thought I was free then." I felt the same way.

My continued communication with the British contacts I made from the staff at Obermassfeld Hospital has been very rewarding. I received information about Dr. Sherman, who performed the skin grafts on me; and the book, *Lasting Impressions*, which I received from the orderly's account at Obermassfeld, is priceless. I often wonder how a guy like that, a prisoner of war like me, just doing his job as an orderly, kept such a magnificent diary of his day to day work in the POW hospital. He describes so vividly just how it was in that hospital. The orderly's name was H.L. Martin and he wrote, "This story is of a very ordinary young Englishman conscripted into the British Army just after the outbreak of World War II and the sequences which led to the long stint of work at Obermassfeld Lazaret. It is intended as a tribute to the many hundreds of POW patients who passed through the often improvised medical provision with much fortitude and stoicism."[11] He preserved history with his fascinating account and I'm grateful that he did.

As part of my research I found a recipe for Welsh rarebit, the dish I enjoyed while in the prison hospital. It's pretty simple – butter, flour, milk, cheese, Worcestershire sauce, mustard, egg yolks, toast, salt and pepper.

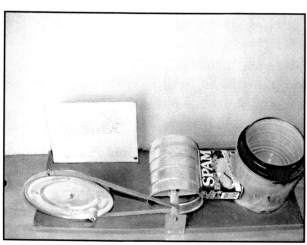

Replica of a POW stove made by Frank

I continued gathering small bits and pieces of history, spending countless hours of research assembling my account. One thing that so intrigued me when I was in prison camp was the handmade cook stove that we used

---

[11] *Lasting Impressions* by H. L. Martin, 1990.

in the barracks. When I returned home, I made one of my own. This is a popular item at speaking engagements and gatherings and generates a lot of interest from not only my fellow former prisoners of war, but all types of audiences.

I was also able to finally meet up with Harold Sturman – the wounded airman who agreed to put a note in his cast and deliver it to my family back in East Pittsburgh. I discovered that he was on the same mission to Merseberg as I was and that he was from Pennsylvania. One day, Harold asked me if I would be attending a big bash being held for all Pennsylvania airmen who had been shot down during the war. My invite came from a fellow I met who was the Mayor of Lancaster and eventually became the Attorney General under Governor Milton Shapp of Pennsylvania. I told Harold I would be attending. It was at this event, many years after the war I finally met him again after our time together in the hospital, and got to personally thank him for delivering that all important message to my family. Harold told me that when he did get back to the States and was having his cast removed, he reminded the doctors to be very careful not to destroy any of the notes that were entrusted to him that were encased in his plaster cast. It turns out I was not the only one who asked Harold to get notes to family members. Harold mailed my note to my family and it arrived on April 1, 1945 – Easter Sunday. As it turns out, my family had found out about my prisoner of war status just prior to the note's arrival.

Eventually, I took ownership of my story and had the opportunity to go to many schools, dedication ceremonies, memorial services – events where I was the speaker. I was able to form my own way of retelling my story that was informative and interesting. But the beginning of my speaking engagements can certainly be traced to those two speaking engagements with Jerry, to Thiel and Geneva Colleges. They broke the ice and opened up a whole new realm of my prisoner of war experience. I can say this with confidence – that Jerry's invitation was crucial to my coming full circle, and for that I'm forever grateful to him. The fact that people now want to hear my story and I am now comfortable with my own life's story allows me to attach pride to my service to my country with no holds barred. I no longer feel guilty about having been a prisoner of war, and when I reached that point a big burden was lifted off my shoulders. It took a friend who said, "Come on, step out of the boat, watch me," to set me free and give me the strength to not hide my story anymore, but to use it to help and educate others.

The ongoing need to inform people about the POW experience came to light when I was asked to be a part of the 'Vietnam Moving Wall' display that was coming to Soldiers and Sailors Hall in Oakland, PA. I was standing on the steps outside of the hall, wearing a baseball cap with the letters, P-O-W, M-I-A on the front of the hat. Someone approached me asking, "What does POW (pronounced like a punch,) MIA (pronounced MY-A) mean?" I was astonished that here, at one of the most patriotic and military settings in all of Pennsylvania, – someone was asking what a POW-MIA was. Even though I was taken aback that someone wouldn't know, I was glad to have the opportunity to provide information about prisoners of war (POWs) and those missing in action (MIA). I found there was a great reward and importance in sharing my story with others. These historical stories must be recorded so that people don't ever forget.

During one of my appointments with a VA doctor, struggling with some of the difficult questions that I still had, I asked, "But why did some guys make it back and some didn't?"

The doctor replied, "Somebody had to live through it all to tell the story." His answer really struck a chord with me and I felt a responsibility; no, *more* than that, an obligation and duty, to speak out; and my confidence grew.

I felt as though I had another mission in my life. I flew missions on my B-17 all those years ago, and now, all these years later, I accepted another mission. As a Director for the American Ex-Prisoners of War for ten years and also a National Service Officer, I was able to speak up on behalf of other former prisoners of war. After ten years of service, I gave up my directorship because now I was beginning a new career. I felt it was vital to put all of my efforts into helping other POW's get their full benefits, which they earned and deserved. Through personal experience, I knew how hard I fought and how many steps I had to take, and how frustrating the process of filing for a service-connected disability can be. I knew I had to share my knowledge with other POW's who were in the same boat. This became my mission and my passion in life. I feel it was divinely ordained to happen and I embraced it, still do.

Chapter Twenty Two

A WIFE LOOKS BACK

I was born on October 29, 1926 the only child of John and Catherine Cerjanic and given the name Anne Catherine. I lived with my parents on Cline Street in Wilkins Township, a wonderful neighborhood filled with many families who came to this country from Yugoslavia to build their dreams.

As a child, I had cousins and relatives who lived nearby and there were lots of kids my age to play with. I'd come home from school, change clothes, go outside, and play until suppertime. We played hide n' seek, hopscotch, marbles – all the old-fashioned games kids played back then. I was a happy child with a loving mother and father, and aunts who doted on me. In the evening, we would sit around and listen to a radio show.

When I was around nine or ten years old I used to take care of the neighbor's cow. I'd place a rope around the cow's neck and walk her to the field nearby, where she could chew on some grass. My pay was 25 cents a week. My parents moved into a small house on Brighton Street in Chalfant Borough, East Pittsburgh, PA.

Young Anne in farmer's field

I knew the war had started because of hearing about the bombing of Pearl Harbor on December 7, 1941, but I had never heard of Pearl Harbor before and neither had a lot of other kids my age. I wondered then what would happen because of the war, but I was just too young to realize all that war entailed. When you're a young teen and something like a war is going on, it just doesn't seem quite real. After all, I was living at home in the United States and the war was taking place "way over there" in another part of the world. The war didn't affect us much on a personal level. It wasn't being fought where I lived and therefore, it wasn't impacting my life.

I attended Turtle Creek High School and I enjoyed spending time together with groups of friends, having fun like most teenagers that age do. It was during one of those times, at a house party in Turtle Creek, that I met Frank. We found ourselves getting to know one another and developing a friendship. All of our friends hung out together; going to dances, parties, and picnics. Frank had already graduated from high school and was making plans for his future by working and attending Pitt part time in an engineering program.

In May, 1943, at age 16, I graduated from Turtle Creek High School; and within a week I went to work at the National Biscuit Bakery in East Liberty, PA. I answered a help wanted ad in the daily newspaper, was hired right away and began working full time.

Frank and I saw each other on occasion, but at this time, we weren't going steady or anything like that. When he could borrow a car, he would sometimes come by and give me and my friends a ride home from work. Then maybe the gang of us would go out to eat and go to a movie. There wasn't anything serious about our relationship at that time.

I became more aware of the impact of the war when, while working at National Biscuit, I discovered what rationing was. Everyone had to use a stamp system, meaning we needed stamps to buy gas for our cars, meat, stockings (what women today call pantyhose), cigarettes and other items. You had a certain number of stamps and when they were gone, you could not get those items, even if you had money to purchase them. The scarcity of items we could formerly buy whenever we needed them brought the war home in a whole new way.

My girlfriends and I would talk about the war at work because some of the boys we knew were enlisting and going off to war. One of the things we did was to make cookies for the boys going overseas, that was a big deal to us. We wanted to help in whatever ways we could.

While working at National Biscuit, I dated a couple of different fellas. Nothing serious, it was the fact that all of us girls dated different guys to have somebody to go out on dates with, just someone to spend time with having fun. Everyone just enjoyed each other's company and nothing was ever serious. A lot of the guys hadn't gone into the service yet, or didn't have to go into the service for whatever reason. Maybe it was just too early in the war at that time.

It was late in the summer in 1943 when Frank told me that he was going to enlist in the Air Corps. In order to do so he had to lose weight because he was about five pounds overweight. He did lose the weight quickly, and as soon as he did he went in to the service. It all happened very fast. I thought, "Well he's going in, and that's that, nothing's going to happen to him." After all, we were all young and invincible.

While Frank was in the service in basic training, we began writing a few letters back and forth to each other. We were in a friendship stage – we were getting to know about each other through our letter writing. When he arrived overseas he wrote a few times. My parents really liked Frank and were silently hoping that he would be "The One." There was a time when I didn't hear from him for seven months. I found out later that nobody heard from him during that time, because he wasn't allowed to send mail.

My friends and I took part in a war bond drive to raise money for the fighting men. We were all excited about seeing the movie stars from that era that came to town. After all, Westinghouse was making a lot of stuff for the war effort, and Westinghouse was right in my hometown – it was where my father worked.

The feelings that all of my childhood friends were invincible began to change in February, 1945. It was at this time that I heard news of the worst kind – I learned of the death of young Dave Cinna, a neighborhood boy whom I had dated. He was killed while fighting on Iwo Jima. At 16, I was completely naive about war and the horrors of war. I remember my parents' reaction to the war was that they hated it, but they never really talked about it.

Not long after this sad news about Dave, in the spring of 1945, I received a call from Frank's sister, Katherine, telling me that Frank had been shot down and was missing in action. Even then, upon hearing the news of his missing in action status, it didn't enter my mind what that actually meant. All I knew was, they didn't call and tell me Frank was dead.

I couldn't wrap my thoughts around what 'missing in action' really was. Not at all. It wasn't until six months after he was missing in action that I found out he was actually a prisoner of war and had been for the past six months.

At that point I was thinking, "Prisoner of war, what exactly *is* a prisoner of war?" I can honestly say I had absolutely no idea what that term meant. I certainly didn't know about how bad he had been injured or what type of ordeal he might possibly have gone through. As these events unfolded my hatred of the Japanese and the Germans grew, and I wasn't too thrilled about Hitler either. But we all waited patiently, hoping and praying that the war would soon be over.

Eventually, the war ended and Frank was allowed to come home on a 60-day furlough, still recovering from his war injuries. He arrived home on June 16, 1945, after being in prison hospitals and camps; surviving forced marches; and healing from his wounds. As soon as he came home we reconnected and began to see each other a lot. That was when we really got to know each other. We spent the entire months of June and July hanging out with friends and double dating, 60 days of great times being together.

Frank and Anne dating
during Frank's furlough

We didn't talk about his war experiences at that time. In fact, I don't remember anyone talking about it. Not one of the boys who were going out with us (one was a Marine, one was a Sailor and one was an Airman) and who all had been through the hell of war spoke about it. That was just common, I guess.

Now, at 84 years old, I can see the differences in the way the military handles young servicemen or women who are wounded while fighting in a war. Today the military arranges to send them home by plane. But it wasn't that way in 1945. I remember Frank having to thumb a ride home from Philadelphia with his leg still festering and bleeding; and then having to thumb a ride all the way to the Westinghouse Bridge where he walked to his home at 110 Bessemer Avenue in East Pittsburgh.

You know a lot of people wouldn't have done that. Most people would be more demanding, saying something like, "I was in the war, can't you get me a cab or something to take me home?" There were so many guys coming home that the military just couldn't do it. But the soldiers never complained. At least Frank Kravetz never complained, I can say that as fact.

We had wonderful times together...the war was behind us...and we felt real joy and happiness reconnecting with each other. We were so compatible, we had lots of friends, and we enjoyed going out.

For me personally, it was an amazing time of reflection and revelation. I had grown older and more mature, no longer just a teenage kid. Of course, Frank had just gone through this horrific time in his life, which sure gave him time to think about what he wanted to do with his life when the time came that he would be fully recovered from his injuries and out of the service.

It was during these moments of spending so much time together that we both decided that we were good for each other and we should make this arrangement permanent.

Marriage was now the topic between us and after discussing it, we decided that September was a nice month in which to get married. I was 18 years old and Frank was 21. My parents absolutely loved and adored him, so there was no problem whatsoever.

Once his furlough was over Frank had to return to the hospital for more recovery, because his wounds were still open. He would spend time in Miami Beach, Florida for rehabilitation and also up in New York before he could be discharged from the service.

Frank mentioned that he also had to have psychiatric evaluations and treatment for his combat experiences...and I still tease him that the psychiatry treatment didn't work! But in all seriousness, with the combat fatigue and shell shock he suffered, as well as dealing with all that he went through, it was a cause for concern and it was necessary for him to get the medical attention for these conditions.

At some point, while he was still home, Frank went to the jewelers on the afternoon of a Pittsburgh Pirate baseball game and bought an engagement ring. He came and picked me up at National Biscuit, took me to the game, and during the game he gave me the ring. I never helped him pick out the ring, but it wasn't a complete surprise.

I did give the ring right back to him to hold on to, because we knew we were going to make a formal announcement of our engagement to our friends and family at Christmastime. So from that ball game until Christmas, it was a secret just between us, and we had extra time to be excited about our plans.

Frank was honorably discharged from the service on November 2, 1945. In December of 1945 we announced we were engaged and that we would be getting married in

September, 1946. My parents were so happy – they thought he was a wonderful man and loved him dearly from the very first time they met him.

Even though we were engaged to be married as an 18-year-old dealing with a guy back from the war, I still didn't feel comfortable asking Frank questions about his experiences or injuries. He really didn't bring the subject up or talk too much about it, either. So, I didn't ask him. Occasionally, when we would go out where he would have shorts on, I would see that horrible wound on his leg and then, little by little, he would tell me about how he got that terrible injury. He told me just enough to explain how he was wounded and how he was thrown out of the plane. After hearing just a small part of his war story, I realized he had gone through so much – I knew this young guy had already lived a lifetime. Yet, with all he had been through, it never made him a mean, miserable person and I grew to respect and admire him as a man even more.

On September 7, 1946 we were married in St. Mary's Church in Rankin, PA by Father Becovac, a Croatian priest that spoke broken English while performing the ceremony and mass. In those days there wasn't much leeway in what you might have wanted to include in your wedding, it was pretty much whatever they told you to do, you did. To this day I joke that I'm not sure we're even married because of the language barrier! Let's just say it wasn't easy. The day we were married was an absolutely beautiful fall day. We had a big, *very* big, wedding with somewhere between 300-400 guests.

I lived on Brighton Street in Chalfant Boro, and as part of the day's events, a tamburitza orchestra came to my house, and they played music while I walked down to the car from my house to go to the church. When I got to the church the tamburitza orchestra played once again while I went up the steps and into the church. As the bridal party exited the church the orchestra then greeted us from the sidewalk, strumming and singing as I walked down the steps, hand-in-hand with my new husband, Frank.

Once the Catholic wedding Mass at church was over, the bridal party and immediate family headed to East Pittsburgh and to Frank's parents' house where we had a nice big lunch. Homemade chicken noodle soup, stuffed cabbage, and all kinds of wonderful food for the wedding party and guests were served.

Our reception was held in the evening at 6:00 p.m., at the Sokol Hall in North Braddock. During this time there was a beer strike going on in the area and that didn't set well with my Dad and his two brothers, my Uncles Joe and Mike Cerjanic. The three of them jumped in a car, drove downtown – somehow getting through the picket lines – and successfully came away with kegs of beer that they delivered to the reception. I don't have all the details of this 'beer run' into Pittsburgh, and don't think I want to know! Thank God for that little excursion though, because the guests were able to celebrate with some drinks. It was a terrific start to our married life, filled with lots of joy and happiness. Then it was on to our honeymoon.

We decided to go to Florida for our honeymoon because when Frank was stationed there he commented when he came back home, "Oh, Miami Beach is *such* a beautiful place – that's where we're going on our honeymoon." I hadn't been there, and it sounded like a good idea to me, because I loved the beach and the sun. I was excited about our plan.

Frank asked for some extended time off for our honeymoon, but Westinghouse wasn't going for his plan. The

Frank and his bathing beauty bride, Anne

secretary down where Frank worked, said to Frank's boss, "He just got back from being a prisoner war and he wants to go on his honeymoon for six weeks. So let him go and when he gets back he can start his program." The boss agreed and that's how we wound up being on a six week honeymoon – with a little gentle persuasion from the secretary of the boss where he worked.

Our honeymoon to Florida was everything we had hoped and planned for. The trip was great from beginning to end, and the perfect start to being 'Mr. and Mrs. Frank Kravetz.'

We returned from our honeymoon and began our married life together, living with my parents for the first six months of our marriage. Then a little three-room house in the same neighborhood went up for sale, because the owners were moving to California. Frank and I looked at the house. It had a nice yard that would be a good place for kids to play, and we saw the possibility of adding an addition at some point, plus it was near both of our parents. We made the decision to buy the house at 105 Elizabeth Avenue, East Pittsburgh, PA and moved in, starting another phase of our life together.

After four years of marriage, at 23 years old, I discovered I was pregnant. On March 23, 1951, our first son, Robert, was born – and what a thrill it was for us to be parents! Three years later, I discovered I was pregnant again – only this time with twins! Our twin girls were born on January 4, 1954, when we welcomed Cheryl and Lynne into our growing family with joy.

Having three little ones in our small little house was an adjustment, but we wanted to have children and we embraced our new roles as mom and dad. Frank, his buddies, and my dad added two rooms and a bath to the upstairs, working almost an entire year on the building project. Getting our house and starting a family were wonderful events in our lives. We were so grateful. As the kids grew a little older, they would always want to scramble up on their Dad's lap. I would hear three little voices repeating, "It's my turn to sit on Dad's lap! No it's my turn to sit on Dad's lap! No it's *my* turn to sit on Dad's lap!" Sometimes Bob would claim he had first dibs because he was the oldest.

As they sat on his lap, the kids were fascinated, but not scared, by the wound and scar on their Daddy's leg. They said it looked like the shape of some part of the world, like an outline of some country. Frank would always gently direct them over to his good leg for lap time. That scar was such a part of our life, but, at the same time, it wasn't a part of our life. I never, ever heard Frank complain about it. Many times I would look at that horrible scar and think how lucky he was to have his legs.

There were times when I would have to shake him awake from nightmares that he would have. He would be hollering and yelling out – I guess reliving his war experiences that were still fresh in his mind. I was so young – and I really didn't know what I could do or how I could help him. We never talked about these incidents. I got used to Frank not wanting to talk about it, so I just took his lead. He never complained about it or said anything. We just moved on.

Our lives were filled with raising children and being involved in community and school activities. Frank and I were in bowling leagues and were part of our kids' involvement in lots of different sports and other activities.

Also at this time, along with his brother Mickey, Frank became very involved in Veterans of Foreign Wars Post 5008, East Pittsburgh, PA. They were among the first ones to get together with a couple of other boys in a little basement in a home to start the organization. As the membership grew, they got a little bit bigger place for their meetings. They purchased a nice lot up in East Pittsburgh and built the building that stands now – Post 5008. The VFW became a good meeting place for serviceman to go for picnics and for parties. It wasn't just a bar, but rather a place that felt like home, where all of the guys could talk, reminisce and get together. Soon the Ladies Auxiliary was formed, which I joined, and we were all there with one thing in mind – how to help our husbands who had been in the service, some with a few more battle scars than others. Some returned home without a leg or an arm, or had some other injury. But the main thing was that everybody was happy the war was over and happy that they had made it home at all. Whoever said, "War is hell" had it right. There were so many lives changed forever. The VFW has been a very nice part of our lives, and it continues to be a thriving community spot for us and many others today.

Back to our story – before you knew it, the kids were grown and began to move out on their own, pursuing their own careers and interests.

It was in the early 1980s that a lot of effort was being put into the recovery of POW's and MIA's from Vietnam. From this, the Department of Veterans Affairs launched an effort to locate prisoners of war from all wars that needed the kind of help the VA was now ready to provide.

Frank invited me to attend the American Ex-Prisoners of War convention in Des Moines, Iowa in 1995 and I thoroughly enjoyed the experience. At this time Frank was serving as the National Director of the American Ex-Prisoners of War in the U.S. East Central Region.

Every convention we went to was enjoyable and we made many lifelong, dear, dear friends all over the United States. We don't get to see them all the time, but we stay in contact by phone, letters, and emails.

This group got started when the *The Bataan Corregidor* mothers got together and asked for help from the U.S. government for their sons, who had suffered so much from their time on the Death March and their imprisonment. From the efforts of these mothers, the original AXPOW organization was formed. It amazes me that some people had the foresight to move this organization ahead. We see so many of these folks in our travels, and get to see firsthand what their hard work has accomplished and how great this organization has been for POWs.

Our involvement with the American Ex-Prisoners of War has turned out to be one of the most important things that has happened in our lives. From the first convention Frank attended, he found out so much about the benefits, medical care, and support that was available to him and other ex-prisoners of war. He immediately took an interest in learning more, serving in the organization as a National Director and Service Officer.

Since his early days of getting involved, up to and including to this day, veterans' benefits have been his life for all of these years. He learned all about the resources available at the veterans' hospitals and the good medical treatment and health care that veterans can receive there. He learned the process about service-connected disability compensations, claim filing, and the benefits to which servicemen were entitled.

American Ex-Prisoners of War is unique among the service organizations, because the members were all in different branches of the service and, of course, they were all so important in helping win the war. The special bond these ex-prisoners share isn't because of what branch of service they were in. Rather, it's due to the fact that they all went through experiencing the hell of many months and years in prison camps in Germany, Japan, Korea, and Vietnam. Then, after surviving something so very cruel and demoralizing, they put that all behind them the best they could, came back home and made a life for themselves. These soldiers are true heroes.

The American Ex-Prisoners of War is one of the greatest organizations I have ever been privileged to be a part of. It is a group that I truly love and have had the great honor of belonging to. Every man I met who was a POW and every woman I met – I never heard them complain about the government, or about anything for that matter. Instead, all I ever hear them say is that they thank God for America, for what being an American means to them, and for the life they have because of our organization. It's the same way with the wives; they are full of gratitude and patriotism. They are a remarkable group of people. The AXPOW allows me to see what an organization can do to help their fellow man.

Frank's story didn't end with him going to war, being shot down, becoming a POW, coming home and making a life for himself… not at all. His story got better when he joined with the American Ex-Prisoners of War organization, and began to help, and continues to help, so many people. I'm very, very proud of him, and I tell him that I'm proud of him and what he does for others. The organization is, sad to say, coming to an end now, due to the simple fact that almost of the members are in our late 80s. This alone will dictate that soon enough there won't be anybody left to serve as a commander, director or any other role that's required to keep it going. Just one of the facts of life. But oh my, what we did accomplish in our heyday!

There has been discussion that next of kin might take over and certainly, if next of kin who genuinely love the POW organization would like to keep it going, I would be all for it. It's difficult to believe that there would be enough next of kin, as most of them are in their sixties now. Would you then consider the grandchildren after that? Would they have enough interest in the cause? I honestly don't know what is going to happen. The fact is, everybody has a life to live. It might just be as we always say, somebody dies and we fold our wings and go on with the next phase of our life. So many, many members are in their later years of life and if they die, their widows get compensated – and that's how it should be. It's sad to think that some of them had to wait so long to receive their just rewards.

Most likely, the ones who did not receive compensation and benefits while they were living did not because they didn't talk about their prisoner experiences and all they had been through. In their modesty, or in trying to forget what happened, or for whatever reason, they didn't bring it to the forefront of any discussions, and therefore couldn't get the help they deserved.

Last year, for example, while spending time with a friend of ours who goes by the name of "Skoogie" I heard his story for the first time. He was 87 years old and we often got together with him and his wife to play cards, yet I had never heard his war experiences before.

About a month after that, we were having dinner at a local Chinese restaurant and he started talking about the war years and the hell he went through being on the ships in the Navy. He would deliver the young soldiers off the ship, dropping of them at some island for combat – putting them right in the thick of things. As he accompanied them down to their landing, he said a soldier said to him, "Sailor boy, you're here just in time to see if you can get your ass knocked off because ain't none of us going to ever come home from all of this."

I've knew this man for 50-60 years and never knew he went through the hell of war, quite simply because he didn't talk about it. This is what I mean when I talk about that generation – they just didn't talk about their war experiences.

Another example is our friends, Morgan and Lorraine. Morgan's job in World War II was taking care of German prisoners of war in Mississippi. It was ironic when we would go visit them and he'd say to Frank, "The guys I took care of sure didn't have it like you had. They had clean beds, food, cigarettes, and there you were sleeping on a straw bed and getting a bowl of soup with bugs in it to get some protein." Again, we never heard Morgan talk about his experiences before that time.

Frank's life began to really move forward, gaining momentum in terms of his recovery and acceptance with all that happened in his life when he began to go to the VA in Pittsburgh. Frank would go to the VA hospital once a month with all of his buddies and it was there, along with his other fellow ex-prisoners of war, in group sessions that they began sharing and talking about their experiences and what they each went through. You wouldn't believe some of their stories, so many of them are so incredible. That's when they all started coming out of their shells. Frank listened to their stories and then he, in turn, told his story. Everybody knew he was POW but no one knew any details because he didn't share them. As the men in the groups listened and accepted him, Frank found the freedom and safety to open up more and more. This is where Frank learned how to talk about what had happened to him.

It was a slow, painful process. You would hear him say something to this fellow, then maybe to another guy. Over time, his story began to be shared more and more down at the VA hospital because that's where he got involved in getting all of his buddies their compensation.

In order to get compensation you had to say what happened to you. You had to describe how you were injured, or starved, or burned, or captured…horrible things, things not easy to share and talk about.

Our dear friend, Pastor Jerry Alexis, captured and taken prisoner in the Hurtgen Forest was instrumental in helping Frank through a lot of his PTSD. Out of all the fellows that went down to the VA, I guess I would say that probably 90% of them received their 100 percent rating because of Frank's work for them. Jerry has always been very supportive of Frank's work on behalf of the ex-POWs, often taking the time to publicly recognize Frank's efforts. He has moved me to tears at some of our gatherings by his kind words and acknowledgment of Frank's efforts. We're so thankful for Jerry's wonderful show of support.

Because of Frank's involvement with the Ex-Prisoners of War organization and the fact he had been interviewed for newspaper and television, he was often referred to by the national headquarters as a contact person for the Eastern part of the country. Someone from Hollywood was interested in his story and asked if Frank would serve as a consultant for the making of the movie, *Memphis Belle*. Frank did provide them with advice, facts and technical support used in the making of the film.

When I saw *Memphis Belle* ... watching the movie on that big screen – I was very emotional. Remember, I wasn't a young teenager watching, but now a mature, adult woman watching. It was very touching. I know there was some Hollywood stuff thrown in there – but it was still a good movie. It brought back a lot of tears for me to see on-screen some of the things my husband went through, and the movie helped me learn more about and understand more of Frank's harrowing experiences.

I found it was a heartwarming movie. A bunch of young kids thrown together for a common cause – to fight a war as an air crew. They were all in their late teens, and early twenties, just kids, really. They learn to fly B-17s and B-24s; to be bombardiers, navigators, gunners, and radio operators. Frank and I talk about this often when we're with our POW friends and with amazement we ask, "Do you realize what these young men were called upon to do?"

I personally knew bombardiers and waist gunners, pilots, ball turret men, and more. But when I actually saw in that movie what they went through, it somehow made it all more real to me. To this day I can see Frank coming down in that parachute after being shot...I can picture it all so clearly.

One person that comes to mind as I think about that movie is Chuck Gialloreto. We knew him all of our lives and our sons played football together at Churchill High School. Yet Frank and Chuck never knew they were both POW's. Even though their sons were both quarterbacks on the team and the families spent a lot of time together, they never talked about it. Chuck was a ball turret gunner and was horribly, horribly burned, then captured, becoming a POW. Yet, never, ever in all the time that I knew this man did he talk about what he went through in the war. Nothing. Not a word spoken. Instead he said, "I can say nothing bad about this government of ours, they have treated me well."

Chuck would always say, "Thanks to my buddy, Frank Kravetz, he got me my compensation, and I knew then that my wife would be taken care of after I'm gone." And that came to pass, since Chuck died a few years ago. Indeed, his widow is now being taken care of due to the benefits he worked so hard for.

There are so many stories like this, about Frank helping people through his involvement with the American Ex-Prisoner of War organization. And when I say helped, I am talking major help – like the times the VA would determine a case was closed, and the veteran wouldn't be given any more than 50% toward his disability. Frank would doggedly pursue the ruling and make inquiry after inquiry about the claim. He would make phone call after phone call, write letters, file appeals, drive downtown to the regional office to speak to an adjudicator or claims representative. He just didn't quit. Those veterans who had given up after being told they'd never get their compensation received what they so richly deserved – Frank was able to get them their claims awarded in full.

I'm reminded of Frank's hard work every time we're out somewhere and we come home to find messages on the answering machine from all over the country, asking for Frank's help with a claim. Frank will take on the challenge of these more complicated claims, working hard and investigating all the details, moving things along, working and working for hours on end.

The next thing you know, Frank will get another call a few weeks later with someone saying, "It's all taken care of, so and so will be getting their compensation benefits starting next week. Thanks for your help, Frank." He doesn't have to do this, there is no pay involved. For him, his reward is a grateful smile and a heartfelt hug from the POW and his wife. The widows of a lot of these guys still send Christmas cards every year with little notes inside saying things like, "I don't know what I would have done without your help, Frank" or "Thanks to you Frank, it's a lot easier on me being alone and making ends meet."

I'm so proud of my husband for what he has done for his fellow POW buddies, in helping so very many of them to get their claims filed, and helping the widows get taken care of. I respect him so much for his work on behalf of others. To this day, at 87 years old, he still wants to help. Just in the last week, he got two phone calls from ex-prisoners of war and their family members seeking guidance for benefits, and jumped right in to help them.

A wonderful event we had a chance to be a part of was the dedication of the National Prisoner of War Museum in Andersonville, Georgia. This was a huge undertaking for The American Ex-Prisoners of War organization and they put a lot of effort into raising funds to have the Museum built. Finally, after many years of hard work and dedication, the dream of the museum became a reality.

The Grand Opening at the museum was held and thousands of ex-prisoners of war were invited, coming from all over the country to attend. Many of our friends that we had made throughout the years came to the event. Shortly after the opening ceremonies, there was one drawback that nobody expected and that was the fact that Frank got sick and was taken to the hospital by our daughter Lynne. He turned out to be fine. Perhaps the sun, heat of the day and all the excitement was too much for him.

We were able to tour the Andersonville Historic site, where the first prisoner of war camp was as a result of the civil war. The stories of what horrors they endured were just unbelievable – it is a wonder anyone survived. We then toured the brand new National Prisoner of War Museum and it was so inspiring – a great achievement and tribute to prisoners of war. So many stories of what they endured during their hardships of imprisonment and the hell these guys went through are immortalized there. It is so important that these stories be remembered and memorialized, so important that our country never forget the brave sacrifices of our soldiers. Frank had contributed some visual displays that were featured in the museum and that was particularly moving for me to see.

I was so proud of our POW Organization and the role they played, especially since I actually knew so many of the wonderful people who were behind such a great effort. The museum is a great achievement and one everyone should take the time to visit.

Being the wife of a World War II combat veteran and ex-prisoner of war, I've had the great pleasure of seeing many of the sights across this country that honor our veterans. One of these visits was to attend the dedication of the World War II

Memorial in Washington DC. Many of the former prisoners of war travelled to the dedication as a group. We stayed together in the same hotel and were provided a police motorcade escort alongside our tour busses to the ceremony. We were treated so wonderfully. They had reserved seats for us right up in front of the main stage. They supplied bottled water, sandwiches, and cold drinks for us. They had nurses and first aid available because they knew we were an older generation. They showed us so much respect.

It was perfect for us because our kids were with us to share in the excitement of the day. My sons-in-law wheeled me all over in a wheel chair because my legs aren't good for walking long distances like they once were. These two strong guys wheeled me around all day – they really took care of me. There was so much time and effort put into the memorial and it showed, it is a tremendous tribute to our World War II veterans.

But the thing that got to me the most was seeing the wall of gold stars, where each star represented 1,000 men who died in the war. As I looked at the wall it was a stark reminder of the tremendous loss and how many thousands upon thousands of our young boys were killed. It was very moving and sad, but at the same time, a solemn tribute; because I was reminded that they lost their young lives so that we all can live in freedom and peace in this great country. The monument is well done; a beautiful, very impressive reminder to everyone of the great sacrifices that were made by so many.

One of the things that Frank has always expressed an interest in doing was going back up on a B-17. I heard him talk about this for many, many years. His dream of doing that came to be in the summer of 2007. The restored B-17, Liberty Belle, came to the Allegheny County Airport and we took the opportunity to go and see the plane. When I saw the plane, I became very emotional thinking about my husband flying in one of them, getting shot to hell and then having to be tossed out of the plane in his parachute because he was so badly wounded.

It was very difficult for me – sad, really, when I saw that small tail section where Frank was located when he was wounded. Just to think that he was in there all alone when he was wounded brought me to tears of sadness, recalling all he went through fighting in the war. We walked around to get a closer look at the plane and took some pictures. Frank was talking to many people, sharing his story with those who were there admiring the giant, silver airplane that helped win the war.

I had to return to the airport terminal section and wait behind the fence with others who would not be taking the flight. When I got to the terminal section, I had been crying from the emotion of recalling all that Frank had been through while in his plane. Someone I never met before began to talk to me. This woman asked me if I was OK. I began to tell her that I was just a little emotional after seeing the plane, then I explained Frank's story to her; shot down over Germany, badly wounded, his crew mates putting the parachute on him and throwing him out of the plane as the crew was bailing out. I went on to explain that he then became a prisoner of war and, now, after all these years, was getting to go on a return flight on a B-17 for the first time since the war. Well, as you can imagine, this lady, her family and others who were near the fence were all crying. They now had a personal connection to this next flight of the Liberty Belle that they would likely never forget.

My daughter, Cheryl, along with a wonderful new friend we had met at the airport the day before, Janice Nielsen, had made all the arrangements for Frank and his friend Jack Tonsic to receive free rides on the B-17.

Shortly before the flight was to begin, Cheryl and her husband Ed walked over to me, hugged me and announced that they, too, would be on the flight with Frank. They had bought tickets and planned to surprise Frank once the flight was in the air. I thought, "Wow, that kid of mine has really planned something extra special for her Dad!" My other daughter Lynne was there and had brought her video camera to record the event and all of the wonderful memories of the day.

Soon they were all aboard, and the shiny B-17 was off into a beautiful blue sky dotted with white clouds day. I can only imagine what Frank was feeling as he boarded that plane again, it was something he has always wanted to do, and now the day was here. He had to be so excited. The flight took a little over a half an hour, and then I could hear the roar of the B-17 and saw it coming in for a landing.

Once the plane landed, I saw the hatch doors open, and then saw my husband and my kids exit the plane, safely landed and back on the ground.

Frank walked over to me with a great, big smile on his face; grabbed me, hugged me, and said, "It was great." I was relieved and happy for him, knowing that getting to ride, once again, on a B-17 was a dream come true for him. I knew he had come full circle. It was a perfect day with a perfect ending.

Eventually, as Frank's story about being a prisoner of war came out, somebody would say to him, "Why don't you come to this school and tell our kids something about your experience? It would be good for them to learn from someone who actually experienced what you did in the war." He started to accept some invitations to speak about his time in the service. He makes a good presentation and became a good speaker.

He still gets invited on occasion to do some speaking, although I don't know how much longer he will continue to do so.

When I first heard Frank speak in public and tell his story, I teared up even though I had heard almost every part of his story from being at conventions and reunions with him over the years. Despite the fact that I have put the pieces of his story together in my mind, every time I go with him, I still get choked up thinking about what he went through.

I remember going to Gateway Middle School for a special presentation that Emily Werle put together to educate her students and honor veterans. I watched Frank speak in front of all of those youngsters. His story was still very moving, even after all the years of hearing it told. I was so proud of him, and proud of and thankful to Emily for inviting him to speak to her students. As it did that day, it still brings tears to my eyes when I hear his story. Emily's husband (our grandson), Mark, was there for the day and we all had a great day together, I would say a *proud* day together. It was very memorable for Frank and me.

After all, his story is one heck of a story. It's unique due to the fact that he was a *wounded* POW – that's a big difference. He wasn't just captured and put in a prison camp. He didn't know if he was going to lose a leg or ever walk again, or even survive his wounds for that matter. Frank's strong faith in God is the thing that I think got him through everything. He has often said, "I knew God would bring me home." He said that because they survived their aircraft being shot down and the terrible injuries, and hospital stays and prison camp, that somehow he just knew he would survive everything he had to go through. And I say, that anybody ingenious enough to make rosary beads out of a little piece of string from his mattress while in a prisoner of war hospital is pretty clever.

Now I'm watching as he completes yet another desire of his, writing his memoirs about being a tail-gunner on a B-17, wounded, bailing out of his plane, being captured and becoming a prisoner of war. Even though I know so much

Standing (l-r): Fritz Ottenheimer – Holocaust survivor, Mark Werle, Emily Werle & Cheryl Werle
Seated: Frank Kravetz and Anne Kravetz (Gateway Middle School)

of his story because I've lived with him for 64 years so far, and we've talked about it, I'm anxious to see the story in print, very much so. I never realized in my youth what he went through, and the older I get the more I realize the horrors he survived. His story became more and more incredible to me with each passing year, and now his dream to capture it in a book is becoming a reality. When others read his book, my hope is that they come away knowing who this man is. Here was a young man from East Pittsburgh, PA, who willingly joined the Army Air Corps because a war was being fought and he wanted to do his part. Initially he wanted to become a pilot, but was unable to see that dream fulfilled because pilot school was filled. That didn't stop him, because he went on to train and work hard to become a crew member on a B-17. He did one heck of a job for six missions, was shot and seriously wounded at the same time his plane was shot, causing the crew to bail out, throwing Frank out of the plane in a last, desperate attempt to save his life.

He was captured and taken to a POW Hospital, worried his leg would be amputated, yet he survived that ordeal, as well as forced marches and two POW camps. He came home and became such a good man, a great husband, a wonderful father and grandfather. He is a proud United States citizen and a dedicated, caring friend to his fellow Ex POW's and their wives.

I want people to realize that he is a man of character, strength and resolve. That he has always been such a good man. He was a good young man that I dated and a good man that I married. After 64 years of marriage I can honestly say I have never regretted a day of our marriage. In all of these years, my admiration for my husband continues to grow, and of course, I have always loved him and always will. I always say when you get married as a couple of young kids who love one another, that's one thing, but if you can stay married for 64 years and like the person you are married to, and you can also admire him for what he does for his fellow man, that's *really* something.

As this book is published, Frank is 87 and I'm 84, and I've grown to like him *and* love him more and more every day. Our marriage brought us such good kids, and that makes our stories and our lives even better. We are blessed with three beautiful children – our oldest son, Bob and twin girls; Cheryl and Lynne. We have wonderful grandchildren and I know they are all proud of their dad and grandpap because they show it every day and in every way.

Frank was happy being a young man in the Air Corp and he was very happy with what he was doing to help win the war. I never, never heard him say to me that he was sorry for joining the Army Air Corps or that he was sorry for what happened to him. No, not at all. All he ever said was "I'm glad I did what I did and I'm glad I survived it." He didn't talk to me much about being on a B-17 as a combat gunner. He would just say things like, "I think I'm a better man for what I went through. I've tried to live the life I thought I'd never have because, when I got shot down and was so badly wounded, and was taken prisoner of war, I didn't even think I was going to live, so everything after that was fine, everything was gravy."

That's how he felt then and that's how he has lived to this day. They all wanted to put the war behind them and go on with their life and that is probably why Tom Brokaw called them 'the Greatest Generation' – because they did not come back home and complain, instead they were thankful for everything they had.

This is certainly the case for my husband and hero, Frank Kravetz.

I Love you, Frank-o.

Chapter Twenty Three

REFLECTIONS:
MY EXPERIENCE; MY PROMISE

I knew there was still one more item on my 'to do' list and that was to go back up and experience being aboard a B-17 in flight one more time.

I visited many B-17s over the years on display at air shows and in museums and always treasured the thought of getting back in the sky aboard one someday.

That opportunity came knocking on July 1, 2008 when the beautiful Liberty Belle came to the Allegheny County Airport in Pittsburgh. My daughter Cheryl asked me to go up and see the plane and Anne and I went along. Jack Toncic, a former prisoner of war and friend from our Physical Therapy group at the VA, had mentioned to me that if a B-17 ever came back to town to let him know. I called Jack and he met us at the airport.

I had no idea that behind the scenes my daughter and another friend, Janice Nielson, had made arrangements for Jack and me to be on board one of the flights scheduled for the day.

It was a complete surprise for both of us to have this wonderful opportunity to go back up in a B-17. It was a beautiful blue sky day and I remember saying: "boy how I wished all of our missions during

Jack and Frank boarding the *Liberty Belle*

the war were like this day." Jack agreed. He recalled how his crew experienced severe winters and they'd have to take off and land in a lot of snow because there wasn't a way to get snow and ice off the wings like there is today.

As I approached the B-17 to get on board, finally knowing that after 64 years I'd be back in the plane that I was shot out of all those years ago, I admit I was getting a little apprehensive. How would I feel and what memories would come flooding back? None of my crew mates were there boarding with me – that was certainly different, and we weren't loading bombs, I wasn't grabbing a parachute or flak jacket and I wasn't going to be shot at! With those realizations, I started to relax.

A crew member of the *Liberty Belle* then gave instructions about the flight and mentioned that if anyone wanted group pictures the crew would be available. He then said, "If anyone has any questions, just ask this guy (pointing to me); as he knows more than I do."

We then were given earplugs and prepared for takeoff. I took a seat right up front and heard the unmistakable roar of the engines getting revved up and it was loud, very loud.

I recalled that on our takeoffs during the war we had such heavy loads – full bomb loads, lots of extra ammunition, the crew and it was always nerve-wracking wondering would we be able to get up with all of the weight?

Next I had the surprise of my life, as I looked and saw my daughter Cheryl and her husband Ed on the plane. I had no idea they would be on board and I was so thrilled that they were making this special return flight with me.

Soon the shiny, heavy bomber was up in the air and we were permitted to unbuckle and move around the ship with the exception of entering the tail. A crew member from the Liberty Belle explained it's just a little too dangerous back there, too old and too fragile.

Not being permitted to go in to the tail section was fine with me. I don't know what my reaction might have been and I didn't want to relive what took place in the tail.

My daughter interviewed Jack during the flight and he had this to say: "When a tail gunner got shot or injured – we would have to crawl through this whole area to get back to the tail to give him assistance. Our tail gunner guy got hit seriously and I had to go back there and give him a shot of morphine and prepare him as best we could before we bailed out if necessary. Fortunately we made it back to the base, the tail gunner went to the hospital and he was OK. When one of the crew members would get injured then you went to their assistance.

Of course that's assuming the radio was working. The pilot or copilot would call and say: "Joe or Jack or whoever, see if the tail gunner's OK" and we'd take an oxygen bottle with us. Last, but not least, you'd say a couple prayers."

My first move was to the bombardier section. I had only been in the bombardier section on a practice flight way back in Kingman, AZ in training – when I got to fire guns for fun. It was a whole new world in the front and quite a thrill to be in the nose. On the day I was shot down, I saw where we were, not where we were going. Sitting behind the pilot and copilot I can remember all of our many preflight check lists and sounds – how it all was prior to combat.

I walked through the plane and saw other passengers enjoying this part of World War II history, gaining an understanding of what it might have been like for us young airmen.

The passengers on board knew I was a former gunner on a B-17 from the crew's introduction and began asking me questions. "What was it like to be on a bombing mission?" I told them we left at 8:30 in the morning and weren't back until 4 or 4:30 p.m. – if we were lucky. That once we were flying over enemy territory, we'd constantly be checking our position, responding to communication over the radio. "Seeing any flak? Any fighters?"

Every position was required to report and we did so in order starting with the bombardier back to the tail. The pilot would repeat his orders: "test oxygen, test guns, report any problems."

The pilot would tell us how many hours until we arrive at our target. We relaxed and enjoyed a candy bar or crackers, tomato juice or hot chocolate. We never overdid it in the food department – as we were always concerned about "relieving ourselves" over enemy territory – *not* a good idea! I enjoyed sharing with the other passengers the brief recap of the way it was for me during combat missions.

I kept moving back and forth from my vivid memories of so many years ago to the present moment of being aboard a B-17 again after so many years. I moved to the narrow cat walk on the plane which was only ten inches wide. It reminded me of all those years ago in the bomb bay, which was only 10-12 inches wide.

We had to pull the pins on the bombs – without a parachute on and the bomb bay doors open. It was part of my duties as a waist gunner to pull the pins and I just held on to the rope that was there to hang on to. Sometimes bombs would get 'hung-up' and you'd have to really work at getting them loose. And if the plane got hit while in that position, well that's pretty daring stuff.

It's amazing how it all came back as I remembered so many things we did as crew members. My first flight on a B-17 was January, 1944 and through all of my training and flying in combat aboard a B-17, ending up on a pleasure ride all these years later was indescribable.

I loved hearing the sound of the plane. There's no doubt any B-17 veteran sitting in their house could recognize the distinctive sound of the B-17 as it flew overhead.

It was so interesting to see how the crew of the Liberty Belle maneuvered the plane down the Monongahela and Ohio rivers turning directly to the Point providing us with tremendous views.

With the flight coming to an end – the pilot gave a thumbs down which meant we had to return to our seats and prepare for landing. As the flight was winding down, I cherished the last few moments aboard what was a thrilling ride. I hope my other daughter and son experience this flight also.

My wife Anne remained at the gate, and she knew what this meant to me being able to go back up. She was very emotional but knew that it was something that I always looked forward to doing and she was glad I was able to go. She and I both knew that I would experience both good and bad memories.

The plane touched ground with a smooth landing, such a difference compared to the landings on the air strips back at the base in England. Back then there were lots of difficult landings for many reasons, sometimes it was flying through bad weather, or parts of the plane were damaged due to enemy fire, resulting in mechanical problems with the plane struggling to get back. And so the landings, at times, were harrowing and once safely back, we'd kiss the ground when we got off. This time, smooth as silk, and I was thankful to be back – safely landed.

My family met me as I got off the plane hugging and kissing me. It was just so altogether different this time around – it was wonderful! Now I don't have to wonder if I will experience flying in a B-17 ever again – I've done it and I'm satisfied.

I still have a small B-17 next to my reading lamp. I don't know why. I guess it's because I still love it. I'm comfortable with it. There's a feeling I got when flying high in combat that somehow brought me closer to God. The poem, 'High Flight' by John Gillespie Magee, Jr. captures that feeling:[12]

High Flight

Oh! I have slipped the surly bonds of earth
And danced the skies on laughter-silvered wings;
Sunward I've climbed, and joined the tumbling mirth
Of sun-split clouds – and done a hundred things
You have not dreamed of – wheeled and soared and swung
High in the sunlit silence. Hov'ring there
I've chased the shouting wind along, and flung
My eager craft through footless halls of air.
Up, up the long delirious, burning blue,
I've topped the windswept heights with easy grace
Where never lark, or even eagle flew –
And, while silent lifting mind I've trod
The high untrespassed sanctity of space,
Put out my hand and touched the face of God.

All the years that I spent collecting different bits and pieces of information led to the natural end product of publishing my story. I didn't expect my research to go as far as it did, but it had to because there was just so much to the story itself, so many components. In the end, I wanted to tell my story – doing so in a book seemed like the logical conclusion.

My life was greatly affected by my trial of imprisonment and depravation, yet I learned to wrap some understanding around the experience to help me deal with it so as to not affect my life negatively. I can certainly understand why so many former prisoners of war do not ever want to share their stories. It's tremendously difficult to relive the struggle and talking about it just isn't worth the pain. And so I wrote to face my demons and move forward, for me – and for others who might benefit from my doing so.

---

[12] http://en.wikipedia.org/wiki/John_Gillespie_Magee,_Jr.

Without a doubt, the saddest day of my life was when I was taken prisoner and the happiest day of my life was when I was liberated. As a prisoner of war – I've had my freedom taken away and I know what that means. If need be though, I would die for the flag and what it stands for – but that's freedom. If you ever lose it and regain it you know what you've lost.

Freedom is more than a word. For me, freedom and life are synonymous – they go hand in hand and they are both blessings.

On the American Ex-Prisoners of War website there is a heading that is listed above the alphabetical line up the biographies of former POW's that reads as follows: 'We take up arms only to protect our country, to throw back tyranny and to defend the cause of freedom. At times the price has run high and never higher than in the last century with so many conflicts. In our country's hour of need, they answered the call. They gave American the best years of their lives and they stood ready to give life itself.'

I've been asked to describe my sense of Patriotism. That's easy. I'm 100% true red, white and blue. I love to fly the flag and proudly do so every chance I get. I love to sing our National Anthem and God Bless America. I love my country – I'm dedicated to it and always will be. I would fight again for it if I had to.

Before I joined the military, I felt that because everyone else was being drafted or enlisting – brothers, friends, neighbors, and classmates, I didn't want to be left out.

The government had a lot of ways to urge young people to 'take up the cause' and fight against the many injustices taking place in the world. My brother John was a Marine fighting in the South Pacific. But it was more than that. The more I learned about the war, I felt it was time for me to do my part. What was happening was so wrong and I felt so strongly about it that I had to act. Being born and raised in a country that has so many freedoms I learned to cherish them.

And as I took my place along with many others by serving in the military, I felt like I was part of saving those freedoms. Part of that effort was being able to also help other nations who lost their freedoms, helping to save people from the tyranny that was being thrust upon them.

I never had any regrets that I volunteered to serve my country. We saved the world from being overcome by evil. Despite losing hundreds of thousands of lives, war was justified for what was accomplished.

Edmund Burke Irish orator, philosopher, & politician said: "All that is necessary for the triumph of evil is that good men do nothing."

Plato is quoted as saying: "Only the dead have seen the end of war." How true.

The bible says there will always be wars – and I know I will always carry war with me.

Around Memorial Day 2007 I was so pleased to be invited to a veterans program being held at Gateway Middle school. Our grandson Mark Werle's wife Emily was a teacher at the school, and coordinated the day's events asking me to be one of the speakers. Mark took time off from work to be with us and hear my presentation and that meant a lot to me as did Emily's interest and hard work to put the program together.

At the conclusion of the program, the students in attendance were allowed to ask me a few questions. A young boy around 12 or 13 years of age asked me: "how old were you when they threw you out of the plane?

I answered: "I just turned 21 six days before."

Another student asked: "What advice can you give if I became a prisoner of war?"

I answered: "Pray. It helps."

Basically, from the time I was shot down out of the tail section of that B-17, I was in somebody else's hands…God's hands. I prayed throughout my ordeal asking Him for help. As I prayed, I promised Him that if He would get me out of this mess, I would never complain about anything again and that with His help I would take care of myself and then take care of others, live my life and be thankful. I think I've lived up to that promise, because I said after my prisoner of war experience: "I'd never be that low again, confined, longing to be home, not knowing if I ever would be."

I can so relate to the following bible verse about my prisoner experience and I treasure its meaning: II Corinthians 1:8-10: "We do not want you to be uninformed brothers, about the hardships we suffered in the province of Asia. We were under great pressure, far beyond our ability to endure, so that we despaired even of life, indeed, in our hearts we felt the sentence of death. But this happened that we might not rely on ourselves but on God, who raises the dead. He has delivered us from such a deadly peril, and he will deliver us. On him we have set our hope that he will continue to deliver us."

My experience changed me because my priorities changed; from wanting things for myself to wanting to help others with their problems and difficulties. To perhaps in some small way make life easier for them, I find that to be very satisfying.

People were there to help me along the way and I'd like to do the same in return. I found a purpose, a strength and a desire to turn negative into positive, but I did not do it alone. No man is an island – isn't a saying – it's the truth. We need each other and we need God. Part of my promise is to love others as God loves me.

So take the time to encourage someone as you journey through life – one person *can* make a difference. Be virtuous and respect yourself and others. Dare to dream and then get busy doing something meaningful and with purpose. It's then that we can find out who we are and what we're made of.

Perhaps my book can serve to inspire someone to reach out to a veteran or someone else struggling along life's journey.

As I've written and seen my own story come to life on these pages, I want everyone to know that I wrote the book because there is nothing heroic about my war experiences. Those who lost their lives for a just cause must be considered the real heroes. Soon there won't be any of us former WWII prisoners of war left; therefore the written history as recorded in this book becomes more important. Many other prisoners of war had unique experiences that perhaps they never had the opportunity to record. I am fortunate to have accomplished this.

I used to question who would believe my story, as unique as it is. Now my hope is that the readers not only believe my story – but perhaps learn from it, too.

And after reading the book I would hope that people would take away with them a reminder to be thankful for the many blessings that life gives you, it will make it easier to accept things you can't control. To not be too concerned about the little things, then when the big problems come along you'll have more time and energy to cope with and solve them. Don't let trivial matters get in the way of living life to the fullest.

Recently, the VA Pittsburgh Healthcare System honored us former prisoners of war by putting a beautiful display in the main entranceway of the hospital in Oakland. We were asked the question: "What did you learn as a POW?"

I answered: "Patience – and not to complain about life. I prayed to the Good Lord, 'If you get me out of this, I'll never complain about anything in my life...' and I've lived that life with my wife."

Cherish your life. Cherish your God who gave you life.

I'm overwhelmed with emotions as I reflect on my 87 years on this earth and how my life turned out. I am so blessed and thankful to have lived the life I lived with Anne being such a big part.

It's been a good life, a wonderful life – blessed with good health to enjoy life and the good things that God has provided for me. I have nothing to complain about. The short relationship I had with Anne prior to going off to war sustained me through my many months without having anyone to love or comfort me and I knew I had to come back to Anne.

I want to let others know that – as a lasting tribute of my love for her – now recorded in these pages.

It was appropriate that on Sunday, July 4, Independence Day 2010 – the B-17, the Liberty Belle flew directly over our house in flight low enough to see her shining in the sunlight and humming across the sky. Anne and I watched her soar majestically in the sky and I like to think it was a fly-over saying "thanks for a job well done."

Photo Courtesy of Pittsburgh Tribune Review newspaper,
May 18, 2006, Photographer Justin Merriman

"The destruction of Germany's great war industries was accomplished almost entirely from the air. No one can stand among their ruins without a feeling of awe for the devastating power of such attacks. The courage and skill of our pilots and their crews in these operations is legendary. They deserve the highest tribute of our people."

– The Honorable Henry L. Stinson,
Secretary Of War 1945

November 2ND, 2010

Frank Publishes His Story

To My Dad

Eleven Two – November 2nd. The same date a young man entered the military in 1943, was wounded becoming a prisoner of war in 1944; and was honorably discharged in 1945. Not an ordinary day in the life of the 'one airman' who is my father.

Frank and his daughter, Cheryl

Dad – It has been such a wonderful privilege, honor and blessing to have worked on this project with you. Throughout the process I learned of your character, determination, strength, compassion and faith. The many hours turned into many precious moments just being together where I not only heard your story but felt your heart. We climbed high with nothing stopping us – and together we did something amazing.

Now these pages stand forever as a testament to the high price you paid while fighting to preserve our freedom. For that I, and many others, say: "Thank you."

I know you won't ever forget Eleven Two… and now… neither will I.   Love, your daughter Cheryl

FRANK'S PERSONAL PHOTO COLLECTION

The next nine pages contain photos that are a collection of some of the fondest memories from Frank Kravetz's life. Thank you for reading Frank's memoir; thank you for learning about or remembering this important time in our history. It is in remembering that we carry forward the lessons learned.

God Bless America
Land that I Love
~ Frank A. Kravetz

Brother Ed

Frank and cousin Mary

Back Row (l-r):
Mother Susan, brother
John and dad George
Front Row (l-r):
Frank, brother Mike

Sister Anna, brother Johnny and sister
Katherine

Brother Tommy and Frank

HEADQUARTERS
EUROPEAN THEATER OF OPERATIONS
UNITED STATES ARMY

RR/ml

APO 887
19 Jan 45

AG 704.02

Cpl Michael A. Kravetz 33109766
G-5 Sect,6th Army Gp
APO 23, US Army

Dear Cpl Kravetz,

Your letter of 7 December 1944 concerning S/Sgt Frank A.
Kravetz, 33706147, has been forwarded to me for reply.

Records of this headquarters still indicate that Sgt Kravetz has been missing in action over Germany since 2 November 1944.
It is regretted that no further information is available at the present time.

As I realize you concern for the safety of your brother,
I wish to assure you that all means practicable are being utilized
to determine the status and whereabouts of our men who are missing
in action and when further information is received pertaining to Sgt
Kravetz, his next of kin will immediately be informed.

Very truly yours

J. S. Owen
J.S. OWEN
Captain AGD,
Asst. Adjutant General.

ST. HELEN'S RECTORY
420 RIDGE AVENUE
EAST PITTSBURGH, PENNA.

February 10, 1945.

BROTHER GEORGE 7-14-40

My dear George:-

Please be advised that your Mass for the safe return of your brother,
Sgt. Frank, will be offered on Wednesday of this week - February the 14th at
8 o'clock.

I can well realized the suspense and bitter feeling you have that
Sgt. Frank is still 'missing in action'. Kindly accept my sympathy.

Sincerely yours in Christ,

Rev. Jn. A. Malic

Response to Frank's brothers Mike and George inquiries;
Photo of brother George

Frank in his flight uniform; Greensboro, NC

Frank and Harold Sturman: shot down same day as
Frank and sent to same POW hospital.
Delivered notes to Frank's family in his cast.

Balloon Launch fundraiser for
WWII Memorial, Veteran's Day 2000

Veterans Day East Pittsburgh Post 5008 Nov. 11, 2008

My son-in-law Ed Werle's old jeep

Another veteran asked Frank for his autograph at the
dedication of Andersonville National
POW Museum

Frank's daughters, Cheryl and Lynne carry the banner in the AXPOW national Convention parade, Atlantic City, NJ Boardwalk

Frank and Anne at Pittsburgh Three Rivers Stadium Former Prisoner of War Fundraiser and Awareness Night

(l-r) Anne, Virgil Smallen, Frank, Cheryl, and Mary Lou Smallen at American Ex-Pow meeting in Tennessee

Newlyweds Frank and Anne

Frank bicycling with Anne

As a National Director and fellow combat veteran, Frank was honored to present his son-in-law Ed Werle with his long awaited Purple Heart for wounds received with the Mobile Riverine Force, US Navy Vietnam

Frank grew the daisies in his garden. The daisy is the national symbol in remembrance of all former POWs. The Military Code of Conduct requires every military person engaged in the defense of the United States that only name, rank and serial number are to be voluntarily divulged to the enemy. American folklore has long deemed that daisies don't tell, making it a sincere tribute to the memory of those who have endured hardships in silence.

East Pittsburgh Postmaster Ed Carr, presenting Frank with a picture of the newly minted POW & MIA: NEVER FORGOTTEN – U.S. Postage Stamp $.32 issued May 29, 1995

One of many speaking engagements as National Director of the American Ex-Prisoners of War

Frank and his family at the premier showing of the movie "Hart's War" in Pittsburgh. Frank served as a technical consultant for MGM Studios, providing information about prison camp life. Lynne seated on Frank's lap, (l-r): son-in-law Ed Hartnett, Rocky Kravetz, Pati Kravetz, Cheryl Werle, Anne Kravetz, and son-in-law Ed Werle.

Washington DC Veteran's Day, November 11, 1997. AXPOWs were the honored guests that year. (l-r): son Bob Kravetz, niece Susan Shaffer, Ed Werle, Cheryl Werle, Ed Hartnett, Pati Kravetz, Lynne Hartnett

Frank and Anne enjoying time at daughter Cheryl and son-in-law Ed's hunting camp in the Allegheny National Forest

Frank and Anne after Frank's induction into Southwestern Veterans Center Hall of Fame, Pittsburgh, PA; May 18, 2006

Frank with Anthony J. Principi, Secretary of Veteran's Affairs (2001-2005) at the VA Pittsburgh Hospital

Frank proudly displaying his license plate

New officers for the 1999-2000 term of the Pittsburgh Chapter of AXPOW being installed by National Director Frank Kravetz. (l-r): are director Bruno Ceccetti, Adjutant-Treasurer Walt Pawlesh, Sr. Vice Commander Fran Tallon, Chapter Commander Howard Lowenberg and National Director Frank Kravetz.

Fellow former POW Rev. Jerry Alexis at a speaking engagement, May 2002

From the front page of the Pittsburgh Tribune Review Newspaper, April 10, 2010: With a reassuring embrace from his daughter, Cheryl Werle, veteran Frank Kravetz recounts his time as a prisoner of war in World War II, at a Former POW Recognition Day ceremony where he and about two dozen others were honored in the chapel of VA Pittsburgh Healthcare System. - Photographer Keith Hoden. Reprinted with permission from the Pittsburgh Tribune Review.

Pictured l-r:
Frank Kravetz,
Jack Toncic and
Janice Nielsen
as Jack and Frank get ready for
an historic flight on the B-17
Liberty Belle, Pittsburgh, PA

Frank with daughter Lynne at local VFW Post 5008, East Pittsburgh, PA

Frank's daughter Lynne and Frank enjoying a family celebration

Frank and Anne with grandson Rocky and his wife Nina

Frank's Pinup Girl

Frank's grandchildren, Anna and Ben Werle (graphic artist Mark Werle's sister and brother) holding Mark's daughter, Aliva

Frank and Mike Clark,
friend and television news anchor

U.S. Congressman Mike Doyle and Frank

Frank and Dr. Jeffrey Peters

Dear Frank,
    This is just a small measure of our esteem for you and appreciation for your dedicated efforts on our behalf in obtaining compensation and keeping us posted on matters important to our welfare. May God continue to bless and keep you and Ann.
        Your ex-POW friends

POW Recognition Day, 2002

Frank's POW friends offer
thanks for all the work Frank
does for ex-POWs.

ACKNOWLEDGMENTS

Maggie Robinson – Silverbear Graphics: Your enthusiasm, commitment, vision, positive reinforcement, professional publishing prowess and unbelievable calm in the 'war room' made this happen. Thank you!

Mark Werle – Werle Creative: Your dedication, resolve, God-given talent, and incredible creativity, gave this book the wings to fly. Love You.

Earl Needhammer and Dylene Cymraes: for embracing not only the story of Eleven Two, but Frank and Anne as well.

American Ex-Prisoners of War National Office; Clydie Morgan, Cheryl Cerbone: Thanks for the research and questions getting answered.

Emily Werle & Joyce Watson: for manuscript help while on vacation.

Ed Werle: Your patience and understanding knew no bounds throughout the many days and nights of 'working on the book'. UDBST!

Special thanks to our book reviewers:

Mike Clark, Television Journalist

Dr. Jeffrey Peters

Congressman Mike Doyle

Robert 'Rocky' Kravetz, Esq.

Additional thanks to:

Jerry Alexis	Elaine Hatala
Ed Blank	Dan Kravetz
Rick Canavin	Pat Lanigan
Ray Capone	Bethany Miga
Linda Crill	Paul Ohrman
Sherri Donnelly	Tauna Perenovich
Lynne Doyle	Living Hope Church

The many friends (you know who you are) who understood what 'hermit status' was for months on end and were OK with it.

AXPOW friends from across the USA.

Eric Zemper and the Eric Zemper Collection for permission to use the B-17 photo used on the front cover.

Brad Bennett and Alan Marsh from the Andersonville National Historic Site for research and photo reproductions.

Amy Lindgren, publisher and editor of *Life After Liberation*.

And finally, thank you to the Pittsburgh Tribune Review for permission to use the photos credited in the body of the book on pages 287 and 298.

A SPECIAL THANKS

To my 'tremendously talented twin'– your capabilities and efficiency never cease to amaze me. Your devotion to the tough parts of this project, the incredible amount of correspondence, computer work, research and 'crunch time' deadlines was nothing shy of remarkable. "I couldn't have done it without you, you couldn't have done it without me." Truer words were never spoken. ~ Love, Cheryl

Once a team,
always a team!

REFERENCES

HISTORICAL DOCUMENTATION

Below are various documents available through the National Archives of the United States that corroborate the timeline and events as told in Frank A. Kravetz's narrative:

Telegram 4 Nov 1944, courtesy National Archives of the United States

Missing Air Crew Report, courtesy National Archives of the United States

Report on captured aircraft 9, courtesy National Archives of the United States

Captured document 2 Nov 1944, courtesy National Archives of the United States

Captured document 7 Nov 1944, courtesy National Archives of the United States

Captured document 18 Nov 1944, courtesy National Archives of the United States

Report on captured aircraft 1, Jan 11, 1945, courtesy National Archives of the United States

Captured document 2 Jan 1945, courtesy National Archives of the United States

WEBSITES

Below are websites that provide additional information about the events that occurred during WWII in the European theatre, especially related to the November 2nd air assault in Germany:

www.14tharmoreddivision.org/

www.100thbg.org

www.303rdbg.com

www.398th.org

www.457thbombgroup.org

www.8thafs.org

www.axpow.org

www.b24.net

www.eleventwothebook.com

www.gunners.net

www.libertyfoundation.org

www.mgm.com/hartswar

www.mohavemuseum.org/kaaf.htm

www.nps.gov/ande/index.htm

www.pittsburgh.va.gov/services/
    (Listing for the Regional Center: Former Prisoner of War Program for Treatment of former POWs)

www.ptsdmanual.com

www.redcross.org/uk/museumandarchives

www.skylighters.org

www.usafalibrary.com

www.vabenefits.va.va.gov

www.vba.va.gov/bin/21/Benefits/POW/index.htm

www.wwiimemorial.com

BOOKS AND PERIODICALS

Flak Dodger, A Story of the 457th Bombardment Group 1943-1945, 8th AAF, Pawpaw Press (Publisher), Lt. Col. Roland O. Byers, USAFR (RET.)

The Fireball Outfit, Out of Publication, Ken Blakebrough (Author), This book has been out of publication. For more information on this book go to www.457thbombgroup.org/Fireball

Lasting Impressions, H.L. Martin, 1990. A copy has been received into the archives of the British Red Cross Society

American Ex-Prisoners of War, Turner Publishing Company, Editorial Staff: W. Curtis Musten, PNC

The Wrong Side of the Fence by Eugene E. Halmos, Jr. ISBN # 1-57249-034-9, copyright 1996.

The Men Behind the Guns: The History of Enlisted Aerial Gunnery 1917-1991 Air Force Gunners [Hardcover] Turner Publishing Company (Editor), Albert E. Conder (Editor) rights to the book is Air Force Gunners Association. www.gunners.net

Fait Accompli, A Historical Account Of The 457th Bomb Group (H), The Fireball Outfit, Compiled By: Homer Briggs and James L. Bass Edited By: John F. Welch, Produced by J M Productions, Brentwood, TN ISBN: 0-9648926-02 (see pages 151-152 for November 2nd events)

One And One Half Missions, Maine to New York the Long Way, by Leland A Dowden, Edited by Maggie Dowden, Western Book/Journal Press Printers and Publishers, San Mateo, California ISBN: 0-936029-41-2

Life After Liberation: Understanding the Former Prisoner of War, by Dr. Guy Kelnhofer, Editor and Publisher Amy Lindgren, Banfil Street Press, St. Paul, Minnesota ISBN: 0-9633008-1-4

MAGAZINES

AF News Magazine of The Eighth Air Force Historical Society

EX-POW Bulletin the official voice of the American Ex-Prisoners of War, www.axpow.org

FYI

April 9 is National Former POW Recognition Day; 3rd Friday in September is National POW/MIA Day. Display your flag and if someone asks you why, tell them.

A traveling replica of the National Prisoner of War Museum is in the making and will soon be touring through the United States.

CREDITS

Photo Cover – High resolution version of the bomber photo for use on the cover of the book – Credit: Eric Zemper collection

LaVergne, TN USA
01 December 2010

206844LV00003BA/2/P